New French Thought: Political Philosophy

NEW FRENCH THOUGHT

Series Editors
THOMAS PAVEL AND MARK LILLA

The aim of this series is to bring to a cultivated public the best of recent French writing in the humanities in clear, accessible translations. The series focuses on the younger generation of philosophers, historians, and social commentators who represent the new liberal, humanistic bent of French intellectual life.

TITLES IN THE SERIES

Mark Lilla, ed., *New French Thought: Political Philosophy*

Gilles Lipovetsky, *The Empire of Fashion: Dressing Modern Democracy*

Pierre Manent, *An Intellectual History of Liberalism*

New French Thought: Political Philosophy

Mark Lilla, Editor

NEW FRENCH THOUGHT

PRINCETON UNIVERSITY PRESS · PRINCETON, NEW JERSEY

Published by Princeton University Press, 41 William Street,
Princeton, New Jersey, 08540
In the United Kingdom: Princeton University Press, Chichester, West Sussex

Library of Congress Cataloging-in-Publication Data

New French thought : political philosophy / Mark Lilla, editor.
p. cm. — (New French thought)
Previously published in French as separate essays.
Includes bibliographical references.
ISBN 0-691-03434-6 (CL)
ISBN 0-691-00105-7 (PA)
1. Political science—France—Philosophy. 2. Democracy—France.
3. Liberalism—France. I. Lilla, Mark. II. Series.
JA84.F8N49 1994
320.5'13'0944—dc20 94-8848 CIP

Publication of this book has been aided by a grant from the National Endowment for the Humanities

This book has been composed in Adobe Bauer Bodoni

Princeton University Press books are printed on acid-free paper and meet the guidelines for permanence and durability of the Committee on Production Guidelines for Book Longevity of the Council on Library Resources

Printed in the United States of America

10 9 8 7 6 5 4 3 2

For Joseph and Marguerite Frank

Contents

Acknowledgments

The publication of this anthology would not have been possible without the inspiration and encouragement of my co-editor of the "New French Thought" series, Thomas Pavel of Princeton University. My thanks also to David Bell and Tony Judt for helpful historical criticism; and to Olivier Nora, Director of the French Book Bureau in New York, for his generous assistance in securing permissions. Editorial and translation support for this project were received from New York University and from the National Endowment of the Humanities, an independent federal agency.

All the articles in this anthology were condensed from longer articles or books, and in all but two cases, from the original French. Permission to reprint is gratefully acknowledged. The original sources are as follows:

Jean-Marc Ferry, "Ancient, Modern, and Contemporary." In French: "L'ancien, le moderne et le contemporaine," *Esprit* (December 1987): 46–48, 52–53, 57–60, 62–65.

———. "Modernization and Consensus." In French: "Modernisation et consensus," *Esprit* (May 1985): 15–20, 22–28.

Luc Ferry and Alain Renaut, "Foucault." In French: *68–86: Itinéraires de l'individu* (Paris: Gallimard, 1986), 79–102, 106–7.

———. "How to Think about Rights." In French: "Penser les droits de l'homme," *Esprit* (March 1983): 70–79.

———. "Kant and Fichte." In French: "Philosopher après la fin de la philosophie?" *Le Débat* (January 1984): 144–54.

Marcel Gauchet, "Primitive Religion and the Origins of the State." In French: "La dette du sens et les racines de l'État," *Libre* 2 (1977): 5–9, 19–28, 41–43.

———. "Tocqueville." In French: "Tocqueville, l'Amérique et nous," *Libre* 7 (1980): 43–76.

Anne Godignon and Jean-Louis Thiriet, "The End of Alienation?" In French: "Pour en finir avec le concept d'alienation," *Le Débat* (September–October 1989): 172–78.

———. "The Rebirth of Voluntary Servitude." In French: "De la servitude volontaire," *Le Débat* (March–April 1990): 145–51.

Blandine Kriegel, "Rights and Natural Law." French version: Blandine Barret-Kriegel, *Les droits de l'homme et le droit naturel* (Paris: Presses Universitaires de France, 1989), 39–40, 46–57, 60–63, 65–72, 98–99.

Gilles Lipovetsky, "May '68, or the Rise of Transpolitical Individualism." In French: " 'Changer la vie' ou l'irruption de l'individualisme transpolitique," *Pouvoirs* 39 (1986): 91–100.

Pierre Manent, "The Contest for Command." In French: "Situation du libéralisme," introduction, *Les libéraux* (Paris: Hachette, 1986), 11–14, 16–18, 24–39.

———. "The Modern State." In French: "L'état moderne: Problèmes d'interpretation," *Commentaire* (Spring 1988): 328–35.

Bernard Manin, "On Legitimacy and Political Deliberation." Originally appeared in English in *Political Theory* (August 1987): 338–55, 362–64. Reprinted by permission of Sage Publications, Inc.

Philippe Raynaud, "Bourdieu." In French: "Le sociologue contre le droit," *Esprit* (March 1980): 83–93.

———. "Constant." In French: "Un romantique libéral: Benjamin Constant," *Esprit* (March 1983): 49–53, 55–62.

Stéphane Rials, "Rights and Modern Law." In French: "Des droits de l'homme aux lois de l'homme," *Commentaire* (Summer 1986): 281–89.

Tzvetan Todorov, "Lévi-Strauss." Originally appeared in English in *On Human Diversity* (Cambridge, Mass.: Harvard University Press, 1993): 60–78.

New French Thought: Political Philosophy

INTRODUCTION

The Legitimacy of the Liberal Age

MARK LILLA

For much of this century a chasm has separated political philosophy in the English-speaking world from that of Continental Europe. As is well known, it did not develop overnight. Its origins can be traced back to the early nineteenth century when distinctly national styles of philosophical reflection first arose in Europe in the wake of the French Revolution. As late as the seventeenth century, European thinkers shared a common language, Latin, which allowed them to communicate directly with their modern contemporaries and indirectly with thinkers of the Middle Ages and antiquity. By the eighteenth century Latin began to fall out of use, but the outlook of the Enlightenment was shared widely enough to permit the works of the *Lumières* to be appreciated across the whole of Europe. Kant read Hume, Hume read Holbach, and everyone read Rousseau. But after the Revolution this extensive community of mind disintegrated, and in its place there developed a number of independent circles defined more strictly by language and approach. The German philosophies of Schelling and Hegel, for example, could not be plausibly translated into the English vocabulary of Bentham and Mill. The two heterogeneous constellations we today call "Continental" and "Anglo-American" philosophy—the one growing out of German idealism, the other out of British empiricism and skepticism—owe their births to this nineteenth-century development which might be called "philosophical nationalism."[1]

The estrangement of *political* philosophy in the two traditions had more concrete causes, however. They were, not surprisingly, political. Here, too, we must turn back to the nineteenth century to understand how they came about. It is a historical commonplace that modern British and American political thought remains within the narrow orbit of liberalism. This certainly is the view of Continental observers ever since Tocqueville, who have long expressed astonishment, whether admiring or critical, at our supposedly incorrigible liberal temper. Over the past two centuries liberal ideas and liberal government have survived the age of revolution, the age of industrialization, and the age of total war. For those of us living in these liberal nations their histories look far less harmonious: we think readily of our radical dissenters and our conservatives. Nonetheless, it is certainly true that even our most radical and conservative thinkers have seldom strayed far from the fundamental principles of liberal politics: limited government, the rule of law, multiparty elections, an independent judiciary and civil service, civilian control of the military, individual rights to free association and worship, private property, and so forth. Our fiercest political disputes—whether over suffrage in England or over slavery and civil rights in America—have been over the application of these principles and the structure of these institutions, rarely over their legitimacy. On this, Louis Hartz's much maligned *The Liberal Tradition in America* (1955) was right. Even today, when the principles of liberty, equality, or "community" are debated by our political philosophers, the basic institutions of liberal government are taken very much for granted. However great the variety and contention we find within the history of our political thought, the fact remains that coherent antiliberal traditions never developed within it.

On the Continent they did. Indeed, the history of Continental political thought since the French Revolution is largely the history of different national species of illiberalism opposed to the fundamental principles listed above, albeit for different reasons. They were all born shortly after the Revolution itself, which had left Continental thinkers bitterly divided over its legacy. In every country there could be found a counterrevolutionary party defending Church and Crown and hoping to restore their authority; opposing them was an equally determined party wishing more radical forms of democracy or socialism to accomplish what the French Revolution had already begun. As time passed the two parties shared little apart from their hostility to liberalism, but this was enough to marginalize it throughout the nineteenth century. Their common attitude also led to the distortion of the original liberal idea, which came to be understood by proponents as a narrowly economic doctrine, or by opponents as a political doctrine meant to defend the economic interests of the rising middle classes. In nineteenth-century Europe, liberalism progressively became a partisan or party label rather than a term employed to describe a type of modern regime.[2] It is true that by century's end, France, Italy, and Germany had managed to construct constitutional regimes that were "liberal" in a great many respects. But this was only accomplished by balancing illiberal political forces delicately against one another, not by making Europeans into liberals. In America and Britain the ground rules of liberal politics were generally agreed upon, while on the Continent they were the result of bitter compromise that left almost no one satisfied. What later would be called liberal "political culture" was absent, and few thinkers promoted it. And by the early years of the Second World War all these quasi-liberal governments had vanished.

The divide within modern Western political thought was thus the effect of, and eventually contributed to, the differing political experiences of America, Britain, and Continental Europe in the century and a half following the French Revolution. "Philosophical nationalism" did not arise in a vacuum. Yet one of the paradoxes of postwar intellectual life is that this "nationalism" persisted, even as the political conditions that originally nourished it began to disappear. In the nineteenth century, differences over political principle also reflected different political histories: Britain and America had unbroken experiences with liberalism, Continental Europe had barely known it. But in the decades following the Second World War, France, West Germany, and Italy all became thriving liberal republics.[3] This was not accomplished overnight, nor was success ever guaranteed. But the political history of postwar Europe now appears essentially to have been the history of its liberalization, a liberalization equally of institutions and of public habits and mores. Whatever challenges governments face in Western Europe today (and they are many), they are not the traditional ones that had dogged European liberalism ever since the French Revolution. They are challenges that arise *within* European liberal polities, and many are to be found in the United States and Great Britain as well.

Nonetheless, political thought on the Continent remained thoroughly antiliberal in orientation after the war. Its right-wing version had been inescapably tainted by the fascist experience and disappeared almost immediately without a trace. But left-wing antiliberalism of a socialist or communist bent emerged strengthened from the war experience. The reasons for this were many and differed from country to country, but its results were similar.[4] In Germany the works of Marxists of the thirties—Georg Lukacs, Max Horkheimer, Theodor Adorno, Ernst Bloch—were revived and later reanimated by younger thinkers like Jürgen Habermas. In Italy the prison notebooks of Antonio Gramsci were published and became the key texts for understanding the relations between Italian politics and culture. And in France Marxism became, in Jean-Paul Sartre's words, the "unsurpassable horizon" of the age and remained so even as it was reinterpreted in light of existentialism, surrealism, structural linguistics, and even Freudian psychology. In short, while the shocks of twentieth-century history had left the liberal idea intact and even reinforced in the United States and Britain, liberal political thought had few champions on the Continent. While in practice Continental Europe was beginning to share the Anglo-American experience with liberal democracy, in theory it still considered liberalism unworthy of sympathetic study.

For decades, then, a sort of Cold War in political philosophy played itself out. Continental thinkers studiously ignored the writings of American and English liberals, and the compliment was returned. Beginning in the mid sixties, though, the contemporary writings of a number of these

Continental figures were translated and began to be discussed in Anglo-American academic circles. While this development might have signaled a wider debate over the character of the liberal age, it only seemed to transfer this Cold War to our domestic front. The differences proved deep between those employing the language of analytic philosophy to treat problems internal to liberalism, and those who criticized contemporary liberal societies from a more historical standpoint using other vocabularies, whether those of Marxism, French structuralism, or German critical theory. Despite repeated professions of mutual respect and understanding, two independent ways of conceiving the tasks and methods of political philosophy have since grown up within the Anglo-American world.

The real casualties of this philosophical Cold War were the antagonists themselves, who gradually became as provincial as the thinkers of the age of high "philosophical nationalism." It is not that partisans of the liberal and Continental approaches in the United States and Britain have not addressed each other; they have, or at least have tried to. Rather, by addressing primarily each other, they both have progressively lost touch with what is currently being thought, written, and experienced on the Continent. European intellectuals frequently express astonishment that a fixed canon of accepted "Continental" authors who became prominent nearly twenty-five years ago are still being quarreled over among us today. Whatever one makes of these works and their value, it is clear to anyone familiar with contemporary Continental thought in the original languages that Europeans themselves have moved on to new questions and approaches. "Philosophical nationalism" is on the wane in Europe. Not only is Anglo-American thought being translated and read more seriously than ever before; Continental philosophers have also been rethinking their own traditions of political thought, whether those of the postwar era or those running back to the French Revolution. This has involved a critical look at the methods, language, and judgment of those traditions—and, in particular, at what Fritz Stern once called (in reference to Germany) the "failures of illiberalism." Though the works that currently exist in English translation give little sense of this, Continental political thought is very much in transition today. One has the impression that the Cold War in political philosophy has ceased to engage the best minds on the Continent, and it is now a strictly Anglo-American affair.

The Rise and Decline of French Illiberalism

Nowhere has the recent reassessment of the Continental tradition been more dramatic and fruitful than in France. To their admirers, French intellectuals have represented a model of critical thinking about politics for most of this century, and a welcome alternative to self-satisfied Anglo-American liberals. In the last decade or two, however, the French themselves have turned a critical eye toward this heritage, provoking a strong reaction against its most representative figures. Such a development could be seen as part of the natural generational flux of intellectual life in France, where patricide has a long, distinguished history. But in this case it also prompted serious reconsideration of a long-standing Continental illiberalism, of which postwar French philosophy is only one recent form. Young French thinkers today sense themselves to be living at the end of something—if not at the end of history, then certainly at the end of *a* history that has defined their national political consciousness for nearly two centuries. They have come to see modern French politics and political thought as one continuous struggle over the character of the society that the Revolution created, a society that has, over the past fifty years, taken on a progressively more liberal cast. Their concern, therefore, has been less to settle accounts with the most recent representatives of illiberalism than to confront philosophically the phenomenon itself, whether in modern French or Continental thought. One can speak of a "revival" of liberalism in France over the past decade, but not in a narrowly doctrinal sense, at least among the most serious thinkers. Rather, one can speak of a revival of political thought *about* liberalism, in an age when the historical tensions between illiberal forces in French political life give every sign of exhaustion, and new tensions are being born within a liberal polity. The character of the liberal age is more seriously and dispassionately debated today, now that the French civil wars over its legitimacy have drawn to a close.

As the French themselves now generally portray their intellectual and political history, their path to liberalism has not been direct, nor does it resemble that followed by Britain or the United States. They correctly point out that French liberalism as a doctrine grew up within the eighteenth-century Enlightenment critique of monarchical absolutism, which gave it a particular cast.[5] While the works of Montesquieu were rather close in spirit to those of English and American liberals, the writings of Voltaire and the other *philosophes* were more exercises in criticism directed against established political and ecclesiastical power than developed theories of government. Disinterested, concrete reflection on political institutions was rare in France in the decades before the Revolution, and hardly more common thereafter. Instead, as the historian François Furet has methodically demonstrated in his writings over the past two decades, French political debate in the nineteenth century soon devolved into contentious struggles over the revolutionary heritage that largely excluded the kind of liberal politics that developed in England and America.[6] The Revolution was seen, much as it is again in France today, as a threshold separating the modern world from all that preceded it. To take sides on the Revolution meant taking sides on modernity itself, which meant that this controversy over the modern age soon displaced strictly political debate over the aims and limits of modern government. This interpretation of the Revolution and its polarizing effect on French political culture lies behind much of the recent historical and philosophical writing about liberalism presented here.

On this account, it is not surprising that in the history of nineteenth-century France, which is littered with republics, restorations, revolutions, and empires, the spirit of liberalism in the English and American sense never really took hold. This is not to say that Frenchmen did not enjoy extensive liberties and periods of relative political stability during this era. Nor is it to say that France did not develop its own liberal tradition of thought. In the first half of the century there was a very important movement that included Benjamin Constant, Germaine de Staël, Alexis de Tocqueville, and François Guizot, who are all much studied today.[7] What distinguished these liberals from their royalist and radical adversaries was that they criticized the means of the Revolution, in particular the Terror, but resigned themselves to living in the society it had created. One reason why they are so widely appreciated now is that they anticipated the current French preoccupation with the Revolution as the threshold to the modern age. For the nineteenth-century liberals, as for their present students, the Revolution had given birth to a new form of society, perhaps even a new human type, that could no longer be understood in the categories of the Ancien Régime but required strictly modern ones. Whether they used the terms "modern liberty" (Constant) or "democracy" and "equality of condition" (Tocqueville) to describe that society, they believed that liberalism as a form of government was more adapted to its dynamics than a restored absolutism or, later, socialism. At the time, however, their works appeared mainly critical and oppositional, reacting to events of the day: the collapse of the Revolution into the Terror, the rise of Napoleonic despotism and empire, and the threat of social upheaval in 1848. They were without wide intellectual influence after their time.

By the middle of the nineteenth century this intellectually important, though ultimately impotent school of liberalism had given way to a distinctively French doctrine called "republicanism." *Républicain* is the least precise and most widely invoked concept in the French political lexicon; even today, after the waning of Marxism, there is hardly a politician or intellectual who does not claim it as his own. The term harks back to the rhetoric of the Revolution, which was deeply imbued with references to classical (especially Roman) republicanism.[8] After the Terror it became common, for those who supported the Revolution but wished to elide its excesses, to refer to the "republic" rather than invoke ideas, such as "democracy," that might have been responsible for those excesses. In the historical writings of a Michelet or in the events of 1848, republicanism meant recapturing and consummating the spirit of 1789. But over time it came to offer an alternative to both radical socialism and democracy, on the one hand, and clericalism and reaction on the other. The central tenets of this doctrine were worked out progressively during the nineteenth century: an austere secular morality to replace that of the church; an active citizenry educated in public schools; a highly centralized, majoritarian government; a homogenous culture, achieved through national education but also through a slow war of attrition against signs of diversity (for example, the campaigns against regional French dialects). In short, republicanism was a syncretic mix of political principles, some universal and some chauvinistic. To be *républicain* came to mean that one defended the timeless principles expressed in the French Revolution, which were valid for all nations, but that one prized France above other nations as the supreme embodiment of those principles. "The republic," Claude Nicolet has wryly noted, "is Gallican."[9]

Republicanism's relation to liberalism is a matter of much dispute today, even among those who have highlighted the dominant illiberalism of post-Revolutionary French politics. Some have asserted that it was simply the form that liberalism took in France, and that the historical parenthesis of the Third Republic (1875–1940) saw the creation of a genuinely liberal political culture after a century of revolutions and reactions.[10] Throughout the nineteenth century there certainly were liberal republicans (Charles Renouvier, Lucien Prévost-Paradol), just as there were more left-leaning ones (Jules Ferry, Léon Gambetta). Others have pointed out the difficulty of reconciling the theory and practice of the Third Republic with the classic theories of liberalism, even those of Frenchmen like Tocqueville and Constant.[11] Indeed, the repeated appeal to the republic and the hostility to individualism confirmed Constant's worst fears about nostalgia for "ancient liberty," just as the glorification of cultural uniformity and political centralization confirmed Tocqueville's concerns about the persistent habits of the Ancien Régime. Much of the Third Republic's early history was marked by conflict over the principles of republicanism, whether over the secularization of the schools or, most memorably, over the Dreyfus Affair. And while it is true that France had established a relatively stable, quasi-liberal constitutional republic in the decades preceeding the First World War, it did so by marking its independence from liberal traditions of thought.[12]

However one views the intellectual genealogy of republicanism, its later development distanced it further from liberalism due to the profound transformations wrought by the years 1914–17. Although the Third Republic would survive for more than two decades, the cultural synthesis it represented in its early years was shattered by the events of this period. The destruction of the Great War seemed to make a mockery of republican civic morality and helped to inspire more radical aesthetic developments in the avant-garde.[13] More important still for political intellectuals was the Russian Revolution. For the European left as a whole this event was decisive; it marked the establishment of "real existing socialism" for the first time. To be sure, it was only "socialism in one country," but that could be remedied. With the Soviet Union now present as a concrete example of a new politics, the patchwork of European socialisms that existed throughout the nineteenth century was overtaken by the aggressive internationalism of the communist parties. In France this development had a very special resonance, however. For the Russian Revolution was not only an advance for the cause of socialism and the socialists; it was also a *revolution*, and therefore seemed to participate in the French national saga. Up until then, the history of the Revolution had been a purely French affair, stretching from 1789 to 1848, then to the Paris Commune, and finally culminating (according to republican historiography) in the founding of the Third Republic. That Revolution was over. But to those intellectuals for whom the Revolution was an eternal process, ever to be extended and reconceived, the Third Republic was a betrayer. Therefore the Revolution was internationalized, with the French Communist Party (PCF) and the Soviet Union now serving as honorary *sans-culottes*.[14]

What this meant during the interwar period was that intellectuals divided politically into two radical tendencies, each appealing to different elements of republicanism, but both hostile to a liberal interpretation of that tradition. On the right one saw the growing influence of reactionary nationalists like Maurice Barrès and Charles Maurras, who began as anti-Dreyfusards before the war. On the left one saw a turn away from the domestic tradition of French socialism and toward German philosophy for an understanding of the revolutionary age. Central in this regard was Russian émigré Alexandre Kojève, who shaped an entire generation of French intellectuals through his lectures on Hegel's *Phenomenology of Spirit*. The core of Hegel's teaching, according to Kojève, was the doctrine of the "master-slave" dialectic in history, which he understood in the light of the early Marx (whose manuscripts had just appeared) and early Heidegger (who was virtually unknown to the French at the time).[15] With this so-called German turn in political thought, French illiberalism also took on a new cast among intellectuals. Whereas in the nineteenth century its language was either that of the church or of radical socialists, now the critique of liberal society was cast in the vocabulary of Hegel and Marx. This would remain its vocabulary until quite recently.

As noted above, the defeat of fascism in the Second World War permanently discredited right-wing illiberalism among intellectuals. Its left-wing varieties, though, flourished in postwar Continental Europe. This was especially true in France, where the humiliations of defeat and collaboration were taken as further evidence of liberalism's "obsolescence." Here, however, the political history of France and that of its intellectuals begin to diverge. For liberalism proved not to be obsolete. Over the next thirty years, which have come to be called *les trente glorieuses*, France built two republics that were fundamentally liberal and a booming economy that utterly transformed the social landscape.[16] This liberalization of postwar French society did not happen automatically. There remained the permanent challenge of the PCF and its unions; there was the untidy process of decolonization whose bloody dénouement was the Algerian War; there were threatened military coups associated with that conflict; and, above it all, there was the unpredictable presence of Charles de Gaulle. But certainly by the mid sixties it was clear that however "exceptional" France was, it was not about to turn either to fascism or communism, if only because the base of such movements had disappeared in the flowering of the affluent society. Nor was it a "republic" in the nineteenth-century sense. The Fifth Republic had a more liberal constitution with a strong executive, a bicameral legislature, a constitutional court to check the legislature, and a welfare state that grew quickly within this framework. The severe secular morality of the republican schools had also disappeared, replaced by greater toleration for religion (which itself was less practiced) and a wider berth for individual self-expression.

This slow process of liberalization, which took place across Western Europe, is easier to see with hindsight today than it was during the fifties or sixties. But what made it even harder to see at the time was that French intellectuals were almost unanimous in their a priori rejection of liberal society and their adherence to some form of Marxism (and to the one party, the PCF, that claimed to offer the authoritative interpretation of Marxism). This history—including the development of Marxist existentialism and humanism in the writings of Jean-Paul Sartre and Maurice Merleau-Ponty, their differing reactions to Stalinism, the ideological changes in the PCF after 1956, the rise of a more orthodox, antihumanist Marxism championed by Louis Althusser in the early sixties—has been told many times before, and need not be rehearsed here.[17] What must be emphasized is how little relation all these intellectual putsches bore to the real social transformations of the time. If anything, as many French writers today maintain, the history of postwar intellectual Marxism must be understood as a series of reactions to these liberal transformations and the erosion of any hope for another revolution.[18]

At the time, however, the grip of Marxism on the minds of French intellectuals was almost complete. There were rare exceptions. One was the group "Socialisme ou barbarie," which was founded by Cornelius Castoriadis and Claude Lefort in 1949, and which published a series of books and magazines criticizing communism from an anarcho-syndicalist viewpoint as a form of bureaucratic totalitarianism.[19] But far more important for the recent revival of liberalism was Raymond Aron. Aron was a unique figure in postwar French intellectual life. Like his *petit camarade* Sartre, he was trained in the Hegelianism of the thirties and had spent a short period in Germany during Hitler's rise to power. But unlike Sartre, Aron took from these experiences an appreciation of liberal skepticism and developed an enduring hostility to all forms of historical determinism, including that embodied in Marxism. He wrote many books on these themes during his long career, was a regular journalist, and helped to launch several important reviews. Nonetheless, Aron was almost entirely without influence among his fellow intellectuals in the postwar decades: "Better wrong with Sartre than right with Aron," the saying went. It was not until the eve of his death in 1983, after French intellectuals had themselves abandoned Marxism, that he began to be read more widely.[20]

The Marxist left of the immediate postwar decade had been shaped politically and intellectually by the currents of the thirties—by the weakness of the Third Republic, by the Popular Front and the Great Depression, by Hegelianism, by surrealism. The generation of thinkers who became prominent during the following two decades, and who participated in structuralism (and what foreigners called poststructuralism), had mostly grown up in different circumstances; their formative experiences were the war and the occupation, the reign of Stalinism among intellectuals in the early fifties, and perhaps most important, *les trente glorieuses*. Here again, there is a large literature on the theoretical perambulations of those associated with this movement, much of it sycophantic.[21] Most of these works treat structuralism as a continuation of the French radicalism that was born in the thirties—as if Claude Lévi-Strauss, Roland Barthes, Jacques Lacan, Michel Foucault, and Jacques Derrida were direct descendants of Sartre and Merleau-Ponty. And there is a sense in which its lineage can be traced back to Kojève, who was the first to announce that "the end of history is the death of man, strictly defined."[22] But in truth structuralism's attitude toward politics has always been difficult to characterize. This was already evident in the early sixties, when the first structuralist works were roundly criticized by the PCF and its intellectual spokesmen, such as Sartre, as an abandonment of Marxism, if not a new form of social conservatism. On the other side, to anticommunists like Aron and Castoriadis, it represented an apolitical radicalization of the historical determinism already present in Hegel's "cunning of reason" and Marx's materialist dialectic. Whatever their differences regarding liberalism, the older antagonists of the intellectual Cold War finally understood what they shared: the presuppositions of a modern humanism that held individual autonomy to be possible, to be the aim of modern politics, and to be discoverable through reason.[23] All these assumptions structuralism denied.

This may be the key to understanding how the structuralist movements, which on the surface did not appear tied to any particular political doctrine, contributed to the long stream of French antiliberalism in the sixties and seventies. Certainly the anthropological studies of Lévi-Strauss, the literary essays of Barthes, and the psychoanalytic lectures of Lacan did not seem to be about politics at all; if anything, they signaled a retreat from the ideologically charged polemics of the fifties.[24] Even the early writings of Foucault and Derrida steered clear of anything that could be construed as political thought. But in another sense they seemed to render everything political. For if autonomous individuals as conceived by the Enlightenment and the liberal tradition do not exist independently, if it is structures that produce them—whether those structures are linguistic, symbolic, cultural, psychological, ideological, "logocentric," or simply those of "power"—then potentially every human experience can be interpreted politically through a political analysis of those structures. Structuralists themselves made a game of protesting such "caricatural" readings of their writings, just as many abjured the structuralist label. Nonetheless, this is precisely how their works were read in France: as profoundly political attacks on liberal bourgeois society. At a time of rising affluence, the decline of the working class, the sclerosis of the PCF—in short, with the disappearance of the political world that Marxism had once described—structuralism seemed to offer new possibilities for resistance.[25] But now, rather than resisting in action the dehumanization of man on the basis of a rational analysis of history, one resisted in theory the ideas of "man," "reason," and "history" as the oppressive products of ideology. After the rise of the New Left and the events of May '68, all this became clear. An idiosyncratic historical work like Michel Foucault's *Discipline and Punish* succeeded in casting a far darker shadow of suspicion over liberal society than Louis Althusser's laborious analyses of Marx's *Capital* in the mid sixties.

The situation of antiliberalism in France after 1968 was therefore highly incongruous. The intellectual reign of structuralism, which called into question every aspect of modern liberal life, also seemed to undercut all hope of escaping the tentacles of "power" through political action. If "man" and the "author" were dead, then clearly so was man as the author of his political acts. Moreover, the events of May not only failed to bring down the Fifth Republic but may have left it strengthened. As Cornelius Castoriadis once wistfully remarked, the last chance for revolution evaporated later in the summer of 1968 when the gas stations reopened, permitting the masses to reach their private vacation homes in their private cars. It is certainly true that the events of May did much to break down hierarchical distinctions in everyday French life, making it less formal, more modern; in this sense it was a real cultural revolution. But the affluence, mobility, and individualism produced by economic growth had already taken their toll on the old idea of a unified left made up of workers, their unions, the PCF, and the intellectuals. If anything, the events of May '68 reflected dissatisfactions with a consumer society that were expressed in the highly individualistic terms of that very society.[26] Politically, May '68 marked the beginning of the end of Marxism, with Maoism and the "boutique" movements of the early seventies (feminism, ecologism, "Third Worldism") left glowing like embers of a dying fire. Intellectually, what remained of the postwar antiliberal tradition was supported by a mélange of structuralism, neo-Marxism, Nietzscheanism, Heideggerianism, and Freudianism—none of it political in the sense that Sartre would have recognized.

It was in this somewhat confused context of progressive political liberalization and persistent intellectual hostility to it that the revival of liberal political thought eventually was to take place in the eighties. The key events were, once again, political. They began in the mid seventies, long before the events of 1989 and the belated rethinking they provoked on the rest of the European left. For some reason, world events that elicited little immediate response elsewhere in Western Europe—the translation of Alexander Solzhenitsyn's *Gulag Archipelago*, the butcheries in Cambodia, the flight of the boat people, the rise of Solidarity in Poland—suddenly set off a profound *crise de conscience* among the French. Why these particular events had such an effect, when innumerable others (Budapest 1956, Prague 1968) did not, is a question that future historians will have to answer. Whatever the cause, the effect was real. In the space of a few years intellectuals who once subscribed to Sartre's view that Marxism was the "unsurpassable horizon" of our time began to concede that communist totalitarianism might fall within that horizon and not be a historical accident.[27] And those who had followed Foucault in seeing classrooms, hospital wards, and offices as thinly disguised concentration camps now confronted the real thing. By the end of the seventies the public record of postwar communism was finally a matter of frank public discussion, and a cooler look at Western liberal societies became possible. The "age of suspicion" was over.

The election of François Mitterrand as president of the republic in 1981, and the simultaneous arrival of the first socialist plurality in parliament since the war, served as a capstone to this development. On one level, the Mitterrand years brought about a liberal normalization of the Fifth Republic, removing it from the long shadow of de Gaulle and the conservative parties who had ruled France in his name since 1958. But on a deeper level they also represented the last chapter in the story of France's struggle over the heritage of the French Revolution. The legitimacy of the Revolution, its interpretation, its possible reanimation, are themes that have coursed through the history of French thinking about politics for two centuries now. For much of this period, partisans and opponents were equally strong; for some of it, a "republican" truce reigned. But after the Second World War, and after the disappearance of the counterrevolutionary party, the PCF remained the sole legitimate representative of those who wished to "complete" the Revolution. The election of Mitterrand and the socialists represented the rapprochement of that revolutionary tradition with the liberal institutions of the Fifth Republic. Rather than heralding *la gauche au pouvoir*, it marked the end of a long tradition of political illiberalism and the birth of a "centrist" republic.[28]

A New Querelle: *Liberalism and Its History*

The changes in the French intellectual climate over the past fifteen years have been as profound as those on the political scene. Most significant has been the almost universal abandonment of the Hegelian, Marxist, and structuralist dogmas that nourished intellectual contempt for liberalism after the war. This shift has also signaled the demise of a certain conception of the intellectual himself, as a "master thinker" whose philosophy of history or theory of power licensed him to deliver ex cathedra judgments on the political events of the day. This image of the French *philosophe* may still have its admirers in certain airless corners of American and British universities, but it has virtually disappeared in France. As a result, space has opened up for more serious and reasoned reflection on politics and the liberal age that France has now entered. During the eighties, discussions of political philosophy centered on books that would have been unwritten, unpublished, or unread ten years earlier: studies of important political thinkers of the past, theoretical treatises on human rights, essays on liberal government and society, even translations of Anglo-American political and moral philosophy of the "analytic" variety.[29] A number of important new reviews were also founded, all concerned with contemporary liberal society and its problems.[30]

Nonetheless, it would be mistaken to speak of anything like a liberal consensus in French political thought today. Few French thinkers consider themselves to be liberals in an unqualified sense, and fewer still in an American or British sense. While it is not uncommon for an American or British political theorist to take up a "defense" of one version of liberalism or another, recent French political philosophy has been by and large diagnostic rather than promotional or programmatic. Indeed, there is an air of strangeness, or exteriority, accompanying French analyses of liberal society, as if they were *in* liberalism but not yet *of* it. This sense of perspective is difficult for Americans or Britons to achieve, which may be why our own "defenses" of liberalism seem so partisan and polemical by comparison.

Another aspect to recent French thought further distinguishes it from our own, however, and its roots go back to the phenomenon of "philosophical nationalism." This is its historical character. The reader of this volume will no doubt be struck by the role accorded to interpretations of modern history, particularly those of the French Revolution. There is a provincial side to this French absorption with the Revolution, an all too ready willingness to see its participants as "nos ancêtres les sans-culottes." But compared to Anglo-American political philosophy, which takes liberalism to be a natural fact or a historical given, rarely asking questions about its social and historical preconditions, French investigations into their own checkered political past have the advantage of raising general questions about the circumstances in which all liberal societies flourish or decline. The fragility of French liberal thought and institutions since the Revolution, their tense relations with the "world we have lost," their character in a world where that Revolution is now said to be "over": these issues resonate more deeply with the histories of most other countries than do the singular experiences of the United States or Britain. Even if one does not take the Revolution to have marked the birth of a global epoch called "modernity," it is not hard to see why that event and its repercussions have been viewed as exemplary and therefore made central to recent political theory.[31]

Ever since the Revolution, French political thought has been "historically conscious." But what is the relation between political philosophy and history? Is political philosophy only possible as systematic reflection on history, including the history of thought itself? Are there historical junctures after which certain political alternatives become literally unthinkable? Or is political philosophy precisely the rational overcoming of such false "historical consciousness"? These questions have been with Western philosophy ever since Rousseau and Hegel. But the French have been forced to confront them again, as they have tried to understand the period of their history that seems to have finished and the one that has now begun.

French thought about liberalism is therefore expressed in two different registers today. One is characterized by what might be called "ordinary" political theory about features of liberal society: human rights, constitutional government, representation, class, individualism, and so forth. Some writings in this line are collected here and will be immediately accessible to Anglo-American readers. In another register, however, the French have been debating the method appropriate to the conduct of political philosophy as such, and to reflection on liberal society in particular. Work of this sort, which defines only one dimension of recent political theory, nonetheless provides a framework for much of the rest, since it explicitly confronts the mode of thinking about politics that was dominant over the past half century. Since its presuppositions and manner of proceeding may be less familiar to foreign readers, a few words of introduction seem in order.

In a sense, it is not surprising that a debate over philosophical method should have arisen from the new experience with liberalism. Beginning in the thirties, political theory in the strict sense—that is, rigorous, informed reflection on political principles, laws, customs, and institutions—progressively disappeared in France and was supplanted by "totalizing" philosophies of history. Either it was absorbed into a rationalist account of history (whether Hegelian or Marxist), or it was ignored in the name of structuralist theories of historical "difference." In neither case, however, did it prove possible to reflect philosophically about liberalism in its own terms. Whatever differences separated these schools of thought, they all agreed that liberalism was illegitimate, as was any "naive," nonhistoricist study of it. To engage in political philosophy in France today and reflect on the liberal prospect therefore require a prior defense of the enterprise itself, in an environment where its possibility has long been denied. Such an undertaking demands a direct encounter with the whole modern historicist tradition running from Hegel to Heidegger, and its French representatives from Kojève to Foucault.

Broadly speaking, three major tendencies in contemporary political thought have engaged this French historicist legacy and attempted either to move beyond it or to redefine it. Each reflects a different approach to thinking about political history in general, and about the liberal experience within it. One examines philosophical and political liberalism in light of the historical contrast between the "ancients" and the "moderns"; a second attempts to develop a modern, nonhistoricist theory of "subjectivity" as a way of reorienting liberal politics; a third analyzes liberalism within the framework of an ambitious historical anthropology of modernity. In general, the proponents of these approaches are sympathetic toward contemporary liberal society, but each has a different notion of what that society is, how it came about, where its strengths and weaknesses lie, and what its prospects might be.

The approach of Pierre Manent, which takes its inspiration from the work of Leo Strauss, will appear the most familiar to American readers and least needs an introduction.[32] Like Strauss, Manent believes that liberalism must be seen as a development within modernity, which in turn must be considered in contrast to the ancient and medieval worlds that preceded it. In other words, modern liberalism must be understood historically as a product of the modern break with the past. However, like Strauss, Manent maintains that this divide was not the product of "history" as an impersonal force but rather was a conscious "project" conceived by the first modern philosophers (Machiavelli, Bacon, Hobbes) and carried out by their epigones in the centuries that followed. Modern history was fathered by modern philosophy. Therefore, to understand modern liberal politics fully, one must go beyond the presuppositions of modern history, escaping its limited horizon, and try to recover and reconsider the original philosophical break making its development possible.

From this perspective, Manent has now written a series of books outlining his own account of this philosophical history, the place of liberal thought within it, and the recurrent tensions in liberal society arising from the modern break. Manent follows Strauss most closely in his history of philosophy and analysis of historicism. In *Naissances de la politique moderne* (The births of modern politics), he maintains that Machiavelli's break with classical thought was responsible for both Hobbes's scientific realism (the cool study of what "is") and Rousseau's utopianism (the restless pursuit of the "ought"). Modern historicism then arose as an attempt to bring the "is" and "ought" together, most compellingly in Hegel's rational dialectic of history. When treating liberalism, however, Manent departs from Strauss by stressing the specifically Christian context in which philosophical liberalism was born. In *An Intellectual History of Liberalism* he emphasizes the fact that the "theological-political problem" in Europe did not arise in a homogeneous city-state or empire but rather out of the tension between universal Christian churches and particular absolutist monarchies. Political power and religious opinion were theoretically separated quite early in European history (the "two swords"), which paved the way for their actual separation by liberalism beginning in the seventeenth century. All the dynamics and problems of modern liberal societies, Manent suggests, can be traced back to this radical separation of realms, which not only rid liberal politics of religion but also cast doubt on any claims to know what is natural and good for human beings. In his subtle study, *Tocqueville et la nature de la démocratie* (Tocqueville and the nature of democracy), Manent pursues this reasoning; however, his conclusions about contemporary liberal society are ambiguous, or at least open to interpretation. On the one hand, he appears to regret the "softening" of human nature brought about by modernity, at times treating democratic indifference to higher things as an authoritarian imposition (Tocqueville's "despotism") and ordinary democratic politics as the end of politics in a pure sense. On the other hand, he considers liberty and self-government to be important compensations for whatever modern man has lost, so long as he uses them wisely and learns, as Manent puts it, to "love democracy moderately." Both sides to Manent's thought are evident in the essays "The Modern State" and "The Contest for Command" translated here.

Luc Ferry and Alain Renaut do not share Manent's appreciation of premodern political thought, stating flatly that "there is nothing to be learned from the Greeks," whose philosophy they consider to be so bound up with a false, hierarchical cosmology as to be alien to our democratic age.[33] They too believe that historicism is mistaken and that it has had a pernicious effect on modern politics. But unlike Manent, they blame this historicism, not on modern philosophy as such but on an "antihumanism" that grew up within it. They wish to remain secular and resolutely modern, yet simultaneously avoid what they see as the dangerous political doctrines that have grown out of certain modern philosophies. Their aim is therefore to find "a modern humanism that is neither naively metaphysical nor flatly historicist," one that would make possible "a modern political philosophy."[34]

Despite their irreconcilable differences with Manent regarding the "quarrel" of the ancients and the moderns, Ferry and Renaut share his view that modern politics and its problems have no history independent of the history of modern philosophy. The philosophical history they recount is fundamentally different from Manent's, however, because it focuses on modern theories of the self—and in particular on a distinction they make between the "subject" and the "individual"—rather than on theories of politics as such. Ever since Heidegger Continental thought has conventionally seen in modern philosophy the relentless rise of a humanist "subjectivity," which Heidegger blamed for the birth of destructive technology, mass society, and much else. Ferry and Renaut argue instead that after Kant and Fichte the idea of "subjectivity" was abandoned in favor of a modern "individualism" that carried with it the notion of a surreptitious order emerging from the interaction of individuals. This "antihumanist" conception of an unconsciously created historical order began as a rationalistic one in Leibniz's theodicy and Hegel's "cunning of reason" but later became an irrational and even more dangerous idea in the works of Nietzsche and Heidegger.[35] Ferry and Renaut have not hesitated to draw political conclusions from this philosophical history. Most contentiously, they have argued that any political movements appealing to Hegel, Marx, Nietzsche, or Heidegger are fundamentally individualistic and antihumanist in nature.[36]

The only way out of this modern individualism, they claim, is to reconceive a "modern humanism" that is neither "historicist" nor "metaphysical"—that is, a philosophy of the subject that makes universal political and moral judgments possible without appeals to religion, tradition, or human nature.[37] However, what they mean by the "subject" is often obscured in their writings, which up to now have mainly been critical and directed against their adversaries.[38] They have yet to develop their own theory of subjectivity or respond to the objections that all such theories inevitably confront.[39] Still, it is clear what they wish such a theory of subjectivity to undergird: a new defense of universal, rational norms in morals and politics, and especially a defense of human rights. (See their "How to Think about Rights," in this volume.) It should be noted, however, that such a defense would not be based on the notion of the isolated individual as possessor of rights and therefore would not be compatible with classical liberalism. Ferry and Renaut appeal instead to the French republican tradition, which they believe can find new foundations in a humanist theory of subjectivity.[40]

Like Manent, Ferry and Renaut believe that political philosophy is only possible today on the basis of a critique of modern historical consciousness, which is to be carried out through a critical philosophy of history. However, a third approach to political theory is being pursued in France today, one that still attempts to reflect directly and systematically about the historical development of modern liberal societies. It is a species of historicism, though it is impossible to place it in a single line of descent from Hegel and Marx, or Nietzsche and Heidegger. Its roots are instead to be found in French historical anthropology. Unlike the Anglo-American liberal tradition, which has been closely allied with economic science since the eighteenth century, French political thought has repeatedly turned to anthropology when seeking a theory of human behavior. Many specifically French reasons underlie this attraction to anthropology, the most important of which is probably the problem of explaining (or explaining away) religious experience after the French Revolution. The "scientific" study of religion culminating in the work of Emile Durkheim and Marcel Mauss actually begins in the nineteenth-century religious theories of August Comte, Saint-Simon, and even Joseph de Maistre. Ever since, French political philosophy has taken on an "anthropological" cast whenever it has had to treat religion directly.

The anthropologist who has most influenced the latest generation of French political thinkers is Louis Dumont, a figure little known abroad outside professional circles.[41] Dumont has become central in France for the simple reason that hc abandoned the Hegelian and Marxist presuppositions that had crept into historical anthropology and focused instead on the problem of modern individualism as first set out by Tocqueville. Dumont began his anthropological research on the Indian caste system. But even his first book on this subject, *Homo hierarchicus* (1966), which begins with reflections on Tocqueville, made it clear that his ambition was to understand the nature of modern life. Dumont's work rests on his distinction between "holistic" societies, whose ideology is "hierarchy," and "individualistic" societies, whose ideology is "equality" (which also, he says, implies "freedom"). Although all societies contain individuals, holistic societies are organized according to principles that do not recognize the individual as the ultimate source of value. Hierarchy is a moral ideology rather than a system of political or economic power, one in which society's claims are placed above those of individuals. Dumont's early writings described the Indian caste system in these hierarchical terms, in an effort to recapture the strangeness of holistic society and contrast it to our individualistic presuppositions.[42]

Since then, his work has centered almost exclusively on the rise of modern Europe, what he calls its "ideology," and lately on the different national forms that this ideology has taken. Assuming that the "hierarchy" of contemporary nonmodern societies is comparable to that of premodern Europe (a very contentious presupposition), he has set forth an influential theory of the development of the modern world out of the spirit of individualism. Dumont believes that individualism was born in early Christianity and with it grew the ideology of equality and liberty that challenged the values of ancient hierarchy. European history from the arrival of Christianity until the French Revolution was essentially driven by the tension between these two ideologies, a struggle that finally produced the modern state and the liberal separation of economic relations from both religious and political control.[43] Dumont does not celebrate this history. On the contrary, he believes that the ideology of individualism ignored the fundamentally holistic nature of all societies, and that modern life is beset by problems arising from its persistant unwillingness to accept this fact. Modern racism, anti-Semitism, and totalitarianism must all be understood as holistic reactions to an individualistic ideology that refuses to recognize the natural priority of social claims over those of individuals.[44]

Like Tocqueville's reflections on America and post-revolutionary France, Dumont's anthropological writings assume a philosophy of history without fully developing it. History is treated as a "thing," a continuous stream of human experience that shifts direction at precise junctures; between those junctures, it is the logical working out of an idea born at one and realized at the next. For Dumont, as for Tocqueville, the birth of Christianity and the French Revolution are such epochal junctures. Since the Revolution, man has become *modern* man, living in an age unlike any other. He has been freed from the power of one idea (hierarchy), only to begin serving a second (equality). These ideas are ideologies, however, not reasoned philosophies of the sort analyzed by Manent, Ferry, and Renaut; they are imbedded in social structures, which in turn shape human consciousness. Contradictions within society can be understood by studying the ideology dominating it, and thereby perhaps moderated, but the ideology itself appears to be inescapable. Faced with the bleak picture of modern democratic society dominated by individualism, Tocqueville appealed to historical providence; Manent, Ferry, and Renaut appeal to the possibility of transhistorical philosophy. Dumont offers no such consolation.

Certainly the most ambitious attempt to incorporate these anthropological insights on ancient hierarchy and modern individualism into a more rigorous philosophy of history is Marcel Gauchet's *Le désenchantement du monde* (The disenchantment of the world).[45] The book's subtitle presents it as a "political history of religion." In fact, it is a speculative history of politics that considers the development of the state as a function of changes in religious consciousness, or what Gauchet calls a "dynamic of transcendence." As readers of his article "Primitive Religion and the Origins of the State" will remark, his treatment of religious experience brings to mind aspects of Hegel's phenomenology and Feuerbach's essays on Christianity. Primitive man, according to Gauchet, organized his world by placing its source outside of himself in unchanging gods, to whom human beings owed everything. This was once the condition of primitive societies everywhere and remains so for those that still survive. But several millenia ago a great historical caesura opened up with the establishment of the great world religions, which presented their gods as changeable and distant, though now approachable. At that moment man for the first time began to exercise control over his own world; once the gods departed from their terrestrial abode, the state grew up to occupy its place. In other words, the new religions and the state emerged together out of this "dynamic of transcendence," in opposition to primitive societies, which had neither.[46] The key to understanding modern history, according to Gauchet, is to understand how man has sought to "possess" himself in politics by slowly "dispossessing" himself of any external debt or meaning in religion.

Previous historical anthropologies have misunderstood this process because they have ignored its paradoxes. The birth of monotheism, with its single, omnipotent God ruling the world through fixed laws, did not represent a lowering of man's status; on the contrary, Gauchet asserts, "the greater the gods, the more man is free."[47] By removing God from our world, by making Him into a "subject," man begins to fashion himself into one as well. One sees this most clearly in Christianity, "the religion of man's exit from religion," the first monotheistic religion founded on the notion of divine incarnation. Seen in this perspective, the "struggle between church and state" in Europe was only a superficial phenomenon; the church and the state are actually twins, born at the same moment of religious world history and working ever since toward the same historical end. Through both of them, man has pursued independence from the pagan gods, eventually separating religion from the state, then transforming the state in the spirit of democratic individualism. Our "democratic, individualistic, statist, historical, technological, capitalistic" world was formed by man daring to fill the void left by the retreat of God.[48] Max Weber was right to see the modern world as "disenchanted," just as Tocqueville and Dumont were right to see the distinctiveness of our modern, individualistic societies. But as Gauchet argues in his article "Tocqueville," none appreciated the psychoreligious dynamic giving birth to modernity and its necessary historical culmination: a world without religion.[49]

The conclusions regarding modern liberal society and its problems that Gauchet draws from this admittedly speculative history are equally ambitious and stand in sharp contrast to those of his contemporaries. He calls his book a "program," a "prolegomenon to a science of man *after* religious man."[50] Gauchet argues in the schematic second half of *Le désenchantement du monde* and in his other writings on psychology and politics, that if liberalism is the product of God's retreat and man's advance in history, it follows that it can be understood primarily, if not exclusively, in light of this process.[51] He maintains that the assertion of human subjectivity has meant the progressive dominance of democratic individualism in politics but also, as repercussions of the gods' withdrawal, the rise of ideology, bureaucratization, nationalism, growing state power, even totalitarianism. The more man is free, it appears, the greater is social power.[52] Gauchet offers no escape from modern man's psychological and political situation in this disenchanted world, only the hope that, having witnessed the death of God, he will cease trying to occupy God's place. "The death of God does not mean man becomes God," he concludes, "but on the contrary that man is strictly obliged to renounce the dream of his own divinity."[53]

The influence of Hegelianism, Marxism, and structuralism may be over in France, but the much debated theses of Marcel Gauchet and Louis Dumont show that the problem of "historical consciousness" continues to haunt political thought. Taken to their extremes, these theses could even be taken to deny both human agency in history and independent philosophical reflection about it. Gauchet criticizes Hegel's historical "cunning of reason" as a secular illusion bred of religion, which once posited an external order established beyond human intentions. But he then appears to replace reason's cunning with the historical "dynamic of transcendence," which drives man from primitive religion to monotheistic religion and an embryonic state, then to a fully modern state in a world without God.[54] Ferry and Renaut reject Hegel's "antihumanist" historicism in the name of a "nonmetaphysical subjectivity" that conceives of man as agent and judge of his historical acts. Gauchet's "subject" is the product of history, not, as it were, its subject. And even at the end of religious history he does not become (in Hegelian terms) a subject "in and for itself."[55]

As Pierre Manent argues in his essay, "The Modern State," the historical-anthropological approach also effaces the distinction between religion and philosophy, and therefore denies the possibility of philosophy.[56] Both Gauchet and Dumont assume that "primitive" or "holistic" societies offer a model for understanding the premodern world out of which liberal Europe developed. But this equation ignores the specific religious experience of Western Europe, which was defined in relation to ancient and modern philosophy. The European "ancients" were not pagan gods; they were Plato and Aristotle, from whom the Christian churches both learned and departed. The birth of the modern liberal world must be attributed to the philosophical "project" of liberating man from the Greek and Christian yokes, not to any merely internal transformation of religious consciousness, says Manent. Gauchet openly denies any possible independence from the "dynamic of transcendence," treating Greek philosophy as a "religion of reason" developed after the break with paganism, and modern political philosophy as contributing to a process already begun in Christianity.[57] In this, as in much else, he appears to be retracing Hegel's steps even as he tries to avoid them.

The debate between Manent, Ferry and Renaut, and Gauchet over historicism in political philosophy defines only one axis of contemporary French thought. It is a central one, however, because it directly confronts the dominant mode of conceiving political philosophy that existed in France from Kojève down to Foucault. Manent, Ferry, and Renaut all reject that tradition outright and have set off in different directions; Gauchet rejects it as well but appears intent on rehabilitating aspects of historicism in his own anthropological fashion. Whether they will finally succeed in escaping Hegel is an open question; they certainly are not the first to try. Indeed, it was Michel Foucault himself who, in his inaugural lecture at the Collège de France in 1970, made the famous pronouncement that his generation, "whether through logic or epistemology, whether through Marx or through Nietzsche, is attempting to flee Hegel."[58] Why they failed is a question that deserves to be posed today. One answer that suggests itself on the basis of these newer works is that Foucault's generation may not have been *sufficiently* Hegelian. Foucault had also remarked in that same lecture that "truly to escape Hegel involves an exact appreciation of the price we have to pay to detach ourselves from him. It assumes that we are aware of the extent to which Hegel, insidiously perhaps, is close to us; it implies a knowledge, in what permits us to think against Hegel, of what remains Hegelian." But to "think Hegel," even against him, means if nothing else to "think the present" in Hegelian fashion; and that present, in the postwar world, has been liberal.

Yet the liberal present was precisely what postwar French thinkers dogmatically refused to think through in its own terms. For all their professed desire to escape the presuppositions of prewar Hegelianism and Marxism, they retained one as an unreasoned article of faith: the illegitimacy of liberalism. This was a political presupposition, not a philosophical conclusion, and it trapped them unwittingly in the French Hegelian web. Perhaps what has permitted these younger thinkers to begin to disentangle themselves is the gradual disappearance of that political presupposition from French life, an event for which they are not responsible but from which they have benefited. Now free to "think liberalism," they are also free to "think Hegel" clearly, and therefore free to begin thinking clearly against him.

An Invitation

The articles in this volume have been collected and translated to give the English-speaking reader a sample of recent French political thought. Since it is impossible to represent every figure in what is now, for the first time in memory, a genuinely heterogeneous domain, certain criteria of selection had to be observed. The first was to limit the collection to a single theme rather than offer a more comprehensive but superficial introduction to the many different lines of inquiry now being pursued. Certainly the central question over the past decade has been that of liberal democracy, its nature, development, potential, and limitations. Earlier debates—over Marxism, structuralism, feminism—continue, though they generate far less general interest in France today, and their participants have dwindled in number. And since such works have been and continue to be translated into English, there was little justification for republishing selections from them here.

The second criterion, in keeping with the aim of the Princeton series to present *new* French thought, was to focus on younger thinkers who have become important in France but are not yet widely known abroad. The authors included here are almost all under fifty and came of age, intellectually speaking, in the post '68 era. The Paris events of May '68 were no less a cultural and intellectual watershed than the Second World War, separating a younger generation from an earlier one shaped by its relations with the Communist Party and "master thinkers," from Sartre to Althusser. This younger generation obviously did not grow up in complete isolation from earlier currents of thought, but its frame of reference is distinctive enough that its work merits separate treatment. Consequently, the writings of older thinkers who inspired much of the recent interest in liberalism—Raymond Aron, François Furet, Louis Dumont, Claude Lefort, Cornelius Castoriadis—have also been excluded from this collection. Fortunately, many of these have also been translated elsewhere and are accessible.

Finally, a word on the motive behind presenting this anthology in English at this time. It is a simple one: to give encouragement to those who would end their self-incurred tutelage to philosophical provincialism, in whatever form it may take today. Ever since the rise of "philosophical nationalism," Anglo-American political philosophy has never lacked reasons for closing its borders and refusing to engage thinkers beyond them. It was said that Continental thought was either too abstract, too metaphysical, too speculative, too historical, or simply irrelevant to the task of "clarifying our concepts and intuitions" about liberal politics. To combat this self-satisfaction and force a *change* in our concepts and intuitions, students of French and German philosophy rightly took it upon themselves to translate and introduce their major postwar representatives to an anglophone audience. Unfortunately, this effort soon bred its own brand of provincialism, which was not only opposed to liberal thought because of unphilosophical partisanship but was ignorant of, if not hostile to, Continental thinkers taking differing paths. "Continental thought" of a particular period and tendency was therefore preserved as if in amber, venerated, and defended with a passionate dogmatism of which only Americans are capable, and of which Tocqueville remains the supreme analyst. This anthology is offered as an antidote to both of these provincialisms, as an unfamiliar example of critical thinking about the liberal age, and as an invitation to engage in it ourselves.

Notes

1. Although Anglo-American "analytic" philosophy had roots in German and Austrian thinkers such as Frege, Wittgenstein, and Carnap, these national differences remained profound. Testimony to their persistence is the periodic reappearance—from Victor Cousin to Richard Rorty—of a philosophical "eclecticism" meant to overcome them.

2. Guido De Ruggiero's comparative analysis of nineteenth-century liberalism still retains its value here. See his *The History of European Liberalism* (Oxford, 1927).

3. Even "social-democratic" governments have been liberal in the sense employed here. For an analysis of postwar social democracy as a form of "pluralist liberal democracy" different from the American model, see Alain Bergounioux and Bernard Manin, *Le régime social-démocrate* (Paris, 1989).

4. These reasons are explored at greater length in my "The Other Velvet Revolution: Continental Liberalism and its Discontents," *Daedalus* (Spring, 1994).

5. The most recent histories of liberalism as a political idea in France are André Jardin's *Histoire du libéralisme politique* (Paris, 1985) and Louis Girard's *Les libéraux français* (Paris, 1985). They are useful reference works and reflect good judgment, but the first is something of a baggy monster and the second is limited to 1814–75. Anglophone readers might still want to rely on Kingsley Martin's *The Rise of French Liberal Thought*, 2d ed. (New York, 1954), for the eighteenth century, and Roger Henry Soltau's *French Political Thought in the Nineteenth Century* (New York, 1959), for the nineteenth.

6. The most concise statement of Furet's interpretation of the revolutionary heritage in French political life and thought remains his *Interpreting the French Revolution* (Cambridge, 1981). His more historical works, in which this interpretation is developed and documented, include *La gauche et la Révolution française au milieu du XIXe siècle* (Paris, 1986), *In the Workshop of History* (Chicago, 1984), *Marx and the French Revolution* (Chicago, 1988), and *Revolutionary France, 1770–1880* (Oxford, 1992). Also worth consulting are the relevant entries in his *A Critical Dictionary of the French Revolution* (Cambridge, Mass., 1989), edited with Mona Ozouf.

7. The rediscovery of the nineteenth-century French liberals began with Raymond Aron's chapters on Tocqueville in his *Main Currents in Sociological Thought*, 2 vols. (New York, 1965–67). The recent French literature on all these thinkers (Mme de Staël remains the curious exception) is now large. As a general introduction, see Pierre Manent's *An Intellectual History of Liberalism* (Princeton, N.J., 1994). On Tocqueville see Manent's *Tocqueville et la nature de la démocratie*, 2d ed. (Paris, 1993), François Furet's preface to *Démocratie en Amérique*, 2 vols. (Paris, 1981), and Marcel Gauchet's "Tocqueville" in the present volume. On Constant, see Gauchet's preface to *De la liberté chez les modernes* (Paris, 1980); Philippe Raynaud's preface to *De la force du gouvernement actuel de la France* (Paris, 1988) and his "Constant" in the present volume. On Guizot, see Pierre Rosanvallon's *Le moment Guizot* (Paris, 1985).

8. The classic study of republicanism as an idea is Claude Nicolet's *L'idée républicaine en France* (Paris, 1982), which ought to be supplemented with Paul Bénichou's study of romanticism, *Le temps des prophètes* (Paris, 1977). For sympathetic interpretations of both see Philippe Raynaud's "Destin de l'idéologie républicaine," *Esprit* (December 1983), and "Aux origines de notre culture politique," *Esprit* (April 1979). See also the recent collection edited by François Furet and Mona Ozouf, *Le siècle de l'avènement républicain* (Paris, 1993).

9. *L'idée républicaine en France*, 504.

10. This appears to be the view of André Jardin in his *Histoire du libéralisme politique* (see chaps. 25–26), while Louis Girard gives a more nuanced view in *Les libéraux français* (266–68).

11. A very effective critique of republicanism as fundamentally illiberal can be found in Tony Judt's *Past Imperfect. French Intellectuals, 1944–1956* (Berkeley, 1993), chap. 12. See also Tzvetan Todorov's treatment of race and nationalism in the republican tradition *On Human Diversity* (Cambridge, Mass., 1993), chap. 3.

Standard works in French on the lack of *alternance* and fundamental liberties under the Third Republic include Odile Rudelle, *La république absolue: Aux origines de l'instabilité constitutionelle de la France républicaine, 1870–1889* (Paris, 1986), and J.-P. Machelon, *La république contre les libertés? Les restrictions aux libertés publiques de 1879 à 1914* (Paris, 1976).

It should be noted that many of the authors represented in this anthology also distinguish liberalism from republicanism because they prefer the latter. For example, in *Le siècle de l'avènement républicain* François Furet and Mona Ozouf defend the republican tradition for resisting the "hedonistic" and "individualistic" tendencies of liberalism (20–21), and in much of his recent writing Furet appears more willing than previously to distinguish the experience of the Third Republic from the persistant struggles of postrevolutionary French history. For a philosophical defense of republicanism against classical liberalism see Luc Ferry's and Alain Renaut's *From the Rights of Man to the Republican Idea* (Chicago, 1992), part 2.

12. As Mona Ozouf recalls, the founders of the Third Republic were more deeply marked by the positivism of August Comte than by the spirit of the Enlightenment. See her essay, "Entre l'esprit des Lumières et la lettre positiviste: Les républicains sous l'Empire" in *Le siècle de l'avènement républicain*.

13. The most influential of such developments was surrealism, which affected not only the arts but also filtered into French philosophy and the social sciences in later decades (as in the writings of Georges Bataille, Roger Caillois, and Michel Foucault). On surrealism as an outgrowth of the war experience, see Maurice Nadeau, *The History of Surrealism* (London, 1987).

14. On the transition from French socialism to communist internationalism, see George Lichtheim's *Marxism in Modern France* (New York, 1966). On the relation of this transition to the revolutionary tradition, see again François Furet's *Interpreting the French Revolution*, part 1.

15. Selections from Kojève's lectures have been translated as *Introduction to the Reading of Hegel* (Ithaca, N.Y., 1969). A superb account of his influence is Michael Roth's *Knowing and History: Appropriations of Hegel in Twentieth-Century France* (Ithaca, N.Y., 1988), which can be supplemented with Dominique Auffret's biography, *Alexandre Kojève* (Paris, 1990). Further light is thrown on Kojève's own thought in his correspondence with Leo Strauss, which has been edited by Victor Gourevitch and Michael Roth and published in Strauss's *On Tyranny*, 2d ed. (New York, 1991).

16. Two classic works giving slightly different accounts of these changes are Jean Fourastié, *Les trente glorieuses* (Paris, 1979), and Henri Mendras, *La seconde Révolution française* (Paris, 1988).

17. A recent history of this period in English, Tony Judt's *Past Imperfect*, also reviews all the relevant literature in a useful bibliographical essay. In addition to Judt's own *Marxism and the French Left* (Oxford, 1986), other standard studies in English include David Caute's *Communism and the French Intellectuals, 1944–1960* (New York, 1964); George Lichtheim's *Marxism in Modern France*; Mark Poster's *Existential Marxism in Postwar France* (Princeton, N.J., 1975); and Michael Kelly's *Modern French Marxism* (Oxford, 1982).

Among more recent books is Rémy Rieffel's *La tribu des clercs: Les intellectuels sous la Ve République* (Paris, 1993), which tries to offer a comprehensive history of the period since 1958 but is so lacking in focus as to be useful only for general reference. A better volume is Sunil Khilnani's *Arguing Revolution: The Intellectual Left in Postwar France* (New Haven, Conn., 1993).

18. See, for example, Pierre Nora's analysis of the term "alienation" in the section, "Mots-Moments," in "Notre histoire. Matériaux pour servir à l'histoire intellectuelle de la France, 1953–1987," *Le Débat* (May–August 1988). For criticism of any one-dimensional reading of the postwar period, see Thomas Pavel's response to this volume in "Empires et paradigmes," *Le Débat* (January–February 1990).

19. Cornelius Castoriadis ran the "Socialisme ou barbarie" group until it disbanded in the early seventies, and since then has written independently on politics and psychoanalysis. He remains an anomaly on the French scene: an anarcho-syndicalist equally critical of communism and liberalism. Claude Lefort first became prominent in the forties as a Trotskyist student of Merleau-Ponty's and a collaborator at *Les Temps modernes*. After leaving "Socialisme ou barbarie" he then slowly drifted closer to the liberal tradition.

Both authors' important works, and English translations, are listed in the bibliography below. English surveys that discuss the history of "Socialisme ou barbarie" include Dick Howard's *The Marxian Heritage* (London, 1977) and Mark Poster's *Existential Marxism in Postwar France*, chap. 5. The full history of French anticommunism—which would include figures such as Boris Souvarine and Kostas Papaioannou, and magazines such as *Le contrat social*, *Preuves*, and *Contrepoint*—has yet to be told.

20. The "rediscovery" of Aron began with the publication of a series of interviews and his own memoirs in the early eighties. These exist in English, respectively, as *The Committed Observer* (Chicago, 1983) and *Memoirs* (New York, 1990), and are a good place to begin studying his thought. Most of Aron's major works in philosophy, history, sociology, and social commentary have been translated into English (see the bibliography, below). A good guide to them is Daniel Mahoney's recent *The Liberal Political Science of Raymond Aron* (Lanham, Md., 1992). Among the essays on Aron's life and thought are Pierre Manent's "Raymond Aron," in *European Liberty* (The Hague, 1983), and Stanley Hoffman's "Raymond Aron (1905–1983)," *New York Review of Books* (8 December 1983).

21. What sets Thomas Pavel's recent *The Feud of Language: A History of Structuralist Thought* (Oxford, 1989) apart from this enormous, largely uncritical, literature are his mastery of the history of linguistics and his detailed understanding of the cultural context in which structuralism grew out of it. (For a review of that literature, see his bibliography, especially pp. 156–57.) For recent French perspectives, see Vincent Descombes's important *Modern French Philosophy* (Cambridge, 1980), Jacques Bouveresse's, *Le philosophe chez les autophages* (Paris, 1984), and François Dosse's *Histoire du structuralisme*, 2 vols. (Paris, 1992).

22. Alexandre Kojève, *Introduction à la lecture de Hegel* (Paris, 1947), 388. On this filiation see Vincent Descombes, *Modern French Philosophy* (Cambridge, 1980), chap. 1.

23. See, for example, their surprisingly parallel attacks on Althusser. Sartre's may be found in the interview he gave in the special issue of *Arc* (1966) devoted to his own work, and in the essays collected in *Situations IX* (Paris, 1972). Aron's

lengthy criticism is in his *D'une Sainte Famille à l'autre* (Paris, 1969), and Castoriadis's is in *La societé française* (Paris, 1979).

24. See Vincent Descombes, *Modern French Philosophy*, chap. 3.

25. On this point, see Marcel Gauchet's analysis of the terms "Discours, Structure" and "Désir, Pouvoir" in the section, "Mots-Moments," in "Notre histoire," cited in n. 18 above.

26. It is Gilles Lipovetsky's provocative and much-discussed thesis that May '68 can only be explained as an expression of a new social individualism produced by postwar liberal life. See his essay "May '68, or the Rise of Transpolitical Individualism" in this volume, as well as his essays in *L'ère du vide: Essais sur l'individualisme contemporain* (Paris, 1983). A contrary view is expressed by Castoriadis himself in his essay in Edgar Morin, Claude Lefort, and Cornelius Castoriadis, *Mai 1968*, 2d ed. (Brussels, 1988). See also the special issue of the journal *Pouvoirs* (no. 39 [1986]) devoted to this question.

27. The first in this line were the "new philosophers." See André Glucksmann's *The Master Thinkers* (New York, 1977) and Bernard-Henri Lévy's *Barbarism with a Human Face* (New York, 1977).

28. See the analyses of the "end of the French exception," in François Furet, Jacques Julliard, and Pierre Rosanvallon, *La république du centre* (Paris, 1988). Although these three authors share a general view of Mitterrand's historical significance, they draw very different conclusions from it—especially regarding the "liberal" and "republican" elements of recent French politics.

29. Certainly the least predictable development in recent French political thought has been the new interest in Anglo-American analytic philosophy. This began under the influence of Jacques Bouveresse, especially his *Wittgenstein: La rime et la raison* (Paris, 1973). Also important have been his critical writings on French philosophy, including *Le philosophe chez les autophages* and most recently *Philosophie, mythologie, et pseudo-science* (Paris, 1991. English translation forthcoming, Princeton, N.J.). Typical works of younger authors working in this are Vincent Descombes's *L'inconscient malgré lui* (Paris, 1977) and *Objects of All Sorts* (Oxford, 1986), and Pascal Engel's *The Norm of Truth* (Toronto, 1991).

Equally surprising has been the reception of political philosophy in the Anglo-American mode. There has been a recent flurry of translations of works on liberalism, communitarianism, and ethics, foremost among which is John Rawls's *A Theory of Justice*. The French, too, have begun to contribute to this literature, mainly through the Centre de recherche en épistemologie appliquée (CREA). Important in this line have been the writings of its director, Jean-Pierre Dupuy, which include *Ordres et désordres* (Paris, 1982) and *Le sacrifice et l'envie* (Paris, 1992).

An excellent summary of recent French work in philosophy that reflects these new interests can be found in the series of essays published in *La philosophie qui vient: Parcours, bilans, projets*, a special issue of *Le Débat* (November–December 1992).

30. The most significant of these are *Le Débat*, *Commentaire*, and *Esprit*. *Le Débat* was founded in 1980 by historian Pierre Nora and philosopher Marcel Gauchet in the hope of moving beyond the ideological debates of the previous decades and opening up new discussions in history, philosophy, and the social sciences. (For a statement of the magazine's aims see Nora's "Que peuvent les

intellectuels?" in the first issue of *Le Débat* [May 1980].) *Commentaire*, which was founded by Raymond Aron in 1980 and is now edited by Jean-Claude Casanova, addresses many of the same themes but has closer ties to the worlds of government and business than the university. *Esprit* was originally founded by the Catholic "personalist" philosopher Emmanuel Mounier in 1932 and has one of the longest (and ideologically most complicated) histories of all French periodicals. It was "refounded," so to speak, by its last two editors, Paul Thibaud and Olivier Mongin, and has since become a friendly critic of the new liberal tendencies.

Two new journals specializing in political thought are *Philosophie politique* (founded by Blandine Kriegel in 1991) and *La pensée politique* (founded by Marcel Gauchet, Pierre Manent, and Pierre Rosanvallon in 1993).

31. If anything, both historical studies and political philosophy have benefited from this focus on the Revolution and its aftermath. The benefits are apparent in the new historical studies of modern French political thought mentioned above, especially those of liberal figures such as Constant, Tocqueville, and Guizot. One also sees them in the philosophical histories of the Revolution and its aftermath, particularly the monumental collective works directed by François Furet and Pierre Nora. On the Revolution, see François Furet and Mona Ozouf, eds., *A Critical Dictionary of the French Revolution*; on public memory in the postrevolutionary period, see the fascinating essays collected in the eight volumes edited by Pierre Nora under the title *Les lieux de mémoire* (Paris, 1984–93).

32. In addition to *Tocqueville et la nature de la démocratie* and *An Intellectual History of Liberalism*, Pierre Manent has also written *Naissances de la politique moderne* (Paris, 1977) and edited *Les libéraux* (Paris, 1986). His *La cité de l'homme* (Paris, 1993) has just been published.

33. Together Ferry and Renaut have written *La pensée 68* (Paris, 1985; poorly translated as *French Philosophy of the Sixties: An Essay on Antihumanism* [Amherst, Mass., 1990]), *Système et critique. Essais sur la critique de la raison dans la philosophie contemporaine* (Brussels, 1985), *68–86: Itinéraires de l'individu* (Paris, 1987), and *From the Rights of Man to the Republican Idea*. Ferry's works in political philosophy include *Rights* (Chicago, 1990), and *The System of Philosophies of History* (Chicago, 1992). Renaut's include *L'ère de l'individu* (Paris, 1989), *Le système du droit: Philosophie et droit dans la penseé de Fichte* (Paris, 1986), and with Lukas Sosoe, *Philosophie du droit* (Paris, 1991). Their statement on the Greeks comes from *From the Rights of Man to the Republican Idea*, 45.

34. Ferry, *Rights*, 19–20.

35. On this account, Nietzsche's and Heidegger's attacks on humanist subjectivity represent not the "end of philosophy" but the culmination of modern philosophical individualism. See Renaut, *L'ère de l'individu*, part 2, chaps. 1 and 3, and Ferry and Renaut, *The System of Philosophies of History*, part 1.

36. This was most effectively, and polemically, done in their essay *La pensée 68*. There Ferry and Renaut put postwar French thought on trial for its attempt to integrate the fundamentally irreconcilable forms of antihumanism found in Marx, Freud, Nietzsche, and Heidegger. This argument was contentious, and not simply because it was directed at the previous generation of "master thinkers": Michel Foucault, Jacques Derrida, Pierre Bourdieu, and Jacques Lacan. The most inter-

esting criticisms were put forward by those otherwise sympathetic to the author's defense of humanism. See, for example, the debate with Alain Finkielkraut and Krzysztof Pomian in "Y a-t-il une pensée 68?" *Le Débat* (March–May 1986).

Ferry and Renaut went even further, however, by suggesting that a corrupting individualism was at the root of many contemporary political movements that seemed, on the surface, to be anti-individualistic and humane. Following Gilles Lipovetsky, they treated the events of May '68 as a "transpolitical," self-referential exercise. They also became central participants in the so-called Heidegger affair, which broke out in the late eighties over new revelations regarding Heidegger's involvement with Nazism. See their *Heidegger and Modernity* (Chicago, 1990). For accounts of the "affair" in the French context, see Mark Lilla, "What Heidegger Wrought," *Commentary* (January 1990); Thomas Pavel, *The Feud of Language* ("Post-Scriptum"); and Richard Wolin's essay in the volume he edited, *The Heidegger Controversy*, 2d ed. (Cambridge, Mass., 1992). A revealing controversy over this last work, involving Wolin and Jacques Derrida, has recently erupted in the United States. See Thomas Sheehan, "A Normal Nazi," *New York Review of Books* (14 January 1993), and the correspondence in the issues of 11 February, 25 March, 8 April, and 25 April.

37. Ferry's and Renaut's conviction that humanism must be "modern" and not "naive" makes it difficult to understand their attitude toward the modern antihumanists. For example, in their introduction to a series of anti-Nietzschean essays that they have collected they announce that Nietzsche helped remove the "scales" from their eyes, and that one must learn to "think Nietzsche against Nietzsche." See their *Pourquoi nous ne sommes pas nietzschéens* (Paris, 1991). A skeptical analysis of their approach can be found in Mark Lilla, "Ni Socrate, ni Jésus," *Revue* (1994).

38. Ferry and Renaut have made two, not always compatible, appeals to previous philosophies of the subject. One is to Kant, and specifically to the *Critique of Judgment*: wishing to avoid the transcendental presuppositions of the First Critique and the rigors of the Second, they have followed the increasingly common strategy of seeking in the Third an "aesthetic" model for reflection on morals and politics. See, for example, Ferry's *The System of Philosophies of History* (part 2, chap. 3) and his recent history of modern aesthetics, *Homo aestheticus* (Chicago, 1993).

A second appeal is to Fichte, specifically to his earliest works: here they discover a "non-metaphysical" philosophy of the subject that makes room for intersubjective experience and permits a critical analysis of history. See Ferry, *Rights* (part 2), and especially Renaut's *Le système du droit*. Their interpretation of Fichte has been strongly influenced by that of Alexis Philonenko, which is developed in his *La liberté dans la philosophie de Fichte* (Paris, 1966), *Théorie et praxis dans la pensée morale et politique de Kant et de Fichte en 1793* (Paris, 1968), and *L'oeuvre de Fichte* (Paris, 1984).

Another path to intersubjective judgment, which Ferry and Renaut do not take (but to which they are not hostile), is that of Jürgen Habermas. A French interpretation and defense of the Habermas alternative can be found in Jean-Marc Ferry's *Habermas: L'éthique de la communication* (Paris, 1987) and in his articles, "Ancient, Modern, and Contemporary" and "Modernization and Consensus," in this anthology.

39. Some of these objections have been put forward in Charles Larmore's penetrating essay on Ferry's and Renaut's work, "Histoire et raison en philosophie politique" in Thomas Pavel, ed., *France-Amérique: Dialogue and Misreadings*, a special issue of *Stanford French Review* (15, nos. 1–2 [1991]).

40. See Ferry and Renaut, *From the Rights of Man to the Republican Idea*, part 2, chap. 3, and Renaut, *Le système du droit*, part 3, chap. 3.

41. Dumont's works in English translation are *Homo hierarchicus*, 2d ed. (Chicago, 1980), *From Mandeville to Marx: The Genesis and Triumph of Economic Ideology* (Chicago, 1977), and *Essays on Individualism* (Chicago, 1986). His most recent work in French is *Homo aequalis 2: L'idéologie allemande* (Paris, 1991).

42. *Homo hierarchicus*, introduction (sections 5–7), and postface.

43. See *Essays on Individualism*, chaps. 1–2, and *From Mandeville to Marx*.

44. See *Essays on Individualism*, chaps. 3–4, and *Homo aequalis 2*.

45. *Le désenchantement du monde* (Paris, 1985). Gauchet's writings in the history of ideas include *La pratique de l'esprit humain*, with Gladys Swain (Paris, 1980; English translation forthcoming, Princeton, N.J.), *La révolution des droits de l'homme* (Paris, 1989), and his recent *L'inconscient cérébral* (Paris, 1992).

46. Here Gauchet relies heavily on another French anthropologist, the late Pierre Clastres. Clastres's most important book has appeared in English as *Society against the State* (New York, 1977).

47. *Le désenchantement du monde*, 53.

48. Ibid., 136.

49. Gauchet's many nuances—regarding the contingency of the transition from primitive to developed religions, the differences between the "great" religions, the possibility of private religious faith in a "disenchanted" world—do nothing to nuance this conclusion.

50. *Le désenchantement du monde*, i, 293.

51. Gauchet believes that human "subjectivity" is a historical product arising out of this process, and that it has carried with it new, problematic concepts (the unconscious), psychological problems (paranoia, schizophrenia), and social institutions (the mental asylum). On these themes, see *Le désenchantement du monde* (238–47), *L'inconscient cérébral*, and *La pratique de l'esprit humain*. The last volume offers a contrasting view of the history of the asylum to that given by Michel Foucault.

52. *Le désenchantement du monde*, 248–91. This also is the lesson Gauchet draws from the history of debates about the French Declaration of the Rights of Man, which begins (he writes) in rebellion against divine right, reaches its peak in the founding act, and ends in the Terror as the sovereign nation tries to replace God. See *La révolution des droits de l'homme* (Paris, 1989). On more recent historical events, see his essay "L'expérience totalitaire et la pensée de la politique" in *Esprit* (July–August 1976).

53. *Le désenchantement du monde*, 291.

54. This is very clearly stated in *Le désenchantement du monde*, 133.

55. Taken together, Gauchet's writings leave the impression that our "exit" from the religious age is followed by our "entrance" into a secular age dominated by psychological conflict, from which a "subject" never emerges. See specifically *Le désenchantement du monde* (238–47), and more generally, *La pratique de l'esprit humain* and *L'inconscient cérébral.*

56. See also the transcript of the debate between Manent and Gauchet over Gauchet's arguments, published in *Esprit* (April–May 1986).

57. *Le désenchantement du monde*, 204–14.

58. Translated as "The Discourse on Language," in *The Archeology of Knowledge* (New York, 1972), 235.

PART ONE

Les Adieux

THE REVIVAL of political philosophy in France has been accompanied by a critical encounter with postwar thought, and in particular with the syncretic mix of structuralism, Heideggerianism, Nietzscheanism, and Marxism that became dominant in the sixties. Tzvetan Todorov, the distinguished literary theorist who himself was once a leading exponent of structuralism, raises doubts about this school of thought in his essay on Claude Lévi-Strauss. Examining the tensions in Lévi-Strauss's approach to ethnology—the search for human universals through the study of cultural differences, the defense of ethical relativism coupled with a preference for primitive over developed societies—Todorov reflects on structuralism's "antihumanism" and its denial of human subjectivity. Luc Ferry and Alain Renaut pursue the same themes in their essay on Michel Foucault, echoing the criticisms developed in their *French Philosophy of the Sixties*. Ferry and Renaut here speculate on the possible political consequences of Foucault's Nietzscheanism, which they consider a raw "vitalism" of power. How can an unjust exercise of power be criticized or resisted, they ask, if the notions of right and justice are themselves taken to be mere manifestations of power? A similar problem is raised in Philippe Raynaud's review of Pierre Bourdieu's *Distinction*. According to Raynaud, the translation of the Marxist theory of alienation into the language of "misrecognition" and cultural "reproduction" drives Bourdieu to a more radical determinism that renders political criticism and action meaningless.

CHAPTER 1

Lévi-Strauss

TZVETAN TODOROV

ETHNOLOGY is a modern discipline whose very object may be identified as cultural difference. Within ethnology, the adoption of an approach to the universal-relative opposition is inevitable—but it may not be a simple matter. To illustrate the difficulties inherent in any undertaking in this area, I shall start with the work of the most influential of the French ethnologists, Claude Lévi-Strauss.

First of all, let us note that in his most general and most programmatic pronouncements, such as his inaugural lesson at the Collège de France, Lévi-Strauss affirms the universalist vocation of the ethnologist. In this connection he recalls the existence of a tradition in French ethnology whose ancestor is Marcel Mauss; it is with reference to Mauss that Lévi-Strauss defines ethnology's "ultimate goal," namely, "to arrive at certain universal forms of thought and morality" (*Anthropologie structurale deux*, in English *Structural Anthropology*, 2:25), and he formulates "a question with which it has always been concerned—that of the universality of the human race" (24). The vocabulary and aspirations of Enlightenment philosophy are recognizable here: there is such a thing as "human nature," constant and universal, which is manifested in forms of thought and knowledge (the establishment of truth and falsity) as well as in forms of judgment (the search for good and evil). In a spirit that remains quite classical, Lévi-Strauss seems to attribute a dominant place to the universal: "The outer differences conceal a basic unity" (59), the base being traditionally deemed more worthy than the surfaces. A description that is only slightly less value laden, but more concrete, presents the relation between the two as follows: "It is as if we were asserting that men have always and everywhere undertaken the same task in striving towards the same objective and that, throughout history, only the means have differed" (*Tristes tropiques*, English, 392). If this formula is combined with the previous one, it becomes clear that the goals correspond to the foundations, the base, while the means correspond to the surface, which is an argument in favor of unity. It could be noted as well that this object and this task, instead of being elements of observable reality, are mental constructions, hypotheses necessary to a comprehension of that reality.

However, no sooner is this hierarchy between the universal and the particular outlined than it seems to be reversed, and the reversal is all the more disconcerting since Lévi-Strauss is the spokesperson not of just any human science but precisely of ethnology—that is, the discipline having as its object individual societies, "a discipline whose main, if not sole, aim is to analyze and interpret differences" (*Anthropologie structurale*, in English *Structural Anthropology*, 14). It is a matter not of denying the existence of features in common beneath the differences but of proceeding to a kind of distribution of labor: one set of disciplines is to deal with similarities, another with differences. "Because such general characteristics *are* universal, they pertain to biology and psychology. The ethnographer's task is to describe and analyze the different ways in which they are manifested in various societies; the ethnologist's task is to explain them" (13). The universal is off limits to the ethnologist *by definition*: whenever a feature is universal, it becomes by that very token a psychic or biological feature and no longer a social one. Such a choice has the advantage of simplicity. But does it not indicate that an a priori decision has been made as to the nature of what is to be studied?

The ethnologist's ultimate goal, according to Lévi-Strauss, is to reach the universal forms of the human mind; but his initial aim (let us forget the term "sole," otherwise we could go no further) is, here, to study differences. Is this not a rather peculiar way to reach a goal, by heading first in the opposite direction? Rousseau had already recommended this approach, however, and Lévi-Strauss is prepared to comply, just as he seems to adopt as his own a conception of the universal that is Leibnizian in inspiration: from the observation of particular facts, one deduces general properties in such a way that each fact appears to be one combination among various possible combinations—of these general and elementary features. This is in fact Lévi-Strauss's structural project: he refers to "that general inventory of societies which anthropology attempts to construct," and the observable data are then nothing more than "the equivalents of so many choices, from all the possible ones which each society seems to make" (11). Only the particular is observed, but the particular is understood only by way of a detour through the general.

Here we have gotten somewhat beyond the opposition between ends and means; but despite some wavering and hesitation, we can say that we are indeed looking at a predominantly universalist project. It is not entirely certain, however, that Lévi-Strauss wants to stick to it. Whatever may be said about ultimate aims and deep structures, what ethnologists have to deal with are the differences among societies; inevitably, this fact inflects their position in the direction of relativism. The first universality Lévi-Strauss abandons is that of moral judgment. If there really were "universal forms of morality," we ought to be able to pass comparative judgments on every culture we encounter; yet even when he preserves the image of the inventory of abstract properties, common to all cultures, Lévi-Strauss denies ethnology any right to judge. "We must accept the fact that each society has made a certain choice, within the range of existing human possibilities, and that the various choices cannot be compared with each other" (*Tristes tropiques*, 385). We are thus confronted with "the impossibility of arriving at any moral or philosophical criterion by which to decide the respective values of the choices which have led each civilization to prefer certain ways of life and thought while rejecting others" (*L'homme nu*, in English *The Naked Man*, 636). Wisdom would dictate that we accept without judging: "No society is fundamentally good, but none . . . is absolutely bad; they all offer their members certain advantages, with the proviso that there is invariably a residue of evil, the amount of which seems to remain more or less constant" (*Tristes tropiques*, 387). Those who do not share this opinion manifest "the absurdity of declaring one culture superior to another" (*Structural Anthropology*, 2:354).

So the general universalist program turns out to convey a radical ethical relativism: every society is imperfect, and no society is better than any other; thus, totalitarianism—to take an extreme example—is as valid as democracy. The same thing is suggested by the famous comparison of cultures to moving trains: there exists no fixed point—that is, no point beyond a culture—from which we can judge others. We have the impression that a culture is *developing*, and we think we are making an objective judgment about it; in reality, all we see is that it is going in the same direction as we are. Or else, on the contrary, we think that another culture is *stagnating*: this is another optical illusion, for we are in fact only designating the difference of direction between its movement and ours. It is at this point in the argument that Lévi-Strauss resorts to the image "used to explain the first rudiments of the theory of relativity. In order to demonstrate that the dimension and speed of the displacement of bodies are not absolute values, but functions of the observer's position, we are reminded that, for a passenger sitting by the window of a train, the speed and length of other trains vary according to whether they move in the same direction or the opposite way. And every member of a culture is as closely linked to that culture as the imaginary passenger is to his train" (340). It is all a matter of viewpoint: if we pass judgment, it is because we are all interested parties. "The wealth of a culture or of the unfolding of one of its phases does not exist as an intrinsic feature; it is a function of the observer's situation in regard to that wealth, of the number or diversity of the interests he has invested in it" (*Le regard éloigné*, in English *The View from Afar*, 10). We have come back to Helvétius.

The image of moving trains may be helpful for visualizing certain elements of the theory of relativity in physics; but does it suffice to justify ethical relativism? In a sense, it is actually absurd to establish a hierarchy of cultures, since each one is a model of the world (just as it would be absurd, in a sense, to establish a hierarchy of languages). But we would have to add at once that that in no way prevents us from identifying good and evil and thus, potentially, from observing that a given society is, at a particular moment of its history, subject to global condemnation (as is the case with totalitarian societies). From another standpoint, is the individual really a prisoner of the train of culture in which he was raised, without any possibility of distancing himself from it (or even of jumping off the train)? Lévi-Strauss manifests a cultural determinism here whose rigidity is no less striking than that of Gobineau's cherished racial determinism, which we shall have occasion to examine later on. It is essential to recognize that one can understand cultures other than one's own and thus communicate with their members. Does not this experience of *detachment* with respect to the customs and values of one's own society characterize the ethnologist himself? But let us not get ahead of ourselves.

Let us forget for a moment the "ultimate goal" of ethnology, established earlier by Lévi-Strauss, and ask rather to what extent his practice provides us with proof of the viability of his system. Does he forgo all transcultural judgment, as he suggests we should? The choices made by societies cannot be compared to one another, he said. And yet a generalist ethnologist like Lévi-Strauss cannot prevent himself altogether from making comparisons and establishing typologies. But perhaps, even as he compares, he manages to avoid passing judgment? Perhaps he succeeds in remaining morally neutral? Let us take as an example the opposition he makes between traditional and modern societies. The absence of writing in the former and its presence in the latter lead Lévi-Strauss to note a difference in the very nature of human relations. What he calls "anthropology's most important contribution to social science" is that it introduced "this fundamental distinction between two types of social existence: a way of life recognized at the outset as traditional and archaic and characteristic of 'authentic' societies and a more modern form of existence, from which the first-named type is not absent but where groups that are not completely, or are imperfectly, 'authentic' are organized within a much larger and specifically 'unauthentic' system" (*Structural Anthropology*, 367). But is contrasting the two forms of society in this way any different from comparing them? And does calling one of them authentic and the other unauthentic still amount to abstaining from judgment?

Another example with respect to which "social anthropology would find its highest justification" (30) is his distinction between "hot" and "cold" societies; the ethnologist's role would now be to identify and to preserve social forms appropriate to each, forms that "correspond to a permanent hope for mankind over which social anthropology would have mission to keep watch, especially in the most troubled times" (*Structural Anthropology*, 2:30). But can one say of such a mission that it implies no transcultural judgment, no moral choice? Has Lévi-Strauss really succeeded in escaping the absurdity against which he sought to warn us? We are obliged to note that his ethical relativism is only another statement of principle, one that is not followed by its own enactment: Lévi-Strauss is no more able than anyone else to keep from passing judgments. More precisely, and in this he resembles Montaigne more than any of his great predecessors, his starting point is a relativism that, however radical it may be, does not keep him from praising primitive societies and criticizing our own. He professes relativism but practices primitivism—that is, an absolute hierarchy of values, even if it is not the hierarchy most commonly adopted by our society.

Lévi-Strauss in fact subjects the Western world, as it has been constituted since the Renaissance, to a discreet but decisive critique. The core aspect of the Western tradition he targets for criticism might be labeled "humanism."

It is true that Lévi-Strauss does not always use this word pejoratively. Sometimes he retains only a specific reference to the traditional scholarly "humanities"—that is, the study of Greek and Latin; this sort of "humanism" is then a first form of the study of cultures different from ours, and ethnology is nothing but the universal expansion, the logical outcome of that older humanism. But even in this rather specialized sense of the word, the critical element remains perceptible in Lévi-Strauss. "Anthropology [was] able to affirm itself as an enterprise renewing the Renaissance and atoning for it, in order to extend humanism to the measure of humanity" (*Structural Anthropology*, 2:32). Renewing and atoning: curiously, if the first term indicates continuity and presupposes the maintenance of the older project, only extended beyond the limits of "our narrow-minded humanism" (51), the second indicates on the contrary that the project itself was a sin rather than a benediction.

What Lévi-Strauss criticizes in Renaissance humanism, which is nothing but the logical outcome of Christian humanism, is thus not simply the fact that it has restricted its sampling of humanity to European cultures alone, while neglecting or spurning the cultures of the other continents: such a reproach would remain compatible with the project of humanism itself, for it would simply show that humanism's accomplishments have not lived up to its initial ambitions. The humanists of the Renaissance or of the eighteenth century saw themselves as universalists, whereas in reality their horizon ended at the edges of Europe; but these limits can be extended without changing the underlying project. What we have to expiate is not the lack of universal extension, which would require only a quantitative correction, after all; we have to atone for a different type of foreshortening, which is "vertical," as it were, rather than "horizontal": namely, the belief that human beings, to the exclusion of all other living species, are the ones who serve as the standard in all things, as the *raison d'être* and goal for every human activity. Humanism—and in this regard its name is not misused—has sought to organize the world around humankind: that is its sin, or more simply its mistake.

In a spirit close to that of other critiques of modernity (sometimes reminiscent of Heidegger, sometimes of ecological manifestos), Lévi-Strauss in fact criticizes, above all, the separation between man and nature, and the subjection of nature to man. "By isolating man from the rest of creation and defining too narrowly the boundaries separating him from other living beings, the Western humanism inherited from antiquity and the Renaissance has deprived him of a bulwark" (*The View from Afar*, 23). Western civilization has favored only the perfecting of purely technical mastery over the forces of nature; it "has been entirely devoted, for the last two or three centuries, to putting more and more powerful mechanical means at the disposition of man" (*Structural Anthropology*, 2:341–42). This is the state of affairs that Lévi-Strauss invites us to question.

It is not overstating the case to say that Lévi-Strauss shows affinities with an antihumanist ideology. He himself does not seem to care for the somewhat aggressive connotations of that label, but he nevertheless confirms the direction of his commitment. "I have often been reproached for being antihumanist," he says in an interview with Jean-Marie Benoist. "I do not believe that is true. What I have struggled against, and what I feel is very harmful, is the sort of unbridled humanism that has grown out of the Judeo-Christian tradition on the one hand, and on the other hand, closer to home, out of the Renaissance and out of Cartesianism, which makes man a master, an absolute lord of creation" ("Entretien" [Interview], 4). Unbridled or not, this is the only humanism we have within the Western tradition; to be against this "sort" of humanism is to be against the only doctrine that, in Europe, has ever been accorded—and rightly so—that name.

Lévi-Strauss (and here is the Heideggerian side of his critique) holds Descartes responsible for this anthropocentric revolution. This is not serious; what is more so is that he would put the opposing, antihumanist tradition under Rousseau's banner. "Exposing the flaws of a humanism decidedly unable to establish the exercise of virtue among men, . . . Rousseau's thinking can help us to reject an illusion whose lethal effects we can observe in ourselves and on ourselves" (*Structural Anthropology*, 2:41). "It is veritably the end of the Cogito which Rousseau proclaims in putting forward this bold solution" (38). Perhaps the reference to Rousseau (essentially to Rousseau the naturalist and autobiographer) gives Lévi-Strauss a better way to express his thought; but it must be said that he comes close to a misreading in his interpretation of Rousseau's position, which is inseparable from the humanist tradition (what is more, this tradition is inconceivable today without Rousseau's contributions). It is indeed on mankind, on human universality, that the Savoyard Vicar, Rousseau's spokesman, bases the exercise of virtue (and the Vicar, as has been noted, owes a good deal to Descartes); but in fact, in order to make Rousseau out to be the father of antihumanism, one has to disregard not only *Emile* and *On the Social Contract* but also the *Confessions* and the *Dialogues*.

It is this narrow Western humanism, an unfortunate amalgam of Christianity (the unity of the human race) and Cartesianism (man at the pinnacle of nature), which is guilty of all the evils that have befallen the world in the last one hundred fifty years. "All the tragedies we have lived through, first with colonialism, then with fascism, finally the concentration camps, all this has taken shape not in opposition to or in contradiction with so-called humanism in the form in which we have been practicing it for several centuries, but I would say almost as its natural continuation" ("Entretien," 4). This hidden continuity can be explained as follows: once one has established a definitive boundary between human beings and the other living species and has admitted that the latter may be sacrificed, in extreme cases, to the former, it is only a short step from here to dividing the human species itself into several categories, and acknowledging that the lowest category may be sacrificed for the benefit of the higher ones. It is in this respect that nineteenth-century colonialism and twentieth-century fascism are the natural offspring of humanism. Communist totalitarianism is not exempt from the same explanation: "The communist and totalitarian Marxist ideology is only a ruse of history to promote the accelerated Westernization of peoples who have remained on the outside until very recent times" (ibid.).

These considerations are undoubtedly marginal in Lévi-Strauss's work, and it is probably no accident that they appear in a newspaper interview rather than in one of his published texts. Nevertheless, they remain perfectly consistent with antihumanist principles, which are also present elsewhere, and they give a concrete meaning to more general propositions. That is why their examination may throw some doubt in turn on the principles themselves.

On the geological time scale, it is legitimate to ignore the opposition between totalitarianism and democracy, in favor of underscoring the common effects of industrialization or urbanization (Heidegger does this as well); it is a different matter if the unit of measure is a human lifetime. Stones and plants suffer perhaps as much under a tyrannical government as under a democracy, and from this viewpoint the one is only the historical ruse of the other; but the same cannot be said from the standpoint of human beings, who are obliged to live either inside or outside a totalitarian state. To say that Hitlerian fascism and the massive extermination of Jews it brought about are "almost natural" consequences of humanism implies not only that the speaker is disregarding or repressing the ideological origins of fascism in nineteenth-century *antihumanism* (in France, the racism of Gobineau, Renan, or Vacher de Lapouge—we shall come back to this point), but also that the speaker is willfully cultivating a logical paradox, since he is complacently deducing the thesis of the *inequality* of man on the basis of human *equality*. Finally, to attribute colonial expansion or the "division of Africa" to the humanist project of exporting the Enlightenment is to take at face value what was only propaganda: an attempt, most often a clumsy one, to replaster the façade of a building constructed for quite a different purpose. The reasons for the colonial conquest were political and economic, rather than humanitarian; if we wanted to look for a single general principle, it would be nationalism—which, as Rousseau understood, is incompatible with humanism (we shall come back to this, too).

The term "antihumanism" designates only the critical side of the doctrine, however; if we were to give it a positive label, we should perhaps speak of "naturalism." Lévi-Strauss in fact wants "man" to get back in line, to find a place—a more modest place than the one he has sought to occupy since the Renaissance—among the other living species, in a general natural order (here we are closer to the ecologists than to Heidegger). In the extreme case we may keep the label "humanism," provided we change its meaning: according to Lévi-Strauss, we must aspire to "a wisely conceived humanism, which does not center on man but gives him a reasonable place within nature, rather than letting him make himself its master and plunderer" (*The View from Afar*, 14). Man will then respect all forms of life and not just his own. But we may wonder whether this label—humanism—is still usable. Man has to be defined, writes Lévi-Strauss, "not as a moral but as a living being, since this is his most salient characteristic" (281–82). However, the term "living" clearly does not suffice to characterize man, since this is a feature man shares with ants; thus, what is in question here is not a new definition of humanity, but the replacement of human beings by living beings. Now one might wonder whether the blurring of the boundary between human and nonhuman does not risk favoring divisions between human groups. "Where shall we stop and draw the line?" Renan asked in the course of a similar meditation. "The animal also has its rights. Is the Australian savage to have the rights of man, or those of the animal?"

Thus, we may be somewhat surprised by Lévi-Strauss's effort to find a new basis for the rights of man, one that would make it possible to dispense with the concept of "man"—namely, the right to life. "These present projects offer France a unique opportunity to place the rights of man on a foundation that, except for a few centuries in the West, has been explicitly or implicitly accepted in all places and in all times" (*The View from Afar*, 284). But it is only during these few centuries, and only in the West, that it has been possible to raise the question of the rights of man, in the strict sense, and with good reason: it is of a piece with the humanist ideology. The new "basis" for the rights of man imagined by Lévi-Strauss consists in denying their relevance and in diluting them into a general right that would apply to living beings—but which would have the singular characteristic of being instituted by a minuscule number of those beings, namely those who speak (ants are not expected to participate in the deliberations that are to lead to the establishment of their rights).

Having rejected the basis for humanism (man's exceptional status in nature and the unity of the human race), Lévi-Strauss also quite logically criticizes its most obvious political consequences—that is, the modern concepts of freedom and equality. What is wrong with our idea of freedom is precisely its relation with universal humanism. "We cannot adopt a rationalist definition of freedom—thus claiming universality—and simultaneously make a pluralist society the place of its flowering and its exercise. A universalist doctrine evolves ineluctably toward a model equivalent to the one-party state" (*The View from Afar*, 285). Similarly, for Lévi-Strauss the affirmation of "the natural equality of all men" is "somewhat disappointing for the mind" (*Structural Anthropology*, 2:330). Let us note at once that a false argument is at issue here: humanism requires equality before the law and leaves open the question of natural equality or inequality. However, it is obvious that equality before the law is no better justified. If society is to improve, we have to maintain "those minute privileges, those possibly ludicrous inequalities that, without infringing upon the general equality, allow individuals to find the nearest anchorage" (*The View from Afar*, 287).

It is along the lines of the same rejection of humanist values that Lévi-Strauss seems to locate his condemnation of cultural intermixing. Here it should be stressed that he does not oppose all cross-cultural communication. A moderate level of communication, maintained within certain limits, even constitutes an undeniable advantage, one from which Europeans, and particularly Spaniards, benefited with respect to the populations they encountered on the American continent in the sixteenth century. Cortés and his companions certainly profited from their familiarity with other European cultures, with cultures of the past like those of the Greeks and the Romans, with cultures of Africa and Asia glimpsed in the course of their travels; conversely, the Aztecs' ignorance of cultures quite different from their own was a handicap, at least at first. This state of limited communication is what Lévi-Strauss calls "the coalition of cultures."

But if communication accelerates, then differences are blurred, and we advance toward the universalization of culture—that is, of one culture at the expense of the others. Now the disappearance of differences would be fatal for all cultures, and not simply for the most easily influenced among them. "There is not—there cannot be—a world civilization in the absolute sense which is sometimes given this term. For civilization implies the coexistence of cultures offering among themselves the maximum of diversity, and even consists in this very coexistence" (*Structural Anthropology*, 2:358). Beyond a certain threshold, communication is therefore harmful, for it leads to homogenization, which in turn is tantamount to a death sentence for humanity; and we have seen that for Lévi-Strauss any sort of universalization raises the specter of a one-party regime. Auguste Comte's utopian dream is for Lévi-Strauss a nightmare.

Gobineau, another enemy of intermixing and homogenization who is mentioned by Lévi-Strauss in the same context, had already faced this paradox. The strength of a culture is expressed through its capacity to influence other cultures; but each occasion for influence is an encounter, and each encounter a weakening. A fatality weighs upon the human race: a society's very strength is its undoing. Lévi-Strauss spells out what was simply a source of internal tension in Gobineau's text: "In order to progress, men must collaborate; and in the course of this collaboration they see the gradual pooling of their contributions whose initial diversity was precisely what made their collaboration fecund and necessary" (360).

Given this "double bind" (if you do not communicate you cannot win, and if you do communicate you are bound to lose), in the text entitled "Race and Culture" that opens his latest collection of essays (*The View from Afar*), Lévi-Strauss chooses the lesser of two evils: he opts against intercultural communication. It is impossible, he says in effect, to desire both cultural diversity and familiarity with cultures other than our own; for familiarity is the first step toward the disappearance of that diversity. It is better to stay home and remain unaware of others than to know them too well; it is better to send foreigners back across our borders than to let them submerge us and deprive us of our cultural identity. Rooting is preferable to uprooting. Lévi-Strauss thus rejoins the tradition of antihumanist French thinkers, from Bonald through Gobineau to Barrès, who are all strenuously opposed to the intermixing of cultures.

One might wonder about the political opportuneness of this doctrine, in an era when the nations of Western Europe are seeking to protect themselves against human invasions originating in the Third World. One might also question its moral rightness—although, as Lévi-Strauss has abandoned the attempt to provide a basis for the exercise of virtue in man, it is not certain that a "natural morality" would find the doctrine defensible. (But how are we to discover what is good for the entire set of living beings? Is it up to the scientists to tell us?) My purpose here is somewhat different: I propose above all to examine the doctrine's truth value and consistency.

Is it true that communication leads to homogeneity and that homogeneity leads to death? So baldly put, such affirmations will never be verified, or even falsified, so great is the distance between the observable facts and the abstract theorem that claims to account for them. It is certain that, as Comte had already seen, today's world is more homogeneous than yesterday's. Industrial society is gradually spreading; Western science is becoming the only science; the democratic ideal and the rights of man are being invoked in all regions of the globe. But must we see in all this an inexorable, irreversible process, with total indifferentiation at the end? I do not think so. Humanity in possession of universal communication will be more homogeneous than humanity without it; this does not mean that all differences will be suppressed. To suppose so implies that differences are the product of mutual ignorance alone: to believe this is to embrace unwittingly the very scientistic thesis proponents of difference would like to combat. If contemporary communications tend to bring people closer together, the weight of history, which will always be with us, pulls us (whatever Comte may have claimed) in the opposite direction. Moreover, the constitution of a universal state is not going to come about overnight, and human populations *need* to see themselves as different if only so they can conceptualize their own identity (the Canadian example comes readily to mind). The differences are displaced and transformed; they do not disappear.

Let me add one further remark. Familiarity with a foreign culture is not the chief reason for the disappearance of native cultures. Local traditions do not need to be subjected to foreign traditions to be destroyed. "Uprooting" is much greater in the move from a village to a suburban workers' enclave within the same country than it is in the case of exile: one is never as conscious of one's own culture as when one is abroad. If there is danger, it does not lurk behind the bush on which Lévi-Strauss has opened fire.

His reasoning runs into yet another difficulty. What he fears is the establishment of a single universal order. What he does, nevertheless, is issue recommendations about how a universal society ought to function. Human migrations and contacts among different ethnic groups are not determined by governments, still less by the society of nations. If Lévi-

Strauss's ideas were put into practice, if humanity were to combat the acceleration of contacts, would that not imply a concerted international effort, a first step toward that unwanted universal state? Is not interventionism, which Lévi-Strauss prefers to the liberal attitude of laissez-faire, the best illustration of precisely the universal decision making he dreads?

We cannot help wondering, finally, whether Lévi-Strauss is right to think that universal uniformity is an inevitable consequence of humanism (the term "universalist doctrine" would thus imply "one-party system"). We find two different types of universalism in Lévi-Strauss. One, which he accepts without hesitation, is the biopsychological identity of the species: this is, in a way, a "starting-point" universalism, unchallengeable but involving no choices at all. "What heredity determines in human beings is the general aptitude to acquire any culture whatsoever; the specific culture, however, will depend on random factors of birth and on the society in which one is raised" (*The View from Afar*, 18). That is what Lévi-Strauss also calls (at least in certain texts) the unconscious—atemporal and universal structural laws—or else the symbolic function, "which is carried out according to the same laws among all men" (203); however, these are pure forms without content. "The unconscious . . . is always empty—or, more accurately, it is as alien to mental images as is the stomach to the foods which pass through it" (*Structural Anthropology*, 203). On the other side, we find the bad universalism, or rather the false universalism, the one that is unwilling to recognize differences, the one that consists in a voluntarist—and, inevitably, unifying—project.

Yet if we look more closely, we find that there are not two universalisms but three (at least!). Alongside the first, which we have already mentioned, there is a universalism that could be called "end-point" universalism: this is the project of a universal State, with a homogeneous population, that we have encountered in certain texts of the Encyclopedists (for example, Condorcet) and their scientistic posterity. But in addition to these two types of universalism there is a third, which might be called a universalism of "itinerary," with the focus not on starting points or destinations but on the approach adopted (on method). If I succeed in communicating successfully with others, I have to imagine a frame of reference that encompasses their universe *and* my own. Aspiring to establish dialogue with "others" who are increasingly remote, we must indeed postulate a universal horizon for our search for understanding, even if it is clear that in practice I shall never encounter universal categories—but only categories that are *more universal* than others.

Lévi-Strauss never bothers to distinguish explicitly between "end-point" universalism and universalism of "itinerary." For this reason, his sometimes justified criticism of "end-point" universalism might seem to apply just as well to the intermediate variety, whereas this is not at all the case—as indeed the entire corpus of his own work attests. The image of trains traveling in various directions over which their passengers have no control does not provide a good description of the human condition. Man should be compared not with an island (*pace* John Donne) but with a fragment of a continent. Cultures are not trains thrust into chaos by a mad switchman. Interactions and even confluences are possible, if not inevitable.

Structural anthropology, as Lévi-Strauss likes to maintain, is at the other extreme from humanist philosophy. Focusing on the differences among societies, the ethnologist instinctively rejects the universal framework that emerged from the Enlightenment. For ethnology to come into being, "the concept of civilization—connoting a set of general, universal, and transmissible abilities—had to give way to the concept of culture in its new meaning: it now signified particular life styles that are not transmissible" (*The View from Afar*, 26). A culture does not transmit itself, any more than it tolerates being blended with other cultures. The two intellectual sources of ethnology are, if Lévi-Strauss is to be believed, equally hostile to humanism: these are the nationalist philosophy elaborated in Germany by Herder and Fichte on the one hand, and the conservative empiricism of Burke and Bonald on the other; all these doctrines are attuned to the differences (of nation, class, rank) that prevail among men, rather than to the unity of mankind.

A further opposition with humanism involves not the discipline as such but its structuralist version, with which Lévi-Strauss identifies. Humanism glorifies man, and in man, his distinctive feature, which is his subjectivity. Conversely, "structuralism reintegrates man into nature and . . . [makes] it possible to disregard the subject—that unbearably spoilt child who has occupied the philosophical scene for too long now, and prevented serious research through demanding exclusive attention" (*The Naked Man*, 687). If we want mankind to take its place in the line-up of species, we must indeed begin by depriving men and women of their specificity—in other words, their subjectivity. What Lévi-Strauss is seeking to eliminate here is not the subjectivity of the scholar (otherwise he would not speak of "reintegrating into nature") but the subjectivity of the creatures the scholar studies. Structuralism, in its Lévi-Straussian sense, is a method for studying human beings that refuses to take their subjectivity into account.

Lévi-Strauss is obviously not unaware of the fact that subjectivity is a constitutive feature of human beings. "The situation particular to the social sciences is different in nature; the difference is to do with the intrinsic character of the object of study, which is that it is object and subject both at once" ("Introduction à l'oeuvre de Marcel Mauss," in English *Intro-*

duction to the Work of Marcel Mauss, 29). In other words, human beings are subjects on the ontological level, but in the social sciences they become objects of knowledge (thus, they are objects on the epistemological level). Now there is no reason to confuse these two levels: the epistemological subject and object are purely relative concepts, synonymous with the observer and the observed, while the ontological subject and object are different substances, either human beings or things. Lévi-Strauss also knows perfectly well that this specific feature of the social sciences (the fact that their object is formed of "subjects") entails a moral precept that does not apply to specialists in the natural sciences: "Our science reached its maturity the day that Western man began to understand that he would never understand himself as long as there would be on the surface on the earth a single race or a single people whom he would treat as an object" (*Structural Anthropology*, 2:32).

If one is attempting to break with humanism, however, one must remove all traces of subjectivity from the object studied; this is the conclusion to which Lévi-Strauss is led. When Sartre uses the label "aesthetes" for those who attempt to "study men as if they were ants," Lévi-Strauss replies: "So I accept the characterization of aesthete in so far as I believe the ultimate goal of the human sciences to be not to constitute, but to dissolve man" (*The Savage Mind*, 247). We have to choose between two meanings of this somewhat enigmatic formula. Either Lévi-Strauss means that science has to analyze rather than accept indivisible entities (but beyond the fact that this is self-evident, it is hard to see how it would oblige us to treat men as if they were ants), or else (and this is more likely) he is suggesting that the practice of the human sciences implies that human beings are to be pulverized, dissolved like chemical substances. Confirmation of this second interpretation of Lévi-Strauss's sentence is provided by his definition of the task of the human sciences: "the reintegration of culture in nature and finally of life within the whole of its physico-chemical conditions" (ibid .).

In his study of myths, Lévi-Strauss puts us constantly on guard against any attempt to introduce the notion of the subject. "The elimination of the subject represents what might be called a methodological need" (*The Naked Man*, 628): myths have to be explained on their own terms, without reference to the will of the subjects who transmit them. Even psychoanalysis is not sufficiently vigilant with respect to myths, for psychoanalysis would allow the subject to be reconstructed on the basis of the concept of the "Other" and a metaphysics of desire; now "there can be no question . . . of smuggling the subject in again, under this new guise" (630). But it is not necessary to see in this exclusion a question of method, and thus of principle. The study of myths has nothing to do with the notion of the discourse-producing individual subject, for the good reason that myths are precisely discourses assumed by the collectivity: what is individual is by definition not a myth. Lévi-Strauss is perfectly aware of this, for he says in the same text: "In order to achieve the status of myth, the created work must cease precisely to be individual" (626). This perspective allows him to maintain the formula according to which men do not think in myths; instead, "myths operate in men's minds without their being aware of the fact" or even "as if the thinking process were taking place in the myths" (*Le cru et le cuit*, in English *The Raw and the Cooked*, 12). Yet when we are dealing with an individual author, the contrary is true: we cannot account for Rousseau's thought without questioning his intentions as a subject (and it is perhaps because he neglected this in his study of Rousseau that Lévi-Strauss produced an image bearing so little resemblance to the original). The exclusion of the subject does not follow from the method, nor does it impose a particular philosophical choice; it is the effect of the matter studied. Myths have no subject, whereas works do.

Sometimes Lévi-Strauss is even more radical, claiming that the need to eliminate the human is a consequence not of the structural method but of the scientific project itself. "Insofar as the human sciences succeed in producing truly scientific work, the distinction between the human and the natural must decrease for them. If ever they become sciences in their own right, they will cease to differ from the others" (*Structural Anthropology*, 2:294). Let us first eliminate a possible misunderstanding: the "human" is clearly opposed not to the "material" but only to the nonhuman. One may be a materialist and nevertheless recognize the difference between human and nonhuman—not in the physico-chemical composition of bodies but in behaviors and structures. With this understanding, it is hard to sympathize with a "truly scientific" work that will result in neglecting the distinctive feature of its object. The task of the human sciences, whatever the particular orientation of the scientist may be, can only be the explanation of what is specifically human; proving that there is no such thing may make the human sciences look more like the "hard" sciences, but it will not give us much insight into human beings, who for their part insist on behaving differently from minerals.

Illogical as it may appear, the elimination of human subjectivity is, in Lévi-Strauss's eyes, a necessity imposed by the very fact that one is practicing a science. But as we have seen, Lévi-Strauss is conscious of the moral and political dangers involved in treating others as objects, and he sees this necessity as something like a tragic contradiction. "Its [anthropology's] capacity to assess more objectively the facts pertaining to the human condition appropriately reflects, on the epistemological level, a state of affairs in which one part of mankind treated the other as an object" (55). His discipline owes its existence to the fact that "exotic cultures, treated by us as mere things, could be studied, accordingly, as things" (ibid.). From this viewpoint ethnology would be an evil, and ought to disappear.

It seems to me that we can reassure Lévi-Strauss and those who share his apprehensions: the evil in question is illusory. It is not because the human being becomes an object of knowledge that he becomes an object pure and simple: no internal necessity of the social and human sciences requires this. If the project of structural anthropology consists in reducing subjects to objects, thus in eliminating the human (but I find this hard to believe), it is the "structural" that is to blame, not the "anthropology." It is true that this discipline got a significant boost from nineteenth-century European colonial politics, and we cannot deny that "anthropology is daughter to this era of violence" (55). However, parents' flaws do not necessarily afflict their offspring; genesis is not synonymous with structure. There is nothing immoral in the attempt to understand human beings. What may be immoral is the use made of this understanding—for example, the reduction of persons to the status of things.

—TRANSLATED BY CATHERINE PORTER

References

Works of Claude Lévi-Strauss referred to in this article:

———. *Introduction to the Work of Marcel Mauss* (1950). Trans. Felicity Baker. London: Routledge and Kegan Paul, 1987.

———. *The Naked Man* (1971). Trans. John Weightman and Doreen Weightman. New York: Harper and Row, 1981.

———. *The Raw and the Cooked* (1964). Trans. John Weightman and Doreen Weightman. New York: Harper and Row, 1969.

———. *The Savage Mind* (1962). Trans. from the French. London: Weidenfeld and Nicolson, 1966.

———. *Structural Anthropology* (1958). Trans. Claire Jacobson and Brooke Grundfest Schoepf. New York: Basic Books, 1963.

———. *Structural Anthropology*, vol. 2 (1973). Trans. Monique Layton. New York: Basic Books, 1976.

———. *Tristes Tropiques* (1965). Trans. John Weightman and Doreen Weightman. New York: Atheneum, 1974.

———. *The View from Afar* (1983). Trans. Joachim Neugroschel and Phoebe Hoss. New York: Basic Books, 1985.

CHAPTER 2

Foucault

LUC FERRY AND ALAIN RENAUT

IN SEVERAL of our writings we have discussed what we have called the *antijuridism* of intellectual endeavors like that of Michel Foucault.[1] In a recent essay Gilles Deleuze denounces the "insults" of those who, not having forgiven Foucault for proclaiming the "death of man," now claim "that he offends the rights of man."[2] (Without naming names, Deleuze attacks those who "in opposition to Foucault . . . invoke a universal and eternal awareness of human rights," an idea that is "feeble or cursory, and [is] even unaware of those elements that might support it (such as the changes that have taken place in modern law since the nineteenth century)."[3] Deleuze does not discuss or refute this idea, but he does briefly respond to it when he asserts, somewhat paradoxically, that "there is no need to uphold the idea of man in order to resist."[4]

In his attempt to restore coherence and depth to Foucault's work, Deleuze maintains that social or political critique is not intrinsically connected to a metapositive reference to the values of the human. But if Foucauldian discourse is not to be viewed as deeply antijuridical, it must be able to account for resistance to power, even resistance to the law, without reference to the man whose death has been proclaimed. But we can see the difficulty of such an enterprise: if "there is no need to uphold man in order to resist," where do we find that dimension of exteriority in relation to power and positive law that can make resistance to the former and criticism of the latter possible? Deleuze's reply: "Is not the force that comes from the outside a certain idea of Life, a certain vitalism in which Foucault's thought culminates?"[5] This is where Foucault's thought connects up with Nietzsche's, as Deleuze correctly says. But the real question is whether there is actually an idea of resistance (particularly resistance to the law) that is compatible with the profound Nietzscheanism that, through vitalism, undoubtedly tinges Foucault's thinking? In other words, can Nietzscheanism as a philosophy of Life ground a political philosophy that makes it possible to resist unjust laws while sparing us a presumably untenable reference to the values of juridical humanism?

To examine the meaning and potentialities of this vitalist option, we can be guided by Deleuze's formulation of Foucault's Nietzscheanism: "Foucault's general principle," he writes, "is that every form is a compound of relations between forces."[6] How is this formula connected with a vitalism of Nietzschean inspiration? The connection is to be found in the following three theses of Nietzsche:

The first is that reality, in all its generality and diversity, has to be conceived in reference to the idea of Life: "Life . . . is for us the best-known form of being," says Nietzsche, and "our only representation of being is the fact of living."[7] Here is the "vitalism" of Nietzsche, who uses the will to attack the metaphysical (Platonic) conception of being as stability/permanence/immutability. In contrast to the ancient distinction between being and becoming, which is metaphysically assumed to be based on that between the real and the apparent, to think of being as life is to think of reality according to the ideas of change, metamorphosis, mutable diversity—in short, according to the idea of History.[8]

The second thesis is that life is to be conceived as the will to power: "My formulation is this: life is the will to power."[9] Or, as Zarathustra proclaimed: "Everywhere I have encountered the living, I have encountered the will to power." Hence it follows that if being is life, and if life is the will to power, then the will to power is "the most intimate essence of being."[10] In other words, all reality is based on the will to power: "The world seen from within . . . would be exactly the will to power and nothing else."[11]

But, as Nietzsche explains, the will to power is actually the will for *more* power. Hence, the second claim is explained by a third, which is that, because life is "essentially the effort toward more power," reality as a whole is understood as a multiplicity of struggles for power in which nothing is ever stabilized by the relations of domination.[12] Thus understood, reality is essentially an infinity of relations between forces in which each struggles to increase its domination or, in other words, its power. This expresses Deleuze's formulation of the "general principle" of Foucault's Nietzscheanism fairly well: "Every form is a compound of relations between forces." Everything that appears within reality (or history), all the forms taken by reality in its constant metamorphosis, are just manifestations of life as the will to power—as the struggle for power and its continual increase.

These three theses could also be applied to the sociohistorical field, which is precisely the dimension that Foucault chose to explore using this idea of life. This explains Foucault's conviction that everything social and historical must be analyzed "in terms of power," that is, using a method that analyzes all historical events as "terminal forms" in which are inscribed "the multiplicity of relations between the forces that are immanent in the sphere in which they operate."[13] We need to have a clear understanding of the representation of the political brought into play by this

Nietzscheanism, and in particular to appreciate the extent and meaning of the changes to which it subjects the traditional approach. In our view, the essence of these changes lies in the explicit refusal to analyze power in terms of right and law.

The rejection of the juridical analysis of power, which Foucault saw as the originality of his thinking about the political, had already clearly appeared in Nietzsche's definition of law as "the will to eternalize the present balance of power, provided one is satisfied with it."[14] Here, law is just one of the social or cultural forms that reflect a certain balance, by definition unstable, in the relations between forces. It is only a moment in the conflict between wills to power, with the advantage resting with those who are "satisfied" with these relations and exploit them in a bid for more power. Thus law is to the advantage of those whom Nietzsche calls the "strong." Here, on new philosophical foundations, we find a conception of law that was also expressed by the Marxist tradition, though with a few minor differences that Foucault very skillfully and carefully tried to highlight.[15]

Unlike the Marxists, Foucault did not reduce the question of power to a "binary and all-encompassing opposition between rulers and ruled at the root of relations between forces, and serving as a general matrix," nor did he root this opposition (ruling class/ruled class) in relations external to the forces themselves (economic relations, for example).[16] As a Nietzschean, Foucault denied that there is any single relation of power, postulating instead a nontotalizable multiplicity of relations that are irreducible among themselves and irreducible to the relation between the ruling and ruled classes. "Power is everywhere," he wrote, "it is produced from one moment to the next, at every point, or rather in every relation of one point to another."[17] Refusing to conceive of power "in a position of exteriority with respect to other types of relationships" in which they have their infrastructure, Foucault thus posited that relations of power are "immanent" in all types of relationships and "are not in superstructural positions."[18] In fact, they produce all the other forms of relationships and social activity (or are produced in them), playing the same role that the will to power played in Nietzsche. Unlike Marxism, however, the project here is said to be one of a "microphysics of power."[19] What is being posited a priori is not the existence of a "macro" relation of power (as between the exploiters and the exploited), capable of absorbing all the others into itself, but an infinity of powers that are intertwined, and beyond (or within) which there exists nothing in the social field that can be identified as their foundation. In contrast to the Marxist desire to "deduce" domination from exploitation, power in Foucault is posited as the alpha and omega of sociohistorical reality.

These refinements are not to be doubted. But they still do not broach the problem of the devalorization of law, which is reduced to one of the forms in which relations of power are said to be crystallized. In this way Foucault preserves the three main effects of any genealogical approach to law, whether the genealogy is done in Marxist fashion or according to the Nietzschean model.

The first such effect is to reduce the juridical sphere to euphemized violence, to the terms of strategy. Foucault, Deleuze imperturbably writes, "shows that the law is now no more a state of peace than the result of a successful war; it is war itself, and the strategy of this war in action."[20] Despite its difference from Marxism, Foucault's undertaking is here inscribed in a common intellectual structure, which is also shared by Pierre Bourdieu in his strategic analysis of social phenomena as techniques of domination and distinction.[21] Just as Deleuze underscored Foucault's understanding of law as "war," Bourdieu devoted a long article—significantly entitled "The Force of Law"—to setting forth "the global position of the juridical field in the sphere of power" and showing how everything in juridical work contributes to "social reproduction," that is, to the perpetuation of existing relations in society.[22]

Another inevitable effect of the genealogical approach to the law, one shared with Marxism, is the refusal to analyze power in terms of the law.[23] In fact, from a "vitalist" perspective, the "juridical-discursive conception of power"—that is, the idea that power should express what is right, in order to pronounce the law, and act according to the law thus expressed—must appear terribly superficial. When, for example, a power is criticized in the name of law for deviating from the rules of law, the rule of law is set up as a principle for evaluating power. But if, as the genealogist insists, law must be understood as merely one component of the relations between social forces, if it is merely one form of Life as the will to power, it cannot constitute the metapolitical standpoint from which to judge and criticize power.

As Foucault logically states, this refusal to analyze power in terms of law must go even further. It must deny not only the analysis and evaluation of power by reference to the rules of its own law but also the "much more radical" approach that attempts to judge power by the standard of "fundamental right."[24] Indeed—and here he is attacking the whole jusnaturalistic tradition—to postulate that "ideally and by nature, power must be exercised in accordance with a fundamental right" is still to grant law (in this case, the idea of law) a normative value that would presuppose its possible exteriority to power.[25] But such exteriority can only be an illusion once we realize that "every form is a compound of relations between forces." This must be true of positive law, and therefore of any idea of a "fundamental right," whether it derives from natural law or something else. In this vitalism, everything that happens is *immanent* in the deployment of life as the will to power and hence *immanent* in the complex web of relations between powers.

Ruling out the transcendence of any authority in relation to the deployment of life, Foucault's profound Nietzscheanism also excludes, by definition, the possibility that right, whether understood as the rule of law or fundamental right, could constitute a moment of escape from the numerous networks of power. Indeed, from this perspective, to analyze a network of power in terms of law or fundamental right would in reality mean to be trapped or mystified by power. Thus the introductory volume of Foucault's *History of Sexuality* attempts to demonstrate that the juridical conception of the political ("the principle that . . . law [has] to be the very form of power and that power always [has] to be exercised in the form of law") actually refers to a very precise stage in the history of power, specifically, the rise of the monarchy during the Middle Ages.[26] When the state as a unitary whole raised itself above the various feudal powers, it did so by giving itself the right to pronounce the law, arbitrating among the local powers, marking out their borders, and establishing hierarchies among them; consequently, the monarch, emerging as the one who expressed the law, developed a certain representation of power as the place of law. But Foucault, convinced that no "form" can be autonomous or transcend life or history, cannot imagine that the thing whose interesting genesis he sketches out could escape the conditions of its genesis. His genealogy convinces him that analyzing power on the basis of the "problem of law and violence, law and illegality" is to conceive of and analyze power only "in terms of a particular historical form that is characteristic of our societies: the juridical monarchy."[27] A "particular" form, and thus a "transitory" one, for although the monarchical power required this representation in order to impose itself, it later evolved and took forms that could not be reduced to the pronouncement of law. In short, the juridical could serve to represent and conceive a certain model of power, a historically specific moment of power, but we have perhaps been engaged "for centuries in a type of society in which the juridical is increasingly incapable of encoding power, of serving as its system of representation."[28] The conclusion is that we must now free ourselves from this representation of power as "a legal system" and thus not "take the law as a model and code."[29] That is, after uncovering its genealogy, we must abandon the analysis of power in juridical terms and analyze the legal system in terms of power.

It is easy to see that for Foucault, this abandonment of a "juridical model" is accompanied by a third effect, again shared with the Marxist tradition, which is the devalorization of the state based on law. If law is "the war itself," then the valorization of the legal state sacralizes the law only within the framework of a strategy, within a process of domination of which this valorization is itself merely one aspect. It is therefore not surprising, as Deleuze recognizes, that "Foucault never took part in the worship of the state based on law" and that, according to him, the "legalist conception" of power "is no more valid that the repressive conception."[30] In both cases, what is at stake are complex strategies of domination, and rather than judging one in the name of the other, one must describe the genesis of both.

It suits Foucault's logic very well that this threefold convergence between his analysis of power and the Marxist one ends up casting doubt on the values of the legal state. But this does not constitute a philosophical objection to such an approach. It is clear that criticism of it must here be internal and not appeal to values (such as those of law) whose soundness is in question. Of course, we are struck by the surprising disparity between the recent return of human rights and the intellectual survival of essentially antijuridical forms of thought. Nevertheless, this disparity does not constitute an argument.[31] The difficulties encountered by vitalism are actually quite different.

The limits of the Nietzschean philosophical option inspiring Foucault's and Deleuze's theses become clear when one considers the problem of legitimate resistance to power, particularly resistance to a law perceived to be unjust. From the vitalist standpoint, everything is power, a will to power that has taken form and crystallized. There is an "omnipresence of power," which Foucault clearly explains: "Power . . . is produced from one moment to the next, at every point, or rather in every relation from one point to another," which means that "power is everywhere; not because it embraces everything, but because it comes from everywhere."[32] But if, according to this "strategic model," everything is immanent in power, how is it possible to understand any social movement as a form of resistance to power? From what standpoint could we point to any "resistance"?

Foucault was mindful of the many faces of social creativity, and in the overall economy of his strategic analysis of politics we would expect him to make a place for the problem of points of resistance. Indeed, he says that the strategic model easily enables one to think of the emergence of resistance. Since power is a relation between forces, and every force struggles for more power and thus resists the power attempting to dominate it, "where there is power, there is resistance."[33] In short, the resistances "are the other term in relations between powers."[34] And if "power is everywhere," it is just as true to say that "points of resistance are present everywhere in the power network." In the analysis of the political, the substitution of the strategic model for the juridical model might thus seem to present no special problem. But if we consider the question more attentively, at least two problems arise.

First, if resistance must be conceived as the mere correlate of power, if it "is never in a position of exteriority in relation to the power,"[35] how can it be shown to be a resistance, and not an expression of power? In other words, the distinction between power and resistance to power seems arbitrary: they are simply two faces of "life as the will to power," with no difference in nature or value that might be grounded in the framework of this model. Faced with this first problem, Foucault might distinguish, as Nietzsche did, between active forces representing the movement of life (the "ascendant" will to power) and the purely reactive or defensive forces that, expressing a "decadent" will to power, attempt to petrify life and preserve their acquired power. Resistance would then correspond to the ascendant will to power, while the decadent one would be embodied in the established position of power. Such a solution, however, creates more problems than it resolves. From a perspective in which everything is "life," how can we valorize "movement" (the "ascendant" will to power) over "rest" (which is held to be "decadent") without surreptitiously introducing a value judgment that the whole analysis was supposed to spare us? This value judgment is revealed in an interview in which Deleuze explains that "if things are going badly in intellectual life today," it is because "all the analyses in terms of movements are blocked" owing to the return to "eternal values" such as those of human rights.[36] But isn't this simply to say that any resistance to power, any "movement," as soon as it is a "movement," represents an "ascendant" moment of life and must in this sense be held legitimate?

An analysis of power exclusively in strategic terms runs into a second problem that stems from its inability to resolve, or even pose, the classic question of legitimate resistance to a power or law that is held to be unjust. If resistance, because it is movement, is more "valid" than the power that is resisted (because the latter petrifies life), how can we judge, for example, resistance to racial laws to be legitimate and the resistance of terrorist groups against Western democracies illegitimate? If resistance is merely the ontologically inevitable correlate of all power, which "immobilizes" the very movement of being, it follows that phenomena of resistance are analyzable only in terms of relations between forces and not in terms of law. In that case, however, the conqueror is always right. Once again, it is history that, through the balance sheet of victories and defeats, becomes the "world's tribunal." Any resistance is then legitimated by the very fact that it is produced by a relation of power. But is this conclusion really acceptable?

According to Deleuze, the whole interest of the Foucauldian approach to the political is to show that "contrary to a fully established discourse, there is no need to uphold man in order to resist." Against the naïvetés of juridical humanism, vitalism now provides a far more insightful interpretation of power: "Life becomes resistance to power when power takes life as its object."[37] This utterance, which is meant to summarize Foucault's main contribution in this area, indicates much more cruelly its narrow limits.

In the modern philosophy of law, the reference to a human natural right had the effect of designating values transcending positivity, both metapolitical and metahistorical values. It thereby made possible the judgment and possible criticism of the historical forms of law by reference to a standard thought to transcend history. The critical function of the ideas of right and law was thus not only preserved but grounded. Within the framework of the vitalism expressed by Foucault, it is unclear what this critical function of right and law is based on. If everything is immanent in history (or life), how can one guarantee the distinction between facts and values, a distinction without which, as Leo Strauss clearly showed, the very notion of right loses its meaning? Faced with the multifaceted return to the idea of human rights in the 1980s, we find it timely to pose once again the question of right—to investigate its conditions of possibility, or, so to speak, its conditions of conceivability. The collapse of the metaphysical systems that underpinned the classic conceptions of natural right seems to us to demand a reconsideration of the question of right. The schools of thought most discussed during these past few decades offer more obstacles than promising leads in such an endeavor.

—Translated by Franklin Philip

Notes

1. See Luc Ferry and Alain Renaut, *Political Philosophy 3: From the Rights of Man to the Republican Idea*, trans. Franklin Philip (Chicago, 1992), 127; and *La pensée 68; Essai sur l'antihumanisme contemporain* (Paris, 1985), 163.
2. Gilles Deleuze, *Foucault*, trans. Seàn Hand (Minneapolis, 1988), 1.
3. Ibid., 90.
4. Ibid, 92.
5. Ibid., 124.
6. Ibid., 92–93.
7. Friedrich Nietzsche, *The Will to Power*, trans. Walter Kaufmann and R. H. Hollingdale (New York, 1968), vol. 2, §41 and §8.
8. Life (or History) is here understood in the Bergsonian sense as the "continual creation of unforeseeable novelties." It is also why Nietzsche wrote that life is a "woman" (*The Gay Science*, §339: "Vita femina"), that is (according to his perception of femininity), the locus of the least foreseeable metamorphoses and transfigurations, and also the locus of an interplay of appearances.
9. Nietzsche, *The Will to Power*, vol. 2, §246. See also vol. 3, §8.
10. Ibid., vol. 2, §4.
11. Nietzsche, *Beyond Good and Evil*, trans. Walter Kaufmann (New York, 1966), §36.
12. Nietzsche, *The Will to Power*, vol. 2, §41.

13. Michel Foucault, *The History of Sexuality*, trans. Robert Hurley (New York, 1978), 92. See Nietzsche, *The Will to Power*, vol. 2, §487.

14. In Foucault's *History of Sexuality*, it is through reference to this rejection that the "stakes" and "method" of the history of sexuality are defined as research on the "type of knowledge about sex" characteristic of our society. See Nietzsche, *The Will to Power*, vol. 2, §487.

15. Foucault, *History of Sexuality*, 121–22. For the most part, these pages repeat an unpublished course Foucault gave in 1973 at the Collège de France on the "postulates of power" in which he underscores his divergences from the Marxist conception (the five postulates demanded are repeated on 93ff.).

16. Ibid., 94.

17. Ibid., 93.

18. Ibid., 94.

19. Michel Foucault, *Discipline and Punish*, trans. Alan Sheridan (New York, 1977), vol. 3, chap. 1.

20. Deleuze, *Foucault*, 30. See Foucault, *History of Sexuality*, 86, 100.

21. Deleuze himself makes the comparison in his *Foucault* (74).

22. *Actes de la recherche en sciences sociales* (September 1986).

23. Foucault, *History of Sexuality*, 107, 120.

24. Ibid., 88.

25. Ibid.

26. Ibid., 89.

27. Ibid., 90. Foucault explains that modern power functions "not for right but for technology, not for the law, but for normalization, not for punishment, but for control."

28. Ibid., 89.

29. Ibid., 88–89: "The legal system of itself was *merely* a way of exerting violence" (emphasis added).

30. Deleuze, *Foucault*, 136–37.

31. In passing, we can only wish good luck to those who have undertaken to find, in Foucault's thinking, material for constructing a "new philosophy of law."

32. Foucault, *History of Sexuality*, 93.

33. Ibid., 95.

34. Ibid., 96.

35. Ibid., 96.

36. *L'Autre Journal*, no. 8 (1985).

37. Deleuze, *Foucault*, 92.

CHAPTER 3

Bourdieu

PHILIPPE RAYNAUD

PIERRE Bourdieu's position within French thought might best be defined as a novel attempt to combine three schools of thought: sociology, the Marxist critique of domination and theory of ideologies, and Gaston Bachelard's epistemology. Bourdieu's originality lies in his intent to confront sociological theory with empirical reality without losing the sharp distinction between science and ideology. This project is what originally set his work apart from that of Louis Althusser and his students.

In an article that seemed to target Althusser, Bourdieu clearly showed how "the claim to dominate empirical knowledge and the sciences producing it leads, in this variant of philosophical ambition, to the claim of deducing the event from the essence, the historically given from the theoretical model."[1] For Bourdieu, this necessarily went hand in hand with "a science without scientific practice, a science reduced to juridical discourse about the science of others." Bourdieu's own desire to produce positive sociological knowledge, not simply elucidate a priori the concepts of historical materialism, established the need for a sociology that could include statistical data not produced by theory. Nonetheless, while Bourdieu challenged the most openly speculative aspects of the early Althusser, it is important to note that he also preserved the core of Althusser's theory of ideology. This theory asserts that although there is a sharp discontinuity between ordinary consciousness and science, it is still possible to account for the irrationality of ordinary consciousness in a theory of ideology that forms an integral part of either the science of history (Althusser) or of sociology (Bourdieu).

Thus, the real effect of moving from Althusser's speculative theory of history to Bourdieu's positive sociology is simply to reinforce the position of the "scientist." However, by displacing the problematic to positive sociology, Bourdieu still preserves the principal benefits of Althusser's project. Because the discontinuity between ordinary consciousness and knowledge is unquestioned, it is possible for both thinkers to reject in advance any objections based on a naive reading of the "facts," since it is assumed that nothing is given, all is constructed. Moreover, both claim that what lies at the root of such objections is a social bias, not a theoretical interest. Althusser's merit was to have made explicit this sort of argument, which sniffs out the bias behind all theoretical objections and dismisses practical ones as nonscientific. Thus, the ability of a work like Bourdieu's *Distinction* to respond in advance to such objections perhaps stems less from the strength of his sociological model than from the epistemological and polemical strategy preceding the model's construction.[2]

In the first two works that established Bourdieu's name we can see how he went progressively from analyzing specific problems in the French educational system to propounding a general theory of that system, employing an original and subtle form of functionalism.[3] The basic idea behind Bourdieu's argument is that the French educational system tends to reproduce social relations, both in their hierarchical structure and in the social recruitment of "agents" for the system. This argument provokes three possible objections: that the educational system has its own rules of functioning and reproduction, which appear to be autonomous; that the educational system, by replacing heredity with the selection of elites through exams, ensures a certain social mobility; and that the scholastic and social paths of students appear to be the effect of their own personal choices and efforts. Bourdieu's response, which crops up in innumerable concrete analyses, is both simple and profound, elegant and conventional. It consists in reversing the terms of the problem and in positing that the system realizes its goal through the very thing that appears to contradict it. That is, the relative autonomy of the educational system is actually the condition for its reproduction. This is so because the causal effects of the educational subsystem are also distorting: the dominating and dominated "agents" of the system reach their social destiny under the illusion of having exercised their individual liberty. The system can therefore reproduce itself precisely because it gives the appearance of not reproducing, thereby masking the real contradictions in reproduction.

What Bourdieu brings to sociology is nothing more than the philosophical scheme that Hegel perfected in his theory of the "cunning of reason." The problem is always the same: if God's work is universally intelligible (Leibniz), and reality is rational (Hegel), or if society reproduces itself as a system (Bourdieu), then how can one explain what does not fit into the system? The answer, from Hegel to Bourdieu, has always been the same: reason realizes itself in its other, in what seems to contradict it.

The scheme of the "cunning of reason" appears frequently in political philosophy: in theories of how private vice becomes public virtue (Mandeville); how the individual "strategies" of economic subjects on the market merge with the general interest (Adam Smith); how humanity must take the bloody road of war to achieve peace (Kant); how the class struggle is the condition for the advent of a classless society (Marx). One might argue that all sociological theory encounters such a scheme once it adopts a functionalist perspective. It must be noted, however, that the validity of the scheme is strictly independent of the empirical material used, which means that it cannot be proved by accumulating examples. Likewise, it is difficult to reconcile this scheme with a theory attributing the logic of the social system to the will of those who dominate, or to make sense of social change.

The "cunning of reason" appears in both Bourdieu's *Reproduction* and *Distinction*, in ways that often make one's head spin. If, as a teacher, I follow a pedagogy that is classic, rhetorical, and structured, I am said to conform perfectly to the model of education invented by the Jesuits to educate elites. If, on the other hand, I adopt a flexible style, I am still said to favor those who have acquired legitimate culture outside of school. If, as an intellectual, I like Schönberg or Kandinsky, I personify the "formalist" spirit of modern culture, which (according to Bourdieu) tries to eliminate the substantial raw material of popular experience. But if I like Verdi or lowbrow novels, it is because I can appropriate popular material and dispossess those to whom it rightfully belongs. Even if I am a gourmet I can no longer innocently prefer beer to vintage wine, or hot dogs to foie gras. The "cunning of reason" is particularly visible in *Distinction*, through the binary opposition "vulgar/distinguished." Bourdieu finds this opposition at work throughout contemporary culture: sensual taste is contrasted to reflective tastes, popular theater to avant-garde theater, substance to form, the simple taste for food to table manners, and so on.

Two lengthy citations from *Distinction* show how Bourdieu's original scheme has found a newly expanded field. Regarding the use of scholastic capital, he shows how subjects "choose" the destiny actually assigned to them by the system:

> The hysteresis effect is proportionately greater for agents who are more remote from the educational system and who are poorly or only vaguely informed about the market in educational qualifications. One of the most valuable sorts of information constituting inherited cultural capital is practical or theoretical knowledge of the fluctuations of the market in academic qualifications, the sense of investment which enables one to get the best return on inherited cultural capital in the scholastic market or on scholastic capital in the labour market. . . . By contrast, the hysteresis effect means that the holders of devalued diplomas become, in a sense, accomplices in their own mystification, since, by a typical effect of *allodoxia* ("misapprehension"), they bestow a value on their devalued diplomas which is not objectively acknowledged.[4]

Regarding contemporary culture, he then remarks:

> Culture is the site, par excellence, of misrecognition because, in generating strategies objectively adapted to the objective chances of profit of which it is the product, the sense of investment secures profits which do not need to be pursued as profits; and so it brings to those who have legitimate culture as a second nature the supplementary profit of being seen (and seeing themselves) as perfectly disinterested, unblemished by any cynical or mercenary use of culture.[5]

Bourdieu's theory of domination is then said to show how formal liberal democracy achieves its real goal (domination) by negating its apparent goal (citizenship). Abstentionism, he writes, plays "a role in the functioning of liberal democracy," "helps maintain the established order," and "is perhaps not so much a hiccup in the system as one of the conditions of its functioning as a misrecognized—and therefore recognized—restriction on political participation."[6]

The particular significance of the "cunning of reason" in Bourdieu's work now becomes apparent. Compared to its use by liberals such as Mandeville or Smith, the scheme he has developed plays a more complex role in the relationship between individual strategies and society. For Bourdieu, each individual's pursuit of his private interests no longer merges with the general interest. That is because the incapacity of the dominated to understand their interests—a failure manifested in depoliticization or in the choice of useless degrees—simply reinforces their submission. Meanwhile, the choice of useful degrees or exercise of "legitimate" cultural tastes appear to the privileged classes as free choices, not as parts of a strategy of domination. Thus what initially appeared difficult to reconcile in Bourdieu's thought—Althusser's theory of ideology and the "cunning of reason"—can now be brought together. Here the essential category is misrecognition (*méconnaissance*) conceived both as the means of reproduction of the system and the general structure of subjective experience, against which "science" constructs itself. The privileged example of misrecognition is the illusion of liberty, whether it be "raw" liberty rebelling against social prohibitions, ethical liberty, or "disinterested" aesthetic judgment.

Here, we arrive at the point where the link between scientific sociology and social criticism is most evident, where the social scientist's subjective "commitment" can be recognized. The illusion of liberty is the ultimate misrecognition that must be eliminated to understand reality. But it also must be eliminated in order to criticize reality with a view to changing it, since misrecognition is both the epistemological obstacle to understanding the social system and the means of its reproduction. It is no wonder, then, that the author of *Distinction* focuses his arguments on the various forms taken by this illusion, which inspires the most brilliant analyses of the work.[7] Undoubtedly, if "the bourgeois claim to the status of the person" has prevented us from seeing that we are automata most of the time, then unveiling hidden determinisms will not be enough. Each time Bourdieu reveals the misrecognized source of our actions, it comes as no surprise that he also invites us to abandon our illusionary subjectivity.

If belief in liberty is the ultimate misrecognition, it remains to be demonstrated how this illusion works. According to Bourdieu, among the old *petite bourgeoisie*, the illusion is embodied in a kind of asceticism that moralizes politics and promotes the abstract universalism of the law, thus dissimulating real social conflicts. The new *petite bourgeoisie*, on the other hand, identifies with the cult of originality, "nature," and personality. They maximize misrecognition by psychologizing their perception of the social, by cultivating as natural the product of cultural inculcation, and last but not least, by supplying the economy "with the perfect consumer, about whom economic theory has always dreamed."[8]

As convincing as these analyses might appear, they always leave a lingering doubt about whether the subjects' perceptions of their own activities have any independent meaning. This doubt is reinforced by the fact that any reductionism showing a value system to be constructed on illusory liberty is potentially applicable to a competing system of values or (in Bourdieu's terms) "habitus." Bourdieu himself is quick to point this out:

> The endeavor to objectify a social ethic—especially a young and therefore aggressively imposed one—of course entails many dangers; lucidity may be no more than the effect of adherence to a contrary ethic. Each of the words used to characterize two antagonistic moralities can of course function as insults for champions of the opposite morality; it is therefore futile to hope to find a perfectly "neutral" tone (the psychoanalytic vulgate, for example, will identify "ascetic" with "masochistic"). In each case, one would need to restore the experimental content of what is sociologically objectified (e.g., the heroic dimension of the ascetic striving for virtue, which takes its pleasure in effort and in the exaltation of self-transcendence, or the generous innocence of the liberationist cult, which is based on an acute sense of the absurdity of social constraints and stakes); and, as has constantly been done here, the dispositions described have to be referred to their conditions of production: repressive dispositions, for example, have to be seen as the product of repression (or social regression).[9]

What is not self-evident is how any meaning could be bestowed on such matters within Bourdieu's system. It appears that the only way the different attitudes described above could pretend to truth would be as moments of reproduction of the social whole. In that case, however, any critique of the social whole itself would have to be renounced. This has been known since Hegel: the "cunning of reason" cannot be used *both* to exclude an autonomous perspective on society *and* to maintain the requirement of systematic rationality. The idea that the real is the rational must be accepted without qualification.

It would thus seem that Bourdieu's project ends with a potentially fatal split between sociological science and the subject developing it. Nevertheless in *Distinction* there are hints at a possible solution to this problem. For Bourdieu, misrecognition is most at home in politics, where the illusion of liberty takes the bourgeois form of the claim to personal opinion, and where the dispossession of the working classes is manifested by abstentionism. Abstentionism reveals the "hidden restriction on political participation" behind formal equality and democracy. But according to Bourdieu, this apparently total political alienation might be the means by which misrecognition can be conquered and domination overcome. For the effect of political dispossession is not only to reproduce domination. It also allows the most dominated of the working classes to evade the illusion of personal opinion, thereby opening the only road possible:

> Even a rapid reflection on the social conditions of the creation of demand for a "personal opinion" and of the achievement of this ambition is sufficient to show that, contrary to the naive belief in formal equality before politics, the working-class view is realistic in seeing no choice, for the most deprived, other than simple abdication, a resigned recognition of status-linked incompetence, or total delegation, an unreserved remission of self . . . , a tacit confidence . . . which chooses its speech in choosing its spokesmen.[10]

If the pseudorationality of the social system is achieved by its apparent contradictions, it is hardly surprising that the road to emancipation for the dominated classes lies in the total and unreserved alienation of their identity to "the party." Using other means, Bourdieu's work thus fits into a continuous current in French culture, one that Sartre depicted in *The Communists and Peace*. Like Sartre in his time, Bourdieu appears to believe that the only alternative to the political emptiness of the proletariat lies in its total submission to "the party," in a "dialectical" reversal that only the theoretician understands. The structure of Bourdieu's sociological reasoning, however, allows him to solve a problem that plagued Sartre's thought. While for Sartre the party should have jolted the people's consciousness from the outside, for Bourdieu misrecognition is the highest quality of the people. Bourdieu's insistence on the cultural dispossession of the dominated classes might now be better understood. Ignoring the symbolic or "scientific" forms once produced by popular cultures, Bourdieu uses the continuity of dispossession to present their current state of decline as the sign of what they embody, a vulgar state of nature to be contrasted with refined culture. Perhaps this is why his work does not treat contemporary social movements sympathetically: they have become too bourgeois for him.

The consequences of Pierre Bourdieu's approach to contemporary society can now be seen more clearly. If any subjective claim is gradually reduced to misapprehension; if rights only reflect the system of domination called formal democracy; if revealing latent determinisms undermines all claim to be a subject with rights—if all this is true, one must simply give up. It is hard to see what other choice remains for the learned but to submit to the objective objectification of sociology, and for the lowly to submit to those who claim to speak in their name.

There is another possibility, of course, which is to change our point of departure, reconsidering the "bourgeois" claim to the status of the person and subjecting it to the discipline of reason and an understanding of the social fabric. Who knows? The idea of rights might still have something to teach us.

—Translated by Ann T. Gardiner

Notes

1. Pierre Bourdieu, "Marx, lecteur de Balibar," *Actes de la recherche en sciences sociales* (November 1975).
2. Pierre Bourdieu, *Distinction: A Social Critique of Taste*, trans. Richard Nice (Cambridge, Mass., 1984).
3. Pierre Bourdieu, *The Inheritors: French Students and Their Relations to Culture*, trans. Richard Nice (Chicago, 1979), and *Reproduction in Education, Society and Culture*, trans. Richard Nice (London, 1977).
4. Pierre Bourdieu, *Distinction*, 142.
5. Ibid., 86.
6. Ibid., 398.
7. See in particular chap. 6, "Cultural Goodwill."
8. Ibid., 371. Translation slightly revised.
9. Ibid., 586, n. 38.
10. Ibid., 417.

PART TWO

Reconsiderations

THE NEW FOCUS on liberal society within French political philosophy has gone hand in hand with a reconsideration of the history of liberal thought. Today there is less interest in simply recounting that history than in learning from past liberal thinkers, and from their mistakes, when engaging in political philosophy. This critical historical approach is apparent in several different philosophical "reappropriations." In their essay on Kant, for example, Luc Ferry and Alain Renaut make the case for a new "critical" philosophy of the subject as an alternative to the dogmatic historicisms of Hegel and Heidegger, who both proclaimed the "end" of philosophy. Philippe Raynaud's thoughtful appreciation of Benjamin Constant is a good example of the recent recovery of nineteenth-century liberalism and its characteristic concern with the era opened up by the French Revolution. Foremost among those liberals was Tocqueville, who today is the object of serious study and widespread admiration. One dissenter in this chorus is Marcel Gauchet, who in his much discussed essay on *Democracy in America* claims that Tocqueville misunderstood European political history by seeing it exclusively through an American lens. Gauchet maintains that the force of the human rebellion against traditional religion that Tocqueville sensed was in fact more profound than he imagined, and that its historical end must be the death of God and a more contentious secular politics.

CHAPTER 4

Kant and Fichte

LUC FERRY AND ALAIN RENAUT

There are three ways of understanding the so-called end of philosophy, each of which is rooted in a way that philosophy understands itself. The first comes directly from the Hegelian conception of philosophy and, correspondingly, from the history of philosophy. When philosophy is conceived as a system of knowledge, its history has the appearance of a progressive systematization of thought, with each thinker since Greek antiquity thus making his contribution to the edifice of philosophy, up to the final closure in which the truth appears as the totality of one-sided moments that have been surpassed. This notion is well known. Everyone, whatever his philosophical outlook, now seems to recognize, if not the "success" of this venture, at least its completion.[1] Even if this notion is sometimes liable to cause confusion and needs to be spelled out in greater detail, on the whole it seems justified: the project of making reality totally intelligible that began among the Greeks really reaches its "culmination" in Hegel's obliteration of any difference between the real and the rational.

A second notion of the "end of philosophy" is most fully illustrated in Heidegger's thought, which then stimulated French philosophy in the 1960s. Paradoxically, this Heideggerian notion also sees Hegelianism as the "height of metaphysics" and thus as the "end of philosophy."[2] For Heidegger and his heirs, however, the point is to show that what Hegel describes as the victory of philosophy is actually its supreme failure. By systematizing the identity of the real and the rational, philosophy in fact "forgets" what its "business" or "task" is: openness to "Being" as the "ontological difference." Consequently, by asserting the rationality of the real—even of what seems to be irrational (war, conflict, contradictions)—through the "cunning of reason," the Hegelian system completes philosophy as a (metaphysical) project of rationality. But in remaining heedless of the dimension of "mystery," of the nonrationality inherent in existence, the Hegelian system leaves open a path for a kind of thinking that would no longer be philosophy, and whose task would be to grasp the enigma of "difference." This way of thinking would rediscover its proximity to poetry or to a kind of writing different from conceptual (metaphysical and scientific) writing, or alternately it would renew a dialogue with the first Greek thinkers, who predated Plato's transformation of thought into philosophy and thus escaped the philosophy of identity. This notion of the "end of philosophy," which gives rise to what Gilles Deleuze called a "generalized anti-Hegelianism," has thus inspired a number of strategies of "avoidance," through which, as Michel Foucault put it, "our whole age, whether through logic or epistemology, whether through Marx or through Nietzsche, is attempting to flee Hegel."[3] The aim is to regain access to an "unthought," to some "other" that the concept vainly attempted to reduce to the "same." We even see this in Leo Strauss's political philosophy, whose theme is a return to the Greeks as an alternative to the Hegelian completion of modernity, which in successive waves has occluded the essence of the political.

There is, however, a third possible notion of the "end of philosophy." It is less familiar than the first two but also less threadbare, since it has been far less present in the debates of the past two decades. We are referring to the kind of philosophical *criticism* that marks the thinking of Kant and the young Fichte and thematizes the project of a systematic and basically completed deconstruction of metaphysical illusions. For contrary to common opinion, critical philosophy does indeed contain the idea of a completion of philosophy. The famous adage that "one does not learn philosophy, one just learns to do philosophy" in no way means that philosophical activity merely consists of a pedagogically valuable method for thinking. Kant is very clear on this point; the *Critique of Pure Reason* set out to unmask, once and for all, the structure of philosophy, which can only move within the framework of *dogmatism* (which asserts the possibility of a true grasp of the whole), *skepticism* (which absolutely denies this possibility), and *criticism* (which tries to resolve the antinomy between the first two models of philosophy). The criticist idea of the end of philosophy, which reaches its culmination in Fichte's first *Doctrine of Science*, appears to be the exact opposite of Hegelianism; Hegel attempted a complete systematization of all that was true, Fichte undertook a no less complete systematization of all false viewpoints.[4]

If we see the status and project of this systematization correctly, it could indeed be philosophically fruitful, insofar as it makes the end of philosophy (as a system) compatible with the pursuit of philosophical activity (as criticism). Such compatibility is necessary if philosophical activity is to escape the difficulties of its present situation. We recognize, however, that this assertion runs into immediate difficulties. From the viewpoint of contemporary historical consciousness, it seems paradoxical to reactivate a philosophical position that predates Hegelianism and Heideggerianism, which today seem to be the unsurpassable horizon of our thinking about the end of philosophy. Critical philosophy appears to have been doubly superseded: first by Hegelianism, in that critical philosophy partakes of Enlightenment rationalism; and then by Heideggerianism, in that its critique of metaphysics still remains captive to this rationalism.[5]

This objection surely merits examination. Explicitly resting on the conviction that the history of philosophy has developed in a linear fashion (whether as progress or decline), it testifies to philosophy's difficulties freeing itself of historicist postulations, even when it claims, as with Heidegger, to escape Hegelianism altogether. Curiously, Hegel's and Heidegger's periodizations of the history of philosophy match up almost perfectly, since both regard as obvious the division between "ancient" and "modern" and the idea of a development within modernity that leads ineluctably from Descartes to the system of identity via Leibniz, Spinoza, Kant, Fichte, and Schelling.[6] It is particularly significant in this regard that a thinker like Leo Strauss, who made historicism a major theme of his work, never questioned this view of historicity as linearity and devoted himself to demonstrating, within political philosophy, how all modernity—despite what "seems" to separate Hobbes, Machiavelli, or Rousseau—merely advances the same destruction of the idea of "natural right." The obsession with the new that characterizes the phenomenological deconstruction of Hegelianism apparently does not guarantee a real break with Hegelianism.

Clearly, reactivating a pre-Hegelian and pre-Heideggerian model of thinking creates a problem only for those who remain immersed in historicism. It is a paradox only from the viewpoint of the Hegelian and Heideggerian conceptions of philosophy's "end." It disappears for the critical viewpoint that sees in these two versions of the history of philosophy an antinomy to be overcome. The fundamental antinomy pervading the whole history of philosophy continues to spark the main contemporary debates and is found most notably in the confrontation between the two noncritical versions of the "end of philosophy."[7] This antinomy opposes, on the one side, the dogmatic thesis of a complete subjection of the real and of history to the principle of sufficient reason, thus making the causal *nexus* the principle of continuity and (logical) necessity of historical processes; it is best expressed in Hegel's statement that everything in history had unfolded "rationally." On the other side is the skeptical antithesis of an absolute resistance of the real and history to being treated according to the categories of identity and rationality; this is expressed in Heidegger's statement that "the rose is without a why, it blooms because it blooms." In this view, historical eras continue to be conceived according to the idea of necessity (since to speak of contingency would be to treat what happens from the viewpoint of reason), but according to a necessity that is more mysterious than logical, a kind of sending (*Geshick*) without sender or receiver.

It is clear that the opposition between these two models of historicism, Hegelian and Heideggerian, can be deconstructed on the basis of the critical analysis of antinomies. In this case the antinomy is between a dogmatism for which (because the real limitlessly conforms to the demands of reason) the totalization of the true is completed to the point of absolute knowledge, and a skepticism according to which (because nothing justifies imagining the conformity of the real with the principles of our reason) the very idea of truth loses all meaning. An analysis that took the terms of this antinomy as its guiding thread would reveal a great deal about contemporary models of thinking, particularly the forms of neoskepticism or neosophistry in which the pursuit of a "generalized anti-Hegelianism" has exhausted itself over the past two decades. For our present purposes, however, it is enough to see that philosophical criticism is not simply a stage that has been superseded in the history of thought, that it remains a way of thinking through the confrontation between the two chief protagonists of its so-called supersession. The critical viewpoint permits the thinking through of contemporary thought and thereby restores a meaning to the idea of reflection.

If philosophy is finished as the attempt to produce systems, it has no chance of survival if it claims to withdraw into itself. It can only open itself to its other, either the various disciplines of knowledge or historical reality itself, without becoming lost in them. From this perspective, two paths currently seem possible for philosophical activity, one aiming through criticism to establish an ethics of communication, the other considering the horizons of meaning implicit or explicit in all empirical study. Given the limited and programmatic nature of this article, we shall confine ourselves (at the risk of fostering certain misunderstandings) to suggesting some possible applications of these two sorts of philosophical activity, with no attempt to sketch their systematic structure. These examples are taken from the historical sciences, but it might be possible to find their analog in the so-called exact sciences.

To grasp the meaning of what we call critical activity, let us return to the antinomy between the Hegelian-Marxist thesis asserting the validity of the principle of reason and the Heideggerian thesis denying it, which is a paradigm of the noncommunication characteristic of current philosophical debates. We can take one of three possible attitudes toward this antinomy. The first would be to follow the logic of one of the two camps and try to show, in a genealogical war, the inadequacy or absurdity of the opposing position. We say a genealogical war, for under these conditions it is indeed a matter of an external criticism that inevitably takes the form not only of a description of the error but of a genetic analysis of its origin. (For example, if Heideggerianism leads to irrationalism, it is no accident with regard to its historical emergence; or if Hegelianism or Marxism forgets the dimension of mystery inherent in existence, this "forgetfulness" is the sign of a naïveté in the face of the task of thinking, and so forth.) If this attempt to appropriate otherness is judged inadequate, a second approach would be to postulate the existence of an irreducible multiplicity of worldviews, any rational discussion among them being absurd, since in the last analysis these views are rooted in an ethical choice that lies outside the sphere of reasonable communication. The antinomy must then be thought of, to repeat the Nietzsche-inspired formula of Max Weber, as an "inexpiable war between the gods."

These two attitudes—that of genealogical war and the war of the gods—have a common ground. They both take the fact of noncommunication as obvious and thus legitimate a kind of violence, so to speak. On the other hand, the third attitude, that of internal criticism, retains the *Idea* of a unity of reason and thus reestablishes the legitimacy of communicational ethics. The critical solution to the antinomy of rationalism and irrationalism may serve as an illustration. In principle it consists in showing that the antinomy is due only to a reification or "ontologization" of reason. A conflict exists only because both the thesis and the antithesis are designed to settle a question that is meaningless or, more precisely, dogmatic: the question of whether or not the principle of reason is truly inscribed in things themselves, in nature or history. (Hence the series of utterly pointless questions, such as whether the emergence of the state is explicable, as the Marxists suggest, or "without a reason," as certain anthropologists assert; whether totalitarianism is the result of some particular historical conditions or an unheard-of, radically novel event whose emergence should be thought of as a "miracle of Being," and so forth.) The critical solution to the antinomy aims to defetishize reason, to conceive of its very principle as purely methodical. The question is not whether some particular historical event has a cause or not, but whether we can succeed, through reason, in constructing its intelligibility. In this sense the critical approach, without ecumenicism, is necessarily synthetic; it leads not to asserting or destroying the principle of reason but to limiting it to the conditions of finitude and temporality. Granting to the "thesis" that one cannot think without using the principle of reason, and to the "antithesis" the radical contingency of reality, the critical approach reestablishes the possibility of an ethics of communication.

The fruitfulness of critical philosophy with regard to the demands of contemporary thought, which surely neither Kant nor Fichte ever could have envisaged, thus appears in a new light. Critical activity manages to think through not only the present situation of philosophy, which is the antinomy between rationalism and irrationalism, or, as it were, between historicism in all its forms and phenomenological neoromanticism. It also can understand the emergence, within other disciplines, of conflicts that are not purely philosophical but also empirical: for example, the antinomy that has appeared in the relations between political philosophy and the social sciences in France. It is clear that the social sciences predominantly adopt a hyper-Hegelian historicist model, which has the logical effect of denying that actors can themselves grasp the intelligibility of their practices, and of claiming these practices must always be explained by a causality external to them. (One thinks, for example, of the sociology of Pierre Bourdieu.) From the viewpoint of this epistemology, the questions of philosophy obviously have no legitimacy, since the horizons of meaning or axiologies through which the actors can possibly understand their own situations are mere objects for a sociohistorical analysis that is supposed to reveal their mode of production. The horizon of meaning within which this historicist genealogy is done escapes interrogation, since it is calmly decreed to be scientific. In the face of this epistemology, the phenomenological model must appear helpful, for it has the advantage that, by destroying the principle of reason, it preserves the autonomy of the political and thereby restores legitimacy to the classic questions of philosophy. Hence the encounter, to our minds sterile, so often characteristic of the relation between a deeply historicist social science and a philosophy that, through a fear of a return to dogmatic causality, takes no interest in concrete research.

Here we touch on the problem of constructing horizons of meaning that we mentioned as among the possible tasks of contemporary philosophy. For to think correctly about historical causality is also to pave the way for a reconciliation of the dimensions of fact and meaning. Once it is limited, the principle of reason is indeed compatible with both empirical research (which cannot forego it without absurdity) and the thesis of the autonomy of the political. The antagonism inevitably engendered between the social sciences and philosophy, when it is inscribed in the antinomy whose model we have just sketched, is calamitous not only for philosophy but also for the social sciences. The human sciences have indeed suffered too long from the illusion that the accumulation of an enormous apparatus of archives, investigations, and statistical data would allow them to escape the problems with which philosophy has long struggled.

From this perspective, it would be interesting to construct philosophically the horizons of meaning of the historical-political movements of modernity. "Constructing philosophically" would mean to show how, on the basis of modern theories of natural right, one can think of only a limited number of political theories that, taken together, form the horizons of meaning for a philosophical understanding of the great political events of modern history. This undertaking would presuppose the prior deconstruction of two illusions.

The first is the illusion, predominant in the social sciences, that political philosophy is essentially concerned with normative, moral questions, while scientific activity demands neutrality and impartiality. This interpretation of philosophy as imagining the "ideal," and of science as working on the "facts," does not stand up to even a superficial examination of the great political doctrines. Though it is valid for a marginal thinker like Leo Strauss or certain great philosophers like Rousseau, it is sharply contradicted in the work of Hobbes, Spinoza, and Hegel. To confine ourselves to Hegel, we only have to read the introduction to his *Principles of the Philosophy of Law* to see that his central theme is precisely the radical criticism of the "moral view of the world," especially when this vision passes itself off as political philosophy. Hegel repeatedly says that the task of philosophy is to "conceive of what is" and not crudely to impose what "ought to be" on the real. In fact, the philosophies of natural right, from Grotius to Hegel, are not, with few exceptions, concerned with the ideal. They aim rather to determine what in the political sphere is of the nature of an Idea, meaning describable a priori, which is not to be confused with the normative. What these philosophies hold to be describable a priori are the various conceivable modalities of the relation between the society and the state, as is shown with perfect clarity not only by Hegel's political philosophy but also in the Kantian construction of right.

A second illusion is the one that the number of possible political theories is infinite. If we take as our first hypothesis that the theories of modern natural right are at the foundation of the political theories of the twentieth century, and our second hypothesis that the chief object of these theories is relations between the state and the society, it becomes clear at the level of what might be called "political ontology" that the relations between the two terms can be conceived in only a finite number of ways: there are political theories that aim at the elimination of society in the state, the elimination of the state from society, or the reciprocal limitation of the two terms. It is also clear that these possibilities were actualized in different ways—in a state socialism, in anarchism and libertarianism, and in the various models of liberalism and democratic socialism. It remains true, however, that these three possibilities are, at the most general level, the only three that are thinkable in modernity—which attests to their systematic structure.

It is from this perspective that it seems to us desirable to write a philosophical history of "human rights" in order to show how the various practices that establish these rights are thinkable in all their diversity only if we take into account solely those conceptions of democracy whose affirmation or negation makes sense. Just as the Greek conception of democracy (understood as an ideal-type) proves deeply incompatible with the whole modern idea of "human rights," so the three fundamental political theories of modernity—socialism, anarchism, and liberalism—give rise to representations of democracy that imply widely differing discourses and practices regarding human rights. It is precisely the logic of these differences that such an analysis—both philosophical and historical—ought to be able to understand.[8]

The current crisis in philosophy proceeded from the still denied desire to produce, under the cover of an antisystem, a system comparable to the great philosophical systems of the past. This was an impossible task that prevented philosophy from opening to its other, notably to the social sciences, or only led philosophy to confound itself with them. In a nearly symmetrical way, the crisis of the social sciences is rooted in the naive positivism that leads them to believe that by riding roughshod over the philosophical tradition, they too can escape the return of the repressed.

—TRANSLATED BY FRANKLIN PHILIP

Notes

1. Martin Heidegger, "Hegel und die Griechen," in *Wegmarken* (Frankfurt, 1978). See Jacques Derrida: "We believe quite simply in absolute knowledge as *closure*," or Heidegger: "By saying 'the Greeks' we are thinking of the beginning of philosophy, in saying 'Hegel,' of its completion."

2. Ibid. See also Martin Heidegger, "The End of Philosophy and the Task of Thinking," in *On Time and Being*, trans. Joan Stambaugh (New York, 1972), 55–73.

3. Gilles Deleuze, *Difference and Repetition*, trans. Paul Patton (New York, 1993), 1; Michel Foucault, *The Archaeology of Knowledge and the Discourse of Language*, trans. A. M. Sheridan Smith (New York, 1982), 235.

4. See the masterful interpretation of Alexis Philonenko in his *La liberté humaine dans la philosophie de Fichte* (Paris, 1966).

5. On this point, see the debate concerning Kantianism that took place at Davos between Heidegger and Cassirer in 1929.

6. See, for example, Heidegger's *Schelling's Treatise on the Essence of Human Freedom*, containing his reconstruction of philosophical modernity as the progressively successful search for system from Leibniz to Hegel, and in which Kantianism appears only as a stage to be superseded on the path to the Hegelian completion.

7. See Luc Ferry and Alain Renaut, "D'un retour à Kant," *Ornicar* 2 (1980), reprinted in *Système et critique* (Paris, 1985); and Luc Ferry, "Sur le dilemme: La raison ou ses marges," *Le Débat* 4 (1980).

8. See Luc Ferry and Alain Renaut, *Political Philosophy 3: From the Rights of Man to the Republican Idea*, trans. Franklin Philip (Chicago, 1992).

CHAPTER 5

Constant

PHILIPPE RAYNAUD

ONE OF THE MOST characteristic aspects of recent intellectual life in France is its disdain for the political works of the great French romantics. While the rich production of Restoration authors has hardly been ignored, it has generally been treated as historical documentation of the intellectual climate of the time. The political thought of a Chateaubriand or a Constant has thus been reduced to expressions of public opinion, or at best viewed as the faint echo of their more worthy literary accomplishments. In a recent edition of Benjamin Constant's major political writings, Marcel Gauchet could thus rightly lament that, compared to "the endless debate over the Enlightenment and the origins of the French Revolution . . . the nineteenth-century bourgeois has been erased from the French intellectual landscape."[1] But now that the principles of modern liberalism—from the necessary limitations of power to human rights—are no longer disdained in France, it is significant that we are finally rereading those who first attempted to reconcile the legacy of the French Revolution with rejection of the Terror.

The fate of Benjamin Constant's political writings is exemplary.[2] Though he explicitly tried to recast the entire liberal doctrine to rehabilitate "the liberty of the moderns," he remains relatively unknown as a political theorist because his thought has been almost completely incorporated into the contemporary liberal credo. Consequently, we have missed more than his extremely acute reflections on modern forms of political sociability. For a close analysis of his *Principles of Politics Applicable to All Representative Governments* also reveals a powerful attempt to achieve a coherent integration of the antinomies that still define modernity. Constant's theoretical writings are not a simple repertory of interesting themes but a crystallized depiction of the antinomies that romanticism was the first to express within European culture.

Constant is best known for his attempt to establish representative government as the best guarantee of individual liberties and his effort to differentiate this regime from Jacobin Terror. This project is what unites Constant's political activities and his political writings. For Constant, it was less a question of supporting one political tendency or another than of defending a contested legacy that seemed to lack doctrinal foundation, and that confused the praise of liberty with vindication of the Terror. As Paul Bénichou once wrote:

> What the liberals rejected above all was the idea of absolute rule over society, whatever the regime. Heirs of the eighteenth century, they had to extract from this legacy a doctrine of political liberty that existed therein only as a potential. The idea of liberty during the revolutionary crisis had been compromised because of the Terror. A doctrine of liberty stemming from the *Social Contract*, which absorbed the sovereignty of the individual through his participation in an omnipotent general will, had served to support a dictatorship. Liberty praised to the skies had engendered its opposite. Faced with the counterrevolution, it remained to show that liberty could be something other than a new kind of despotism in France.[3]

What French liberals of all shades thus had in common was an ambivalent, double-edged attitude toward the Revolution. Their defense of the Revolution's results was combined with a critique of the revolutionary process. Constant's originality and particular strength was to move beyond an analysis of contemporary circumstances to focus on the principles of political philosophy and constitutional law. Such an undertaking, unusual among French writers of the period, links Constant to Kant and Hegel. We see this especially in his famous discussion of Rousseau, which later formed the matrix of all liberal critiques of the *Social Contract*.

A confrontation with Rousseau was inevitable for anyone hoping to distinguish the liberal heritage of the French Revolution from the excesses of the Terror. Rousseau had defined "the contract passed between society and its members as the total alienation of each associate, together with all his rights, to the whole community."[4] According to Constant, Rousseau had thus "made of his *Social Contract*, so often invoked in favor of liberty, the most formidable support for all kinds of despotism."[5] Disassociating the liberal concept of liberty from the doctrine set down by Rousseau (considered the Jacobin's forefather) was a commonplace of postrevolutionary literature. Burke's diatribes against the spirit of the system and the use of abstractions or "metaphysics" in politics very quickly found imitators in France.[6] Counterrevolutionaries who worried about defending the traditional order, or liberals trying to keep individuals alive, took as their primary target the paradoxes of the *Social Contract*. Constant's merit was to show that the legal foundation of modern liberalism could not be laid if the spirit of Rousseau were totally abandoned. Likewise, since criticism of the revolutionary moment had to distinguish what Constant called "our happy Revolution" from the excesses of the Terror, the defense of individual liberties against despotism could not help adopting two crucial aspects of the doctrine of the social contract. The first was that "the principle of the sovereignty of the people, that is, the supremacy of the general will over any particular will," was the incontestable principle of all legitimate political authority.[7] The second was that the idea of law, which established the very idea of legitimate power, had to be reaffirmed against force. Rather than try to eliminate all the "metaphysical" aspects of the *Social Contract*, Constant aimed to define the limits within which the principle of popular sovereignty was legitimate, and in so doing justify the validity of the liberal concept of liberty.

The kinship between the democratic principle of popular sovereignty and the liberal defense of individual liberties seems obvious today. For Restoration authors, however, it was not at all self-evident. On the contrary, for historical and theoretical reasons, they saw a conflict between the two principles. On the one hand, the liberal's linking of individual liberty to limited political power seemed aristocratic, since in France it came from a class intent on defending its prerogatives. On the other hand, the idea of popular sovereignty associated with the "Roman" or "Spartan" fanaticism of the Jacobins appeared risky, since it might submerge the individual in "the people" and lose those who best represented liberal values.

In choosing to open the *Principles of Politics* with an acknowledgment of the legitimacy of popular sovereignty, Constant immediately adopted an original position. In effect, he aimed to show that the preservation of individual liberty was indeed compatible with the supremacy of the general will, that is, with popular sovereignty. What distinguished his position from the democratic-liberal vulgate in French political culture was his keen perception of the novelty of the riddle represented by the Terror. While announcing a new era of liberty, the French Revolution also extended the law to all aspects of social life, which can be seen less in the Terror itself than in the Convention's legislative activity. Herein lay the most difficult problem of the Revolution, since it meant that one could not depend on the state's conformity to law as a criterion of a just regime.

The outlines of this problem had already been sketched out in Constant's 1814 pamphlet, *The Spirit of Conquest and Usurpation and Their Relation to European Civilization*. This short work introduces a recurring theme in Constant's thought: that "the modern imitators of the republics of antiquity," in trying to restore classical liberty in a world where it was impossible, had established the possibility of a new despotism. Liberty had come to be defined not as the enjoyment of individual liberties but as the active participation of each and every person in the body politic.[8] One source of this idea is Rousseau. But it is Mably, "less eloquent, but no less austere in his principles than Rousseau, indeed, even more extreme in applying them," for whom Constant reserved his sharpest criticism:

> The Abbé de Mably, like Rousseau and many others, had mistaken authority for liberty, and to him any means seemed good if it extended the action of this authority upon that recalcitrant part of human existence, whose independence he deplored. The regret he expresses everywhere in his works is that the law can only cover man's actions; he would like it to cover the most fleeting thoughts and impressions; to pursue man relentlessly, leaving him no refuge in which he might escape from his power. No sooner did he learn of any oppressive measure, no matter by whom it was practiced, than he thought he had made a discovery, and proposed it as a model; he detested individual liberty like a personal enemy; and whenever he came across a nation deprived of it, even if it had no political freedom, he could not help admiring it.[9]

Beyond the "terrorist" episodes of the Convention, this attempt to absorb social life and individual liberty into the law explains the passionate desire for uniformity that the Empire was to inherit. As Constant characterized it, "Variety is what constitutes organization; uniformity is mere mechanism. Variety is life, uniformity, death."[10]

Thus we can see how Constant was able to understand the ambiguity of the Revolution and the paradoxes of the *Social Contract*. A legitimate government or regime that depends on consent rather than force cannot challenge the principle of popular sovereignty; but in itself this principle cannot guarantee individual liberty, whose development may conflict with the demands of politics. The doctrine of sovereignty and that of individual rights cannot therefore be reduced to a single principle. On the contrary, they each have to be formulated independently, in order to show that they limit and mutually condition one another.

The liberal tradition had long defended the notion of the irreducibility of individual liberties to the jurisdiction of political authority but still maintained the harmony between individual rights and social requirements. Constant's individualism is more radical, since it posits individual rights as absolutes which, transcending social obligations, can be guaranteed only if the powers of the political association are limited from the outside:

> The universality of citizens is sovereign in the sense that no individual, no faction, no partial association can arrogate sovereignty to itself, unless it has been delegated to it. But it does not follow from this that the universality of the citizens, or those who are invested with the sovereignty by them, can dispose sovereignly of the existence of individuals. There is, on the contrary, a part of human existence which by necessity remains individual and independent, and which is, by right, outside any social competence. Sovereignty

> has only a limited and relative existence. At the point where independence and individual existence begin, the jurisdiction of sovereignty stops. If society oversteps this line, it is as guilty as the despot who has, as his only title, his exterminating sword. Society cannot exceed its competence without usurpation, nor bypass the majority without being factious.[11]

The attempt to reconcile individual rights and the Rousseauistic inspiration of the French Revolution thus leads to an important reformulation of liberal doctrine. This reformulation poses two new problems, which might be posed as questions. First, if Rousseau's doctrine of the social compact made it possible to conceive the formation of the sovereign as the expression of political liberty, what is the status of political liberty in Constant's system? Second, if the individual and society are posited from the outset as autonomous, without mediation through a contract, how then can relations between individuals within society be envisaged? Let us take up these questions in order.

We have already discussed how in *The Spirit of Conquest and Usurpation*, then in *The Liberty of the Ancients Compared with That of the Moderns*, Constant was able to disassociate the liberal concept of liberty from revolutionary practice by contrasting ancient and modern liberty. Concerned with defending "our happy Revolution" while simultaneously condemning the 1793 Republic, Constant attributes the excesses of the Terror and the project to regulate social life through law to a disdain for the character of liberty. Inspired by ancient republicans, the revolutionaries planned to compensate severe restrictions on individual liberties with active participation in the exercise of sovereignty. However, the development of modern states, the abolition of slavery, and the love of independence implicated both the need to respect individual rights and the impossibility of regularly exercising political rights. "Among the ancients," wrote Constant, "the individual, almost always sovereign in public affairs, was a slave in all his private relations. . . . Among the moderns, on the contrary, the individual, independent in his private life, is, even in the freest of states, sovereign only in appearance."[12]

Given the opposition between ancient and modern liberty, it would initially seem that the essential characteristic of modernity is the continuous decline of political liberty; "sovereign only in appearance," the citizen is actually trapped in the private sphere. The price of political liberty would seem to be the alienation of individual rights, while the cost of individual freedom in the modern world would be political alienation. More romantic here than his fellow compatriots, Constant is in fact far from an unreserved admirer of the modern world:

> We can no longer enjoy the liberty of the ancients, which consisted in an active and constant participation in collective power. Our freedom must con-

> sist of the peaceful enjoyment of private independence. The share which in Antiquity, everyone held in national sovereignty was by no means an abstract presumption as in our own day. The will of each individual had real influence: the exercise of this will was a vivid and repeated pleasure. Consequently the ancients were ready to make many a sacrifice to preserve their political rights and their share in the administration of the state. Everybody, feeling with pride all that his suffrage was worth, found in this awareness of his personal importance ample compensation.[13]

Constant did not establish this opposition in order to make the political freedom proclaimed by the French Revolution appear illusory. Instead, he reversed the relationship between individual and political liberty as conceived by classic liberal doctrines. If political liberty for the moderns cannot have the concrete richness that it had in ancient republics, it remains no less necessary for guaranteeing the preservation of individual liberties. "Far from renouncing either of the two sorts of freedom which I have described," Constant writes, "it is necessary, as I have shown, to learn to combine the two together."[14]

Political liberty thus plays a necessary role in modern society. But as Constant's critique of the contract doctrine shows, it has an essentially negative function of limitation with respect to power. Since the supremacy of the general will is linked to the necessity of consent, our participation in the body politic is reduced to "the eternal rights to assent to the laws, to deliberate on our interests" without actually instituting them.[15] In fact, the principal function of political liberty, besides maintaining an explicit separation between civil society and the state, is to preserve individual liberty in its entirety. "Individual liberty, I repeat, is the true modern liberty. Political liberty is its guarantee, consequently political liberty is indispensable."[16] If, by renouncing the Rousseauistic reconciliation of the individual and the body politic, Constant predicts a retreat of individuals into the private sphere, he also shows that this relative "privatization" of social life can only be preserved if individuals remain citizens.

From the deductive analysis in the *Principles of Politics*, we have seen that individual rights are formulated independently of the association. It would be wrong to conclude, however, that Constant dismisses all examination of the relations between the individual and society. The question has simply shifted from political philosophy to a philosophy of history, as Constant moves from Rousseau back to Montesquieu.

Fundamentally, the *Social Contract* tried to posit the conditions for an autonomous society: if the sovereign merged with the association as a legislative body, this was because liberty could be envisaged only as society determining its own laws. By reintroducing a separation between the sovereign and society, Constant is led to abandon a voluntaristic conception of law in favor of deterministic objectivism. Constant's aim is both to eliminate the traditional figure of "a causal agent" (*pouvoir-cause*) unifying society from the outside, and to abandon voluntaristic modern philosophy. If the problem of law is no longer seen from a voluntaristic perspective, and if civil laws are modeled after natural laws (as in Montesquieu), one must dismiss as despotic the conscious revolutionary attempt to transform society. In the political philosophy of the *Principles*, the supremacy of the general will is transformed into mere external regulation of its political power. Moreover, as with Montesquieu, laws here are not products of a sovereign will but the "necessary relations deriving from the nature of things."[17]

A double problem emerges, however. On the one hand, in order to avoid voluntarism, Constant must show how society comes together without external intervention and becomes a self-regulating system. On the other hand, since this critique of voluntarism is still supposed to defend individual rights and human liberty, it must simultaneously avoid a purely mechanical representation of society. Formulated in this way, the problem no longer lies in choosing between a "sociological" approach stemming from Montesquieu and the "normative" approach of Rousseau. Rather, it marks the appearance in French political thought of a classic problem found in German philosophy since Leibniz: how to reconcile the existence of human liberty and that of a real equilibrium between particular wills, an equilibrium necessary for society or history to be conceivable.

The rejection of Rousseauistic (or Jacobin) voluntarism did not lead Constant to promote positive law as an alternative to natural law. Rather, it led him to formulate in elementary form what Hegel would later call the "cunning of reason." Comparing the doctrine of the *Principles* to the analysis in *The Liberty of the Ancients Compared to That of the Moderns* is revealing in this respect. Whereas a natural-law conception of rights makes such rights appear to be transcendental, established without rational justification, and opposed to society, Constant's historical analysis shows individual liberty (and its corollary, political liberty) to be a rational necessity, functionally adapted to the requirements of modern life. The power of opinion, the development of commerce, the increase of wealth: all these are elements of the new bourgeois society that render individual liberty and protections against arbitrary power socially necessary. Moreover, the advent of the modern individual in postrevolutionary France contributed to a paradoxical process, Constant believed. In trying to revive ancient liberty, the revolutionaries paved the way for the advent of modern liberty. It is thus through the "cunning of reason" that Constant simultaneously validates the results of "our happy Revolution" and criticizes its excesses.

It would seem, therefore, that the schism between individual and society, between society and state, is resolved by Constant in a new philosophy of history. Modern society, seen as a necessary product of the free actions of individuals, also constitutes the environment necessary for the promotion of individual liberty. Nonetheless, Constant allows a certain nostalgia for ancient liberty to color his thought and considers inevitable a relative decline in political liberty. In modern society, individual liberty can perhaps fully maximize private enjoyment, but the citizen is no longer at home in the body politic. This trace of dissatisfaction with modernity, this truly romantic nostalgia, has an obvious cause. For if the social equilibrium is achieved without constraint through the spontaneous participation of particular wills, the individual necessarily sees this equilibrium as foreign to him. Constant characterized this feeling thus: "Lost in the multitude, the individual never perceives the influence he exercises. Never does his will impress itself upon the whole; nothing confirms in his eyes his own cooperation."[18]

Constant's *oeuvre* represents the highest achievement of the program put forth by French liberals of the Empire and Restoration. In it the defense of the French Revolution is based on the perceived harmony developing in the new representative regime between the necessities of modern life and the principles of natural right. Nonetheless, Constant's political philosophy, like his interpretation of history, reveals a lingering problem: the modern individual seems to have lost the possibility of identifying with a global political project or of being fully at home in the body politic. Constant tirelessly defends individual liberty by defining a "private" sphere outside of society. It is thus significant that he presented the defense of individual rights as an ethical duty rather than as social necessity. Constant chose not to explore this ethical path systematically. Instead, he was able to show, perhaps better than anyone else, how achieving the greatest aspirations of subjectivity in bourgeois society can still leave society as a whole dissatisfied. This liberal's awareness of the difficulty in identifying fully with modern society, even though it produces the conditions for individual emancipation, is perhaps one of the great embodiments of the romantic spirit, where radical modernity goes hand in hand with unappeasable dissatisfaction and anxiety.

—Translated by Ann T. Gardiner

Notes

1. Marcel Gauchet, Préface, in Benjamin Constant, *De la liberté chez les modernes*, (Paris, 1980).

2. In English, see Benjamin Constant, *Political Writings*, trans. Biancamaria Fontana (Cambridge, 1988).

3. Paul Bénichou, *Le temps des prophètes* (Paris, 1978), 33–34.

4. Jean Jacques Rousseau, *The Social Contract*, in *The Social Contract and Discourses*, trans. G.D.H. Cole, revised and augmented by J. H. Brumfitt and John C. Hall (1973; rpt. London, 1986), 191.

5. Benjamin Constant, *Principles of Government Applicable to All Representative Governments*, in *Political Writings*, 177.

6. Edmund Burke, *Reflections on the Revolution in France* (1790; rpt. London and New York, 1986).

7. Benjamin Constant, *Principles of Government*, in *Political Writings*, 175.

8. See *The Spirit of Conquest*, part 2, chap. 7, in *Political Writings*.

9. Benjamin Constant, *The Spirit of Conquest and Usurpation and Their Relation to European Civilization*, in *Political Writings*, 107.

10. Ibid., 77.

11. Benjamin Constant, *Principles of Politics*, in *Political Writings*, 176–77.

12. Benjamin Constant, *The Liberty of the Ancients Compared with That of the Moderns*, in *Political Writings*, 311–12.

13. Ibid., 316. Translation slightly revised.

14. Ibid., 327.

15. Ibid., 324.

16. Ibid., 323.

17. Montesquieu, *The Spirit of the Laws*, trans. Anne M. Cohler, Basia Carolyn Miller, and Harold Samuel Stone (Cambridge, 1989), book 1, chap. 1, 3.

18. Benjamin Constant, *The Liberty of the Ancients*, in *Political Writings*, 316. Translation slightly revised.

CHAPTER 6

Tocqueville

MARCEL GAUCHET

In the pages that follow, I will not consider Tocqueville's thought in and for itself but rather for its present application. What is democracy today? What has it become, and what must be said about it henceforth in relation to what Tocqueville taught us? His great work on America, which I will specifically examine, continues to be an incomparably wise and living source, always surprisingly relevant upon examination. In it, Tocqueville placed his finger on what he calls the "equality of conditions," one of the sources of the irrepressible dynamic of contemporary societies. But beyond its deceptive simplicity, the profound nature of this term remains to be elucidated. Only rare authors have had the good fortune to be right against themselves and history, penetrating beyond limits that they could not have imagined crossing and justifying themselves at the cost of their own naïveté. It is all the more instructive, given Tocqueville's unique insight, to ponder the other side—the limits, obstructions, and blind spots of his reflection.

For in retrospect, we see that Tocqueville also has a certain systematic blindness to appearances that have for us become essential to the democratic phenomenon; their true historical significance seems to have escaped him. It is a limitation that exemplifies and sums up, as it were, the American detour itself. Having studied democracy in the New World, Tocqueville lost sight of the twisting paths by which another type of democracy became established in the Old World. He was unable to discern that America's political novelty was essentially contrary to the normal march of modernity. Tocqueville considered the peculiar historical experiences by which the Old World finally forged the democratic order to be obstacles to the true manifestation of democracy. Confronted with the continuing struggle between the antagonistic European forces of reaction and revolution, Tocqueville tended to ignore the ultimate significance of the advent of democracy for the history of all societies, when he considered the American laboratory. What he brilliantly observed, and what is a central and universal trait of modern societies, is the multiform work of equalization. But this is only one of the many possible faces of democracy, and, in the final analysis, one of its least predictable and most singular developments. It takes this form only when circumstances are such that the principles of the political regime precede the formation of society and literally shape it. What remains outside this overly clear matrix is the Old World's transformation of its own organic-hierarchic unity and the difficult task of adjusting principles to function effectively in a desperately rebellious society, principles by which democracy was formed on Europe's side of the Atlantic. This is a model of democracy more as a mode of social being than a political system—or a political system as the expression of, and mode to manage, the latest developments of society that did not take place within the special American model. The European model of democracy inseparably carries with it the totalitarian menace, a potential specifically absent from the American situation, at least in its original form, whereas European history of the last century is unintelligible outside of this context.

Tocqueville did not completely ignore this crucial divergence in lines of evolution. We sense this in the concluding part of *Democracy in America*, which represents Tocqueville's return to Europe and to himself. There we see the shift in perspective, the portrait of an unprecedented despotism that democratic nations now have to fear. Now we must prolong his reversal as much as our present history permits and measure how far the American difference led Tocqueville to drift away from our own European world.

There is an underlying problem conditioning Tocqueville's thought that justifies his look at America and reveals the reasoned key to what appears to us as a certain blindness. This problem, which is all the more paradoxical given Europe's destiny, might be called the "reconciliation" or "harmonization" of democratic society with itself. At its heart is the scandalous incapacity of the Old World nations to recognize and accept their ineluctable democratic evolution. Tocqueville cannot find words strong enough to express this idea. The democratic revolution proceeds in an irresistible movement. Its advance is "the most continuous, ancient and permanent tendency known to history."[1]

Only the language of religion or the categories of the absolute are capable of furnishing a correct notion of the force indubitably yet subterraneously affecting societies over time. How could one not recognize in it "certain signs" of the will of God himself? "The gradual progress of equality is something fated. The main features of this progress are the following: it is universal and permanent; it is daily passing beyond human control; and every event and every man helps [*sic*] it along."[2] Such a phenomenon was hitherto concealed from human intention; so that it grew equally from the efforts of "those who intended it" and "those who had no such intention," from "those who fought for democracy" as well as "those who were the declared enemies thereof."[3] All partisanship aside, what other position can one adopt toward it other than to be a humble witness content simply to record it? "The whole book has been written under the impulse of a kind of religious dread inspired by contemplation of this irresistible revolution advancing century by century over every obstacle and even now going forward amid the ruins it has itself created."[4] All minds must bow before such resounding, historically irrefutable logic. After understanding that the "effort to stop democracy" would amount "to fight against God himself," nations should coldly resolve to "acquiesce in the social state imposed by Providence."[5]

But they have not. And here one must speak of a scandalous, perhaps even blasphemous blinding of the "Christian nations" before the fate that the "Sovereign Master" assigns them. Although "the gradual and measured advance of equality," which Tocqueville sees as the salient trait of the democratic age, is obviously "the past and the future of . . . history," the peoples of Europe and their governors are incapable both of forming a clear consciousness of the movement carrying them along and guiding themselves accordingly.[6] None of the heads of state was able to detect the social revolution about to occur: "All have worked together [toward it], some against their will and some unconsciously." At times they are stupid enough to believe that it is in their power to oppose it; at others, their lack of understanding prompts them only to yield before it. Because of this ignorance, inextricable confusion arises, and those who should be the natural friends of democracy become its enemies, unwittingly undermining its foundations and fortune. By an inexplicable perversion, European societies remain obstinately unconscious of their democratic truth. They tear themselves apart to see if they need a social state that is largely already in place, and against which all are impotent. They remain strangely powerless to set up and organize themselves openly in a democracy and channel its force. "Hence we have our democracy without those elements which might have mitigated its vices and brought out its natural good points. While we can already see the ills it entails, we are as yet unaware of the benefits it might bring."[7] Such is the situation that requires Tocqueville's American detour. To understand even the fundamental principles of democracy, we must look beyond the complete intellectual and moral disorder that conceals its true nature in the Old World, to a society that lives in fundamental accord with its socially democratic state.

For Tocqueville, American society is thus a concrete providential response to an abstract demand. As a model, it is contingent and not in the least constraining: "I am very far from believing," says Tocqueville, "that they have found the only form possible for democratic government."[8] Yet it illustrates what we must dare to conceive: a society that coincides with the democratic principle and accepts, espouses, and deploys the social and political order linked to the equality of conditions. Thus, it is the "one country in the world in which this great social revolution seems almost to have reached its natural limits; it took place in a simple, easy manner."[9] There is no need for speculation: only one reading is possible of the essential harmony between institutions and mores and their generating principle, equality, to which our history destines us.

Discovering what exactly constitutes Tocqueville's "complete and peaceful" correspondence or continuity of a society governed by first principles proves less obvious than one might expect. On one level, certainly, this correspondence is not difficult to understand. It refers simply to the free unfolding of the principle of popular sovereignty that follows directly from the recognized equality between individuals. In the United States, it is "put in practice in the most direct, the most unlimited, the most absolute manner. . . . It spreads with freedom and attains unimpeded its ultimate consequences."[10] Tocqueville's formulations are famous: "The people reign over the American political world as God rules over the universe. It is the cause and the end of all things; everything rises out of it and is absorbed back into it."[11] On a second level, with the absence of a significant and organized public dispute over democratic rules and forms, there is a positive and general adhesion, symbolic as much as effective, of the community to its mode of functioning. The American principle of popular sovereignty, says Tocqueville, is "recognized by their [the people's] mores" as well as "proclaimed by the laws."[12] Society knows itself in all its parts for what it is; it understands itself without obscurity, drama, or violence. At a third level, however, we discover something decisively more problematic. The harmony of society with the fact of democracy, as Tocqueville understands it, essentially signifies civil peace and unity of community—things that, despite their apparent empirical irrefutability, involve a view of democratic societies and history that must be questioned. It is here, on the most solidly factual terrain of his inquiry, that we discover how America deceived Tocqueville.

In 1848, Tocqueville added the following lines to his book:

> While all the nations of Europe have been ravaged by war or torn by civil strife, the American people alone in the civilized world have remained pacific. Almost the whole of Europe has been convulsed by revolutions; America has not even suffered from riots.[13]

During the preceding sixty years, he wrote in the same foreword, the American people were "not only the most prosperous but also the most stable of all the peoples in the world."[14] There were no supporters of revolution in the United States, or only very few, which was not the case in

Europe. The prospect of revolution appeared empty and lacking in popular appeal. Tocqueville saw nothing fortuitous in this and devoted a chapter of his second volume (published in 1840) to demonstrating that, contrary to what a superficial view would suggest, the social state of democratic nations does not carry them toward brutal transformations of laws, doctrines, or mores but "wards it off."

> I must . . . make it perfectly clear that a nation is not safe from revolution simply because social conditions are equal there. But I do think that, whatever institutions such a people may have, great revolutions will be infinitely less violent and rarer than is generally supposed. I can easily, though vaguely, foresee a political condition, combined with equality, which might create a society more stationary than any we have ever known in our Western world.[15]

The concrete mechanisms of stabilization, of standardization ("Men's main opinions become alike as the conditions of their lives become alike"), indeed of perpetuation of the established order and beliefs, suggest that by its nature an authentically democratic society excludes the peril of internal discord that only a revolution could resolve.[16] A deeper revolution, unavowed but discoverable, arises from something like Tocqueville's latent "metaphysical" presentation of the establishment of democracy. Time and time again the remarks flowing from his pen indicate a certain relativism. "Equality forms the distinctive characteristic of the age," he says at one moment without further explanation: it does simply because it does.[17] Tomorrow, therefore, another notion of the relationship between individuals could impose itself in an analogous manner and substitute itself for democratic values. It suffices, however, to take this idea to its logical conclusion to sense how little it accords with the dominant orientation of Tocqueville's work. In fact, the author clearly leans in the opposite direction. His overwhelming tendency is to hold democracy in its modern form as something other than an accident of history or a revocable contingent decision of providence. In the background, one discerns the insistent idea that democratic equality is fundamentally the realization of the overall plan of history as expressed by divine will.

The fashion in which Tocqueville understands religion disposes him to this position. The profound meaning of the Christian message is equality: "Christianity, which has declared all men equal in the sight of God, cannot hesitate to acknowledge all citizens equal before the law."[18] The democratic age, as the American example powerfully confirms, is the blossoming of the religious ideal. But Christian revelation itself only speeds societies to the realization of this immanent principle, long relegated to obscurity. Thus, Tocqueville views the advent of democracy as the deployment and materialization of a truth that society had hitherto carried secretly within it. "The principle of popular sovereignty," he writes at one time, "*which is always to be found, more or less, at the bottom of almost all human institutions*, usually remains buried there"—just look at "the intriguers and the despots of every age" who claimed legitimacy through popular sovereignty to better usurp it.[19] The peculiarity of the modern world is not that it invented such a concept but that it allowed it to manifest itself fully. Tocqueville says more to support the impression that the socially democratic model brings perfection with his notion that it is formed on the basis of equality. This implies that it cannot be had beyond equality, since it is with equality that the relations between men find a logically perfect and definitive locus in resemblance, and individual self-sufficiency finds fulfillment. The true peril in democracy does not reside where appearances would suggest: not in the subversion that Tocqueville rightly dreads but in the relentless immobilization caused by restlessness. What I fear, says Tocqueville, is

> that mankind will stop progressing and will dig itself in. I fear that the mind may keep folding itself up in a narrower compass forever without producing new ideas, that men will wear themselves out in trivial, lonely, futile activity, and that for all its constant agitation humanity will make no advance.[20]

How can democratic society be at peace with itself under these conditions? Since it lives in conformity with the most profound demand that ever traversed and united a society, it is devoted by nature to interior tranquillity. Democracy essentially reconciles society with itself, and revolutions rarely appear in this perspective other than as the inevitable effect of the democratic wave that unforgivingly breaks over all it encounters. Tocqueville makes this point forcefully clear. The end of the socially democratic state's violent effort to impose itself is, he says, fatal. As a result,

> even when this great revolution has come to an end, the revolutionary habits created thereby and by the profound disturbances thereon ensuing will long endure. As all this takes place just at the time when social conditions are being leveled, the conclusion has been drawn that there must be a hidden connection and secret link between equality itself and revolutions, so that neither can occur without the other.[21]

But temporal coincidence is not an intimate link, and in reality, what one first observes to be revolutionary, far from being a part of democracy itself, constitutes no more than the residual heritage of the process from which democracy issues. As such, egalitarian democracy signifies the entrance of humanity into an age when great revolutions have ceased to be necessary, even if "small ones" remain possible. Moreover, the internal logic of social functioning tends to proscribe them.

Thus the United States has the privilege of exhibiting the true face of democracy: *the privilege of commencement*. In Europe, popular sovereignty had to overturn the existing order to establish itself, and the aftermath of this pitiless struggle continues to blur maps and lead minds astray. In the United States, democracy arose without the need to destroy a secularly entrenched aristocratic regime. "The Americans have this great advantage, that they attained democracy without the sufferings of a democratic revolution and that they were born equal instead of becoming so."[22]

What Tocqueville found in the United States appeared to be a satisfactory resolution of the problem posed by the destiny of European societies, subject to the inexpiable struggle between "two contrary principles," and thus a confirmation, in the first place, that the democratic state is completely acceptable to society. The conflicts of the Old World lend support to the view that the specter of equality ushers in an indefinite era of civil discord, with each step toward popular sovereignty bought at the cost of aggravating the social war, as if democracy could never establish itself free from questions about its principle. But to Tocqueville, the American example is a unique and probably transitory situation, revealing a society fully adapted to its democratic nature, organized in accord with the imperatives born of the equality of conditions. In this way, a democratic society is destined to acknowledge and embrace itself as such. And what it discovers about itself in the process is evidence of what conceals the potential for profound collective peace, harmony, and authentic social unity. The society that aspires to be democratic and presents itself as such, and that liberates itself by granting its members equal rights to participate in it—an apparently inexhaustible source of discord—in fact turns out to be a society tending toward fundamental moral and spiritual agreement with itself. Hence the risk of conformity.

Here is the precise point of divergence between the respective dynamics of American and European politics, and the blind spot in Tocqueville's vision. Tocqueville's thought is limited by his obstinate adherence to the perspective of *democratic coincidence*, which is founded on the postulate of the social world's necessarily positive cohesion. Tocqueville's remarks on that point are not in the least equivocal:

> What keeps a great number of citizens under the same government is much less a reasoned desire to remain united than the instinctive and, in a sense, involuntary accord which springs from like feelings and similar opinions. I would never admit that men form a society simply by recognizing the same laws; only when certain men consider a great many questions from the same point of view and have the same opinions on a great many subjects and when the same events give rise to like thoughts and impressions is there a society.[23]

And he showed how the inhabitants of the United States satisfy these very conditions. The same idea recurs in his second volume:

> It is easy to see that no society could prosper without such beliefs, or rather that there are no societies which manage in that way. For without ideas in common, no common action would be possible, and without common action, men might exist, but there could be no social body. So for society to exist, and even more, for society to prosper, it is essential that all the minds of the citizens should always be rallied and held together by some leading ideas.[24]

In other words, no society can exist without a living intellectual unity. The misfortune of Europe, and especially of France, always inheritor of revolutionary ruptures, is to have lost this unity and acceded to the rise of a generalized anarchy in which "human opinions were no more than as a sort of mental dust open to the wind on every side and unable to come together and take shape."[25] Unity does not always signify flat unanimity or colorless identity: "Although there are many sects among the Anglo-Americans, they all look at religion from the same point of view." They differ among themselves about the form of government, but "they agree about the general principles which should rule human societies."[26] On a number of points, their public opinion "fractionalizes to infinity." And a shrewd observer discerns, behind the diverse "political factions" where they gather, "the two great parties which have divided mankind since free societies came into existence," one "working to restrict the use of public power" and the other "to extend it."[27] Nevertheless, there is a domain of shared presuppositions, within which none among these parties attacks "the actual form of the government and the general direction of society." Tocqueville makes a comparison here that helps to clarify why he places such emphasis on a comprehensive congruence of minds:

> Nowadays the republican principle is as dominant in America as that of monarchy was in the France of Louis XIV. At that time the French not only loved their monarchy, but could not imagine the possibility of putting anything else in its place; they accepted it as one accepts the sun's course and the succession of the seasons. There were neither advocates nor adversaries of the royal power. In America the republic is in just that position, existing without contention, opposition, or proof, being based on a tacit agreement and a sort of *consensus universalis*.[28]

The spontaneous convergence of souls is not sufficient. It must also be mixed with another necessary factor, the intervention of a spiritual power that limits human pretensions, religion. In addition to intellectual unity, and in order to reinforce and embody it, intellectual constraint is needed, which only faith in the divine can furnish. In truth, the role Tocqueville assigns to religion is not easy to determine. No matter how strongly he links the standardization of opinions to the equalization of conditions—which logically should establish the consensus—that he judges indispensable, one has the distinct impression that he believes that only a body of dogmatic beliefs, sheltered from the disputes of experience concerning the afterlife, can ultimately assure a firm conjunction of minds. "Equality puts men side by side without a common link to hold them firm" so that "among democratic peoples all the citizens are independent and weak."[29] Does a similarity of ideas suffice to counterbalance the tendency of individuals to scatter and withdraw among themselves, or have they lost a unanimously held conviction with which they can *explicitly* and almost visibly commune? Tocqueville in effect suggests this: "How could society escape destruction," he asks, "if, when political ties are relaxed, moral ties are not tightened?" But the question that follows carries us again higher in the hierarchy of necessities: "What can be done with a people master of itself if it is not subject to God?"[30] Other ways besides identical beliefs regarding final ends exist to make individuals aware of their feeling of community. They begin with daily participation in local affairs and participation in an intensely associative life: "The free institutions of the United States and the political rights enjoyed there provide a thousand continual reminders to every citizen that he lives in society."[31]

On the other hand, religion fulfills an irreplaceable function: the containing of human activities within boundaries, outside of which these activities cease to be viable. For it is inconceivable to abandon people entirely to themselves. The human mind relies exclusively on ideas, an element of radical dissolution that must be kept out of bounds. Normally, reason stops its own movement in order to bow before a superior power. Again, Tocqueville imputes the transgressions of the Old World on this score to the excesses of the revolution. It is an "accidental and particular cause," he writes, "preventing the human spirit from following its inclination and driving it beyond those limits within which it should naturally remain"—in this case, "the close union of politics and religion."[32] Narrowly associated with the princes in power, Christianity became the enemy of the popular power that was about to impose itself, in such a way that the triumph of equality seemed to go hand in hand with the eradication of faith. Whereas the United States, with its strict distinction between domains that sheltered revealed truths from the vicissitudes of public debate, not only allowed "the natural state of man with regard to religion" to blossom; by the same stroke, it permitted religion to exercise its indispensable task of morally constraining the soul, which is necessary for the maintenance of a republic.[33] "For my part," Tocqueville states, "I doubt whether man can support complete religious independence and entire political liberty at the same time. I am led to think that, if he has no faith he must obey, and if he is free, he must believe."[34]

But this does not make the organization of society subordinate to a religious jurisdiction. On the contrary, it is advisable to abandon all there "to the discussion and to the trials of men," which is what equality imposes, at least in principle. But wanting to contain, within the sphere of collective administration, the liberties of judgment and movement attached to individual independence would be as vain as wishing that a set of rules be established, or a sphere of "certain and immutable" moral rules be recognized as emanating from the divine will. Thus, limited by the "truths it accepts without discussion," and confronted in the moral world with intangible imperatives thanks to which "everything is classified, coordinated, foreseen, and decided in advance,"

> the human spirit never sees an unlimited field before itself; however bold it is, from time to time it feels that it must halt before insurmountable barriers. Before innovating, it is forced to accept certain primary assumptions to submit its boldest conceptions to certain formalities which retard and check it.[35]

These last sentences, indicating the distinction between the political world and the moral and religious world, do not signify the absence of interaction between the two. The political effect depends on the faith invested in the afterworld, but this effect can only be produced under conditions created by the principle of popular sovereignty, in which church ministers expressly refrain from intervening in public affairs and recognize it as a field entirely shaped by human initiative. The autonomy of religion with regard to the political renders it politically effective. Tocqueville summarizes this point in a particularly thought-provoking statement: "While the law allows the American people to do everything, there are things which religion prevents them from imagining and forbids them to dare."[36]

The need for both intellectual unity and intellectual constraint before the decrees of a divine intelligence: these are the two conditions that Tocqueville finds in the United States and judges to correspond to the "natural" inclination of the socially democratic state. They are closely interdependent, and not simply because the common belief in certain truths, which are sheltered from debate, has the effect of uniting individuals. Man's radical questioning of the foundation of the moral rules that govern his relations and of the deeper meanings that order life in society bring irreconcilable division to the community; conversely, antagonism between social groups cannot emerge except when the overall meaning of the human universe and its ends are questioned. Tocqueville is led to distinguish between free management by citizens of all that pertains to their interests, and the consented servitude of individuals regarding the transcendent master of their destinies—precisely in order to exclude the prospect of a total administration of the world of men by men, even in ultimate legitimation. This intuition had an exorcistic value, the result of the author's horror before the chasm opened by revolutions. There is an intimate connection between the establishment of society through a limitless interrogation with itself, which is a decision to traverse "the empty and practically limitless space" that opens when its members recognize no other master but themselves, and civil conflict, even revolutionary struggle. Tocqueville sees in "irreligion" the passion that, above all else, marked the peculiarly extreme character of the French Revolution. He observes,

> Thus even in the most violent social upheavals people had anyhow something of the past to cling to. In the French Revolution, however, both religious institutions and the whole of government were thrown into the melting pot, with the result that men's minds were in a state of utter confusion; they knew neither what to hold on to, nor where to stop. Revolutionaries of a hitherto unknown breed came on the scene: men who carried audacity to the point of sheer insanity; who balked at no innovation and, unchecked by any scruples, acted with an unprecedented ruthlessness. Nor were these strange beings mere ephemera, born of a brief crisis and destined to pass away when it ended. They were, rather, the first of a new race of men who subsequently made good and proliferated in all parts of the civilized world.[37]

It is unquestionably because of this total power to put things into question which it liberated in society, that the French Revolution marks the beginning of an epoch. The astonishing thing is that the same man who so clearly discerns the link uniting the social conflict with the extension of the human problematic, who moreover notices the permanence of these "new beings" who surpassed the limits of the thinkable, this same man nevertheless refuses to see this phenomenon as anything but a "fortuitous and temporary" deviation in the course of history. The man so convinced of the irrepressible character of the movement to equalize conditions, when faced with the workers' uprising in 1848, could only regard these proletarians as strangers, as other. For as we see in the *Recollections*, in Tocqueville's eyes there was no question but to contain or crush them; he was unable to consider it as an instance of the integration of the excluded, as another inevitable step in the progression of history that he himself described and that has indeed occurred. From the viewpoint of subsequent developments of European democratic societies, these blind spots are all of a piece. If the past century established anything, it is that one must reverse Tocqueville's terms and take as essential traits of democracies what he imputed to the consequences of the revolutionary accident—whether with regard to internal discord concerning forms of government or to debates over the fundamental values. Since the day in which Tocqueville wrote, neither intellectual unity nor constraints on intelligence have appeared as irreducibly original contributions of the democratic universe. To hold men together by means of their opposition, to engage them in an endless appraisal of the signification uniting them in society: in the final analysis, these are the crucial properties of democracy in the Old World, under the contradictory pressures of the revolutionary will and the republic's retrograde refusal to acknowledge equality. Contrary to Tocqueville's earliest American vision, democracy is not the profound agreement of minds; it is the merciless dissolution of meaning and the antagonism of ideas. The democratic age, to return to Tocqueville's formula, is the age in which society makes men conceive of everything and allows them to dare everything. Insofar as it is a society of conflict, it is a society structuring itself outside of the unity that Tocqueville put beyond the divisions of the revolutionary age.

The distinctive feature of democracies in Europe is precisely that they have developed with a great misunderstanding of their cause, without being reconciled with themselves through their political forms. And this is precisely the result of the heavy emphasis on the connection between unity and identity in Tocqueville's thought. Tocqueville's originality was to have placed the general adjustment of the collective process within the notion of the free deployment of equality, for which the social state and the institutions of the United States served as a model. But this preoccupation was not uniquely his: it was shared by all the minds of his century, especially the adversaries of democracy, who are Tocqueville's principal targets. They insisted with alarm that the substantial, indispensable unity of the social body was menaced to its foundations and led Tocqueville to believe that once equality was completely established the unity had to be sought by different means. Only going backward to the reestablishment of ancient hierarchies permitted him to recover the organic solidarity of men, outside of which there is no society worthy of the name. The preoccupation that dominates authentically reactionary thought draws from the same source as Tocqueville's search in the United States for a society capable of enduring without discord the absence of the explicit links that once produced collective cohesion.

What is remarkable is that this resolute rejection of the republican regime in the name of the indispensable unity of the social body played an equally determining role in placing society into political conflict. What we know today as democracy was fashioned in part by the opposition to democracy. The presence of a party hostile to popular sovereignty had already created a space for radical social debate concerning the very essence of the collective order; within this space could be expressed not only the conflict of ideas about the political system but also the conflict of interests internal to society. Far from weakening with the advancement of equality and its institutions, as Tocqueville believed, the "struggle of contrary principles" furnished a mirror to society that reflected a division that was more serious than the tension between the hierarchic past and the egalitarian present: the gulf between the propertied and the propertyless, between the owners and the proletariat (which, significantly, Tocqueville notes, "does not exist in the United States").

The inevitably open debate imposed by the existence of a reactionary plan eventually furnished the framework within which there developed an endless reconsideration of the reasons and the ends of human community, out of the report of a complete contradiction between the interests of some and those of others. Let there be no mistake: the resulting antagonism between reactionary conservatism and republicanism is necessarily revolutionary. Tocqueville deplores the perverse effects of these forces and longs for a reasonable acceptance of history's movement. But this antagonism in fact revealed the central aspect of the democratic process, which is the conflict itself. Indeed, as a result of the new symbolic framework thus installed, the contingent battle between supporters of the ancient order and partisans of the new one inevitably took on political meaning as a social conflict—above all, as a conflict of classes. The system of modern democracy then established itself around this representation of a nonaccidental division that was taken to be inherent to the structure of society. As Bergougnioux and Manin observe, the creation of the workers' party marks the crucial moment of crystallization.[38] The entrance of the party of class brings with it a reorganization of the whole political spectrum, beginning with a redefinition of the nature of the other parties, whose correspondence to socially defined forces now becomes decisive. The competition for power through the mechanisms of delegation is thus transformed by the process of legitimate expression of recognized antagonisms whose potential violence is reduced by their symbolic materialization. The struggles of the democratic principle as it came to predominance in Europe were powerfully influenced by this evolution. They gave shape to what democracy itself organized: the existence of the irreconcilable within society.

The slow formation of the battlefield was not consciously completed, nor did the system of pacification resulting from it arise from a deliberate calculation. Quite the contrary. By opposing the social disintegration it saw in popular sovereignty, the reactionary or counterrevolutionary party unwittingly gave the democratic division its initial form; by seeking a society delivered from its former antagonisms, the revolutionary labor party helped to structure the political system in the terms of social conflict. And the major consequence of both strategies was to allow the separation of the state from society to manifest. On one side was now the sphere of private interests and collective groupings; on the other was the sphere of legitimate representation of social divisions, translated in terms of power applicable to the social whole, now conceived as a moving play of forces.

Since the rise of the modern republic and the notion of autonomous individuals deliberating on the form of the contract uniting them, politics has tended to appear as a locus of indistinction between power and society, power understood ideally as the society in action. The unanimous character of ancient democratic politics inspired the desire for unity that obsessed the French Revolution and that tends to proscribe factions and parties, even to the point of erasing the differentiation between the people and its representation. From there, primitive democratic voluntarism easily slips into the mold of ancient representations of power as necessary to maintain the collective cohesion and conformity of men. In both cases, power appears as that through which the social body coincides with the plan justifying and animating it. Historically, the representation of the conflict is the lever that allows the society to function, despite the tenacious remnants of the archaic scheme of instituting political will. At the instant it becomes conscious enough to be the keystone of politics, the autonomy of civil society is thrown into question: a domain independent of human activity, organizing itself, producing its own cohesion, and handing down its decisions as a function of the cleavages crossing it. The mechanism of representation, far from reconciling the collectivity with itself, instead affirms the distance separating the place where the conflicts take root and develop (society) from the place where they exhibit themselves and reverberate (the state). And just as the social conflict is pacified through its symbolic recognition, the difference of the state is neutralized through its symbolic manifestation. The representative operation is not only the recognition of the autonomy of politics in relation to civil society; it is simultaneously a demonstration that power issues from society and only exists due to it, even if power later separates itself from society.

And so we find ourselves in the presence of a system that allows the divisions which, on the surface, the players within it deny, refuse, or try to suppress. Because the state, if symbolically separated by the very mechanisms that provide for its occupants, is never in its official discourse anything other than the immediate and organic expression of the general will and the specialized executor of the collective interest. Similarly, the forces and groups in conflict have no respite from the dangerous effects and the artificial character of democracy—and yet at the same time feed on this fact. They deny reality, or declare it about to be overcome. In short, *democracy does not imply that one must know oneself to exist.* Democracy results from the interaction of parties, all equally ignorant of the democratic truth, although they are not all ideologically antidemocratic. The parties make sure we understand this. I do not deny the existence of effectively "democratic" parties, which call themselves republicans or liberals, that accept competition among a plurality of currents of organized opinions. I only suggest that the final reality of democratic action, if it passes through the open but rule-bound struggle for power, arises (whatever the political regime) from the shadowy logic of a social trial that contradicts the ideology of institutional principles. For what does the confrontation of the parties, as conceived by Tocqueville from the American cases on, presuppose if not general consent to the "generating principle" of the law and to the present state of society, and a common intellectual unity that exists despite divergent views? It presumes that society always reflects a state of unity and ultimate harmony with itself, without the "natural and permanent dissidence between interests" of the diverse classes of citizens, and correspondingly, without any questioning of the foundation of the social structure.

It is indispensable to break with all such notions if one wants to grasp the real operation, not of "regimes" but of the democratic societies that arose in the Old World, where even the most well-grounded democratic institutions were in constant debate concerning the terms of the communal bond. Contrary to the conciliatory illusions of liberal republicanism, class criticism borne on the wave of the workers' movement, has been a major element in the formation of this symbolic arena for irreconcilable differences that constitutes the heart of modern democracies. Within the "normal" spectrum of the parties, the proletariat, organized into a party, introduced the supplementary dimension of an irreversible deviation. Simultaneously, the illusion of an imminent abolition of presently reigning divisions also arose—an illusion guided by the same postulate guiding the other parties: the necessity of cohesion and the destiny of social unity. One can argue that democracy arose independently of the democratic parties' efforts to advance it, but only if one understands by that those parties which discerned and sought real novelty. Democracy has advanced and situated itself in the shelter of a general denial of the actual articulations of its own social agents. It has established itself unbeknownst to its creators, either as a result of their respective blindness or from the intersection of enterprises that are contrary to the authentic democratic spirit. All were inspired by the idea of society's final reconciliation with itself, a scheme that dominates the entire history of humanity, and with which the democratic age marks an essential rupture. True democracy, in our societies, falls far short of what these social protagonists envisioned and hoped for. Without a doubt, it has been materialized in rules, forms, and institutions that make it seem an explicit form of practice. However, as a social process, it has engendered itself and continues to unfold largely unaware of itself.

But is it destined to remain unaware of itself as a process? Will the shock of a return from totalitarianism act as a decisive transformative factor? For it appears that democracies inherently bear the potential for their own negation in the form of totalitarianism. This possibility was inscribed from birth in the democracies that developed in the Old World, and it accompanies them as their inseparable double. It arises from the contradiction that it forged between their explicit and implicit parts, between the ideologies confronting each other and the underlying reality of the symbolic system in which they fit. Democratic society is formed out of deep conflict, yet it is populated by people who conceive of it solely in terms of social unity. It is therefore continuously menaced by the discourse borrowed from reality and ideology, which materializes at the expense of the truth. This conflict can take the counterrevolutionary form of a society with a strong organic solidarity guaranteed by the re-establishment of a hierarchical structure (fascist variety), or the "progressive" form of a society supposed to produce a superior and definitive type of unity thanks to the absorption of class antagonisms and the separation of the state within an achieved historical totality (communist variety). It can even take the form of a hard republicanism in which popular sovereignty is invoked in its unanimous aspirations against the artificial cleavages created by parties. Although this leads more to plebiscitarian authoritarianism than to totalitarianism proper, the reconciling aspect of the regime places it within the totalitarian perspective.

The essential point to note here is the historically regressive character of the totalitarian enterprise. Totalitarianism fundamentally proceeds from a reaction against democratic novelty and is revealed in a fanatical will to return to the explicit cohesion of the human community, whose instituted ideal dominates history from its origins to our day. Since the advent of the state and of classes, this includes the conformity of society to a pre-established plan that it authorizes. It is almost as if humanity faltered before the unbearable spectacle of its own trust, which arrives with the retreat of religion and open debate over the organization of society. It is almost as if society was incapable of supporting the manifestation of its internal contradictions, which are discovered to shape the social terrain once religion ceases to conceal them. Totalitarianism is the return of the religious principle to rule within a world about to abandon religion and reflects the vain mourning for the concealment that religions offered from their origins, the senseless perseverance of what democratic modernity renders impossible—that is, the full and entire reconciliation of society to a predetermined truth. This fierce, unanimous, and obstinate refusal to consider what the existence of religions attests is assuredly the most unfathomable mystery of human societies. Its roots are inscrutable. What is clear is that the phenomenon of totalitarianism represents the virulent re-emergence, within a world extricating itself from religion, of an ignorance materialized in the arrested unity of the social body, which we at least know is powerfully rooted in the unconscious order of human groups. At the same time, it is true that totalitarianism is inseparable from modernity, that it was inconceivable in the age of religion—for the good reason that religion played the same role, though at a lower cost.[39] Totalitarianism is not religion, but it tends to reestablish the type of collective cohesion that religions once assured in a universe where religion, though it still exists, has ceased to have an effective connection with the social. Strangely, it allies the most ancient and the most new. With the state, the instrument par excellence of its realization, totalitarianism employs a social factor whose rise is strictly correlative to the decline in religious transcendence. It is with the complete reintegration in human space of justifications, until then supposed to depend upon the beyond, that the project of an exhaustive seizure and integral restructuring of society by detached power becomes imaginable. In this sense totalitarianism signals the advent of modernity, in that it carries the potential of the modern to the limit.

Still, one must not neglect the other side of the phenomenon and must ask what the omnipotence of the state serves. If the means of totalitarianism fall within the horizon of modern politics emancipated from religion, the plan it follows is thoroughly reactionary, representing a nostalgic return to an ideal social form that arose from a religious vision of human destiny.

It seeks the good old days in which everyone thought alike, in which everyone's place was clear while his membership in the community was fully tangible, days when the convergence of interests, the symbiosis of different agents, the cooperation of everyone and everything toward one unique and manifest goal formed the solid framework of community existence. Totalitarianism is radically unable to free itself from this original religious model of social life yet is fundamentally affected by democratic rifts. It is in order to recover a lost or about-to-be-lost world that the new power contained in the state is mobilized—alas, in vain. If there is an actualization of the phantasmagorical plan of domination inscribed in our societies' pretension to possess themselves, it is the dreamy appeal to collective identity that produced the ancient transcendent divesting of meaning. It is the ghostly reincarnation of an evanescent or dead past.

This hypothesis at least has the merit of adhering to the effective conditions in which totalitarianism actually appeared. Totalitarianism did not appear in countries where a secular process of construction of the national modern state occurred. On the contrary, it emerged in contexts of archaism or insufficiently developed state structures, where the national state had only feeble roots, on account of its recent constitution (Germany or Italy), or where the historical vitality of the old imperial model was at odds with the modern state (Russia or China). It established itself following periods of political liberalization, sometimes overtly in reaction to the disintegration that followed such liberalization, sometimes thanks to the agitation resulting from it, but always in order to shut out the authentically democratic possibility that had been glimpsed. It was almost as if totalitarianism had to establish a mirror state of the nation and in its absolute sovereign strength return to the other side, to the intangible coherence and mystic solidarity of the momentarily shaken society. Entry into the era of state monopoly over the definition and organization of the society is always violent. But with totalitarianism, the monopoly is meant to re-establish an exact reconciliation of society with itself, where no contradiction makes people oppose one another, where the state coincides with society and indeed absorbs it. Religion once guaranteed this reconciliation, but the social opposition of democracy, separating the state from society and class from class, represented an unheard-of rupture.

In such conditions, no "political spirituality" or "monotheism" can possibly offer protection against the totalitarian peril inscribed in social atheism. One does not guard efficaciously against totalitarianism by returning to religion but rather by finishing the process of removing it. Totalitarianism is not born from a defect in religion; it is born from its insufficient eradication and a powerlessness to escape its hold. The totalitarianism episode, a formidable symptom of the inherent tensions within our societies, is a pathological transition between two historical epochs. On the deepest level, it is the reactive sign of the human race's difficult break with the primordial reflex that prevents it from seeing itself for what it is. The democratic age has undertaken to undo and detach us from this reflex, and the stakes are high.

For such is the new dimension that introduces democracy and of which totalitarianism is in conspiracy: the absorption of society in a question about itself, through the very division within it. All earlier societies, by the process of explaining and justifying themselves, created nearly unanimously accepted responses to totalitarianism before being faced with its threat. These responses varied infinitely in their content but were uniformly constructed on the following model: if things are as they are, it is because the Others, the Gods, the Absolute Other, the one and omnipotent God, wanted them that way. The radical originality of democratic society, on the other hand, is always to question itself—a factor that is the result of its own organization, which furnishes it with antagonistic responses. On the one hand, with the separation of the state, one sees the paradoxical possibility of a complete seizure of society by itself, which permits it to model and organize itself (through "revolution," for example) and simultaneously remain dispossesed. This power becomes operational only outside of and against itself. On the other, with class divisions and the constant structural divergence of interests that they impose, an interrogation about the nature of a just (or simply acceptable) order emerges at the heart of collective existence, though now with the certitude that the response is to be found within society and nowhere else. This is not a society in which everyone is constrained to pose questions. It is a society in which the social process is itself a kind of question, so that although the visible actors oppose what seem to be ready-made responses, they actually continue to dig deeper, rendering any closed debate impossible.

Without a doubt this concealed dynamic of incertitude, this inexorable destabilization of what millennia of tradition settled upon as unquestionable, and these infinite possibilities for questioning that flow from the very structure of democratic societies are dimensions that Tocqueville did not accept. He discerned them. He speaks exceedingly well of "an almost limitless empty space" into which "every revolution" launches the intellect of men.[40] It is thus more significant that he rejects them consciously, as contrary to the normal movement of societies and destined not to emerge except in a transitory manner. In retrospect, his repugnance for revolutions is not surprising when one considers the feverish reactions of rejection that even in our century were unleashed by the progressive entrance of the human race into debate unbounded by "natural" foundations or "self-evident" markers. Everything is contestable, everything can be established or instituted otherwise than it is; far from becoming acceptable through use, in comparison to the time of a Tocqueville, this perspective as it deepens becomes only more painful. It can even revive the totalitarian idea of an assured collective foundation. Today, newly delivered from our totalitarian temptation, our intelligentsia finds nothing to propose other than an exchange of faiths, so as to continue to avoid seeing into the abyss of social possibilities. Man "abandoned to himself," as Tocqueville says, remains unbearable for man.

Nevertheless, if there is in our universe a phenomenon, "universal, durable, which escapes each day from human power," that "all the events" like "all men" conspire to develop even when they oppose it, then it must be the irresistible settling of societies into an interrogation about themselves. We are probably arriving at a turning point, where the previous economy of ignorance is breaking apart, and conscience is gaining an ineluctable character. The return from the cataclysmic clash of totalitarian illusions with reality no doubt plays a role. But there is also the historical exhaustion stemming from the blindness of all parties regarding the meaning of their conflict. Each denies the other the right to exist, calls for its elimination, and strives to impose its own vision of a society that would be unified as a result of the absorption of the other. Blindness permitted the confrontation to take the radical form of the collusion of two worlds, and thereby extend to all aspects of human activity without exception. If we are witnessing the collapse of these virulent confrontations, it is also because they have exhausted their usefulness; there remains nothing in our world, or nearly nothing, that is not open to discussion. As a result, the problematic dynamics of democracy no longer imply the aggressive affirmation of an integral and exclusive representation of the good society. It is now taken for granted that life in society is legitimately subject to debate, and that the oppositions that make up the debate are inevitably affected by it. This is not to say that they tend to disappear; they are simply acknowledged tacitly and no longer need to impose themselves to be accepted.

But with the total power of the society over itself henceforth symbolized in the state, and with the internal antagonism among different visions of social and human destiny, history is not over. On the contrary, collective atheism, which is perfectly compatible with private faith, is just now being inscribed in the social logic of democracies after more than a century of gestation. For contrary to what Tocqueville believed, democratic society does not need the ultimate limits traced by divinity. By organizing itself to permit free questioning, it is destined to turn individuals away from the divine. The disappearance of God is built into the social mechanism itself. If the powers of rejection, whether totalitarian or religious, do not win out in a generalized burst of reaction—a possibility that cannot be excluded—the development of democracies following their "natural inclination" will be the tomb of religions.

—Translated by Kenneth Weinstein and Eric Ward

Notes

1. Alexis de Tocqueville, *Democracy in America*, trans. J. P. Meyer (Garden City, 1969), 9.
2. Ibid., 12.
3. Ibid., 11.
4. Ibid., 12.
5. Ibid., 12.
6. Ibid., 12.
7. Ibid., 13.
8. Ibid., 18.
9. Ibid.
10. Ibid., 58.
11. Ibid., 60.
12. Ibid., 58.
13. Ibid., xiv.
14. Ibid.
15. Ibid., 639–40.
16. Ibid., 641.
17. Ibid., 504.
18. Ibid., 16.
19. Ibid., 58 (emphasis added).
20. Ibid., 645.
21. Ibid., 634.
22. Ibid., 509.

23. Ibid., 373.
24. Ibid., 433–34.
25. Ibid., 433.
26. Ibid., 373.
27. Ibid., 178.
28. Ibid., 398.
29. Ibid., 514.
30. Ibid., 294.
31. Ibid., 512.
32. Ibid., 300.
33. Ibid., 299.
34. Ibid., 444.
35. Ibid., 47, 292.
36. Ibid., 292.
37. Alexis de Tocqueville, *The Old Régime and the French Revolution*, trans. Stuart Gilbert (New York, 1955), 157.
38. *La social-démocratie ou le compromis* (Paris, 1979), esp. 43–49.
39. I have developed this point in "Politique et société: La leçon des sauvages," *Textures*, nos. 10–11 (1975), esp. 67–78.
40. Tocqueville, *Democracy in America*, 432.

PART THREE

What Is Modernity?

French theories of modernity have always had as their subtext long-standing national quarrels over religion and secular politics. This subtext has come to the surface in recent years as political philosophy once again began to consider the French Revolution, which is almost universally considered the threshold of the secular modern age. What distinguishes Marcel Gauchet's work is his search for the roots of modernity within religious experience. In an early essay on primitive religion that outlines the principal argument of his book, *Le désenchantement du monde* (The disenchantment of the world), Gauchet offers a speculative account of the state's development out of the first religions, seeing their common source in man's original sense of "indebtedness" to forces outside his power. The end of this history, he asserts, will be a modern secular state without religion. In "The Modern State," Pierre Manent takes issue with Gauchet's (and Louis Dumont's) anthropological history of politics for ignoring the distinctive "theological-political" struggle that gave birth to the modern age. Modernity was a project of European philosophy, which defined itself against religion; it therefore cannot be considered an outgrowth of religion. Manent maintains that the problems and prospects of the modern state can only be understood in terms of modern political philosophy. Jean-Marc Ferry, by contrast, says that we live in a "contemporary" age that is neither "ancient" nor "modern." What distinguishes our epoch is that it is governed by communication rather than by the gods or objective natural laws. Pointing here to the theses of Jürgen Habermas, Ferry argues that intersubjective communication offers the only means of justifying action in a world "disenchanted" with both religion and science.

CHAPTER 7

Primitive Religion and the Origins of the State

MARCEL GAUCHET

Meaning: what men throughout millennia professed to owe to the gods, what societies nearly always believed they owed to something "beyond" for their workings. This term represents both the most elementary form of, and most general reason for, religious belief. In what follows, I will argue that the key to understanding the state should be sought in the deepest roots of the religious act. To understand why men have always felt a need to be *indebted*, why societies have relied upon something alien to themselves to justify their existence, is to comprehend why the state became possible at a certain moment in human and social development.

Since prehistoric times, man has striven for structured social organization. The state is only one manifestation of this structure, just as religion is another. Religion claims that we owe what we are to the gods, that is, to beings who by nature are different from us. This is an eminently political proposition which is, in a sense, the basis of every society; it is a feeling of obligation that arises directly out of the primordial logic dictating society's existence. By going back in time to the religious tie between supernatural founders-givers and human heirs-debtors, we can elucidate the system of primitive links that produces the social space. With regard to the social universal, not only does the affirmation of religious otherness appear as a secondary and derivative institution but so does the system of managing the differences in power as such. Two things can be obtained by exploring this obligation toward the sacred: first, the apparatus that prevents power from being divided up within the community; and second, the reason for the potential deployment of this obligation by the state itself. Thus, what is common between societies without a state and those dominated by the state can be grasped by studying this debt.

The question can be formulated as follows: does the advent of the state mark an absolute caesura in human history? Is the appearance of this separate power a radical creation, an ex nihilo invention in the annals of society? I argue that it is not, precisely because of the interpretation of the religious phenomenon that follows. If the universal story placing the source of meaning outside the human world is examined, if one studies its causes and effects, it becomes clear that the founding of the state is not the construction of a completely new social dimension but simply the transmutation of a dimension already present within society. Although this is a significant transformation, it is not a radical one. The state is simply the new face of the partition that cuts across society, the partition that can be considered the condition for the possibility of society itself.

The immense disparity resulting from the emergence of a partition in society separating dominators and dominated should not be minimized. It implies a relationship of subjection between members of the same community and an authority within the collectivity that monopolizes force and legitimacy, thereby holding the power to decide for all. Enormous differences ensue from this single stroke, bringing incalculable effects and opening a new era in human existence. But this asymmetry between masters and subjects, this distance placed suddenly between rulers and ruled, this dispossession of community in the name of a separate power arises from pre-existing conditions; it has a hidden precursor in the societies that precede it. This precursor is to be found in the dispossession and prolonged subjection to which man acquiesces by accepting the belief that he is indebted to outside forces for the order of the world. This religious subjection and dispossession is quite distinct from acquiescence to the commands of the state and to the state's power of confiscation. This initial split between masters and common mortals does not take place between men, but between living beings and the rulers of the afterlife, in such a way that the subjects are all equally subjected to the rulers.

Significantly, this subjection prevents a division in society between those with power and those without it, since everyone is equally dispossessed by and subjected to these forces. Still, there is real dispossession and subjection; we find that the state did not arise in unstructured societies that were their own masters and were capable of altering themselves via general consent. The state supplanted societies that viewed themselves as lacking effective control over their way of being; these stateless societies did not acknowledge a right over their internal order, since they believed it to be dictated and legitimated by an external source. The advent of the state represents a total metamorphosis in the manner in which society manages its separation from the source of its meaning and legitimacy.

But the state itself does not bring about this separation. Before the state, all societies transferred outside themselves their founding principle, i.e., the origin of their mode of organization, the foundation of their sentiments, the reason for their rules. The externality of the social foundation predates the state and is the first act in its history, a history in which the state's appearance is only one manifestation—a decisive one, certainly, but one that arises from something already present. The state transforms society by openly giving shape to the social division, by bringing otherness inside the human community until it makes men think they have different natures, depending on whether they rule or submit. The state introduces such a fracture in the way individuals acknowledge each other in the midst of the same space that it gives the impression of being an unprecedented invention. In effect, the state is another kind of meaning for men, giving them a sense of strangeness between those who command and those who obey. But the otherness that the state injects into the social fiber already existed in another form. The state merely places it within society, whereas before it regulated relations between society and beyond. If the state is possible, it is because there is already a mysterious imperative within the society to see itself in something other than itself, to conceive its meaning to be a debt. We must search for the origin of the state not in the separation of a unique locus of power but far beyond, in that which could necessarily give rise to the heteronomy that has haunted human groups since the dawn of time.

I am not saying that the state emerges from the development of a potentiality present at the origin of societies and that develops in their histories. Rather, it is founded on an exterior component of society's vision of itself that may be seen in all earlier societies. This externality need not deploy itself as a division of power. It is fruitless to look to primitive social structure, manifested through this feeling of obligation, for a dynamic principle that brings about the transformation of one economy of power to another. In primitive societies, the debt toward the external is mobilized in service of keeping power within society; in developed states, the obligation to the other serves to legitimate the difference in power between those commanding and those obeying. These are two similar systems, between which there is no logical, a fortiori passage in which one brings about the other and one marks a clear progression with regard to the other. But the two systems represent two heterogeneous modes of assuming and managing the same primordial articulations that allow society itself to exist. The state is neither an absolute social creation nor part and parcel of a normal and predictable linear development of history. Instead, the state should be recognized as one of those unpredictable predictabilities, founded upon necessity, which is not itself necessary. It is from eternity, but not necessarily for eternity. Because, given the recapitulations of human experience, human consciousness eventually wakes up to the constraints that society obeys and that allow it to persevere. If we were to bring these constraints to light and learn to recognize them, might we not begin to dissolve the invisible limits they have always placed on the human enterprise?

Objective conditions do not enlighten us about the origins of religion. On this, Durkheim was right: one must not look to the ways society places itself in nature but rather to society itself and the imperatives it follows through its organization. One must begin with the social space to understand the religious decision to free the human world from its first cause. There is a place where the thought of otherness in the society first arises. We must also understand the exact meaning of the religious fact and its *political* function. For religion is not just a mystical way to illuminate the universe and the connection of phenomena. It also constitutes a veritable social structure, an effective piece of the social reality that fulfills a strategic role in the actual workings of society. Religion is how society relates to the external; it arises politically from the establishment of society's exterior perception of itself. Through religion, a line of division is established between men and the modes of their societal organization. The reasons directing the organization of society exist outside of society. This prevents anyone from questioning the legitimacy of collective life from its very founding—that is, it prevents anyone from exercising power. The philosophy of primitive religion speaks to the symbolic externality of the social foundation rather than the effective division of political authority.

Implicit in this proposition is the exchange of one form of externality for another. For if there is no difference between the living and the legislators of the invisible, there is a distance within the community of men between those who command and those who obey. This distance will be embodied in religion or the state; that is the alternative. Moreover, society exhibits a distance from itself, an internal rupture of the social fabric without which it could not exist. Religion both expresses and neutralizes this split. Religion has its foundation here: if the thought of religion arose, it is because a virtual separation of meaning with regard to the social already existed.

But the separation of society is not random; it corresponds precisely to the original political structuring of society. That structuring placed outside of society the point from which society could conceive of itself, provide itself with meaning, and act upon itself. Religion's consecration of society to something other than itself serves to neutralize the detachment of one instance of power until it is stripped of all meaning. This religious language affirms, on the contrary, that it is the source of power from which man takes his origin as well as his reason for being, the location from which the invisible powers command the visible. But in primitive societies at least, this place is set so far above men that none among them can hope to occupy it. Power exists but is not for men; to attain it, man must cease to be man. No political separation is possible inside society; no man can make himself separate from the rest, utilizing the split between men and the powers to whom mortals owe their way of life to command. As a result, men are united and made equal through this common dispossession. "Our ancestors taught us": behind this positive assertion lies a negative one: "No one among us can teach us." There will be a crucial turn in this arrangement later in history, when the religious fracture from the supernatural comes to justify the division between men. On one side will be those who participate in the essence of supernatural powers; on the other side, the ordinary masses who bow down before the supernatural truth embodied in society. Here the man of power is born: a being created within society but through the sovereign difference with the external and, by his very nature, placed at an infinite distance from the common man. This is an enigmatic moment in the separation of the state, the alienation of men with respect to each other according to whether they have the right to obey or to command. We know nothing more of the reasons that brought about this decisive turn. But by taking the religious dimension into account, the conditions that authorized it can be perceived. The birth of the state corresponds to a reversal in the relation to externality that existed at the social foundation. Once an instrument of equality, the fracture between the living and the founding ones who rule their existence now becomes the source of subjection. Societies before the state could all invoke the wisdom of ancestors, the endeavors of mythical heroes, and the will of gods; no one within those societies could claim to be them, to represent in person the final ends of the universe and impose submission to them. The advent of the state requires and is marked by the advent of the representatives of the invisible and masters of meaning among men. One always owes meaning to the gods, but now debt to the gods is expressed through the mediation of other men.

The state arises by turning this arrangement of difference, originally destined to preserve society against the state, against society itself. The state does not create the externality through which it justifies its own separation from society. It only exploits the already immemorial recognition that the law of things is not within the grasp of men. It entirely transforms the mode by which the society relates to its reason for being and its regulating principles. It introduces within society a separation between the exclusive representatives of the law and the masses whose destiny is to submit, but once again, it does not institute the separation of society from the supposed powers thought to understand it, will it, and rule it. If this earlier separation had not occurred, the state could not have subsequently appeared. In other words, religion was historically the state's condition of possibility. The state could not have been established had it not reflected the earlier division between society and its foundation. If it was able to appear necessary and legitimate, despite the rupture of political equality that it represents, this is because it put a new face on a very old faith in externality: the feeling that we owe society something other than ourselves. Of course, religion was not an institution created out of nothing, whose substance was afterward transmitted to the state. As I have suggested, religion arose out of a still more primitive social structure, which it both expressed and neutralized. If religious thinking was possible, it was because society could not establish itself without dispossessing itself of meaning or placing outside of itself the point from which it could control, understand, and found itself on reason. It is perhaps more precise to say that the foundation of the state is the same as that of religion.

Once this is understood, it then becomes possible to analyze the relations between religion and the state: the symbolic separation of society from its foundation and the political separation between the possessors of legitimate authority and their subjects. At least one thing is clear: no state can be born without a major transformation of primitive religious discourse. This is not to say that changes in the religious sphere are the cause of the state's coming into being. Rather, the appearance of a universal order or the definition of collective ends is absolutely inconceivable without a thorough reformulation of the vision of the "beyond." That men might participate in the divine and themselves represent ultimate wisdom was precisely what the religious arrangement of primitive societies was meant to prevent. We have seen how this was accomplished. What must now be examined in detail are the paths by which, in contrast to what occurs in the primitive world, a human identification with the divine viewpoint emerges, a passage to the externality of the establishing significations. How does a man take on the face of the faceless other thought to command the destiny of all things—and bring himself to be recognized by others as such? How does what is above and beyond men come to take a human form?

However one answers such questions, one thing is clear; the state cannot triumph without the liquidation of religion. If the first states were rooted in religion, it is necessary to the internal development of the state's power that it demolish any reference by society to something other than itself. So long as it presents itself as the representative and agent of divine power, the development of the state is arrested and fails to reach its full potentiality. Its natural destiny is to achieve this externality by which society's organization was hitherto understood, justified, and defined. Where God was, there the state shall be. Or, still paraphrasing Freud, we might say that the state is called upon to dislodge God. The logical conclusion of the state's self-affirmation is its eventual monopoly of the legislative externality that was thought to be beyond the grasp of men—society is now able to think of itself in its entirety through the state, and the state shows itself to be capable of constituting society.

Human history is nothing but the history of a long, victorious battle against political alienation, that is, against an original separation of power, then a defeat that continues to grow larger. But it is also the history of the state, right down to the totalitarian attempts to complete state control that have characterized our epoch. The manifestations of domination are also the stages of a truth, that of the social bond itself. The advent of the state, the liquidation of the religious legitimation of the social order, the affirmation of man's total power over his society, and the dream of absolute domination: these key moments in the genesis of political alienation are also those of a discovery of what man does with man, of what it means to be a social being. The choice of the society against the state, after all, is a prejudice born of an illusion, while to choose the state reflects a willingness to come face to face with the nature of the bond that holds societies together. Do we have a choice, then, between a liberating illusion and the implacable truth of oppression? Or should one perhaps believe that a certain epoch is over, an era characterized by the refusal to ponder the social enigma—the enigma of the division that unifies? Has a new epoch opened, one in which the rejection of domination will be matched by the will to ask what creates and nourishes it?

Indeed, it seems as if man, moved by an obscure intuition that subjection is ingrained into his deepest inner self and makes him what he is, can refuse domination only by simultaneously turning away from fundamental questions. In the rejection of servitude lies a passion for ignorance that tricks man and leads him astray. Men seem to enter history backward, choosing not to see themselves for what they are, refusing to emancipate themselves by seizing control of the power that separates them into masters and slaves. They turn away from the truth that they are the creators and agents of their history. But perhaps we are at the moment when all that is changing, when the desire to be free from masters is matched by the understanding of why we have them. In fact, only masters, worried about justifying themselves, have ever asked why some give orders and others obey. The slaves have always maintained that there is no reason for subjection to exist. Alas, there is a reason, one with more profound energy than their despair. But what if this question—why there are masters and slaves—became the slaves' own question? What if, after millennia of refusing to see the true origins of submission, men began to confront the reasons for power with a will not to fight but to dominate the principle, a will not to stop the master but to become the master? Perhaps we have reached the historical point where we will finally realize the truth of power, the only truth capable of preventing it from being exercised.

—Translated by Kenneth Weinstein

The translator wishes to acknowledge editing assistance from Jacob Scholl and Dwight Cruikshank.

CHAPTER 8

The Modern State

PIERRE MANENT

WHEN SPEAKING of the modern state we speak of the *modern* state, presupposing its distinctiveness. Since the end of the seventeenth century there has been the growing conviction that a group of economic, social, intellectual, and political developments in Europe is changing the setting or regime of human life. But these developments are not thought to have their cause in human reason and will, that is, in human nature. Instead they have been subsumed under other terms: first commerce and enlightenment, then civilization, and finally history. It would seem that European man improved his condition without trying to, or even knowing it.[1] But understanding this rational human development—rational because its effects must be considered good and desirable—forces us to resort to a new inclusive element, no longer nature but history.

At the end of the eighteenth and the beginning of the nineteenth century, the conviction that Europe was entering a new epoch was so strong that philosophers were principally occupied with thinking about, justifying, and celebrating this transition. This period began with Montesquieu and came to a kind of close with Hegel, though their accents were different. Montesquieu's task was essentially critical. He wanted to show that the ancient authority opposing the new authority of "commerce, knowledge, and gentleness"—in short, the authority of Greek philosophy and the Greek city-state—had an insufficient foundation. Therefore the thrust of *The Spirit of the Laws* was the progressive substitution of the modern criterion of liberty for the ancient criterion of virtue. Hegel's task was more purely contemplative. With the French Revolution and the Napoleonic Empire, the triumph of the modern was complete and definitive, and a new reign of reason had been established. For Hegel, it was less a matter of criticizing the ancient than of showing the historical necessity that implied its being overtaken by the modern.

Our view today also differs from that of Montesquieu, but it cannot be identified with Hegel's. We have lived too long under this new reign of reason, we have witnessed too many of its perverse effects to share his assurance. Simultaneously, we cannot, nor do we wish to, renounce the modern faith and go back to some version or other of ancient authority. We want to live and think according to modern reason without having it lead to the progressive historicism that Hegel most coherently and profoundly represented.

Refusing the historicist complacency that placed us at the summit of human history and consciousness, some are now being led to rehabilitate different versions of the "ancient" much more completely than Hegel did and judge the critique to which the Enlightenment subjected it as radically insufficient, almost scandalous. The ancient and the new appear to many interpreters rather like poles of human life, equally conceivable, equally (although antithetically) sensible, regardless of which pole the interpreter favors. Two striking examples of this new "polar" thought are provided by the works of Louis Dumont and Marcel Gauchet.[2] Gauchet thinks about politics and history in terms of the autonomy/heteronomy polarity. Dumont approaches them in terms of individualism and holism. But revealingly, the social type used as a foil to modernity by Dumont and Gauchet is exterior to the European or Western region. For Dumont, the "ancient" is represented by the Indian caste system; for Gauchet, it is "primitive religion." The antithesis or polarity they claim to discover (or at least to reconstruct) is not the one discovered or constructed by the moderns in their struggle against the ancient.[3]

But how is it possible to ignore that the ancient so often spoke Greek? How is it possible to ignore, in other words, that the only truly available antitypes of the modern state and modern philosophy are the Greek city-state and Greek philosophy? Since the world began, there have been only two regimes or political orders that were truly conceived: the Greek city-state and the modern state. Therefore, only this polarity will help us get our bearings and orient ourselves in history. And it is according to this polarity alone that we must do it, since it was through the critique of Greek philosophy and the Greek city-state that modern philosophy and the modern state became aware of and constructed themselves.

The founders of modernity—Machiavelli, Hobbes, Descartes, Spinoza, Locke, Montesquieu, Rousseau—had one thing in common: a radical and often fierce critique of Aristotle. It can indeed be assumed that this "pagan" target was chosen simply because it was safer than attacking Saint Thomas and the onto-theology of the Christian tradition. But one can hardly imagine that in so serious a matter these great minds were mistaken in their target. Aristotle's philosophy was definitely the strategic bolt that had to be sprung. If the modern project was to be intrinsically possible and profitable, then Aristotle's philosophy had to be, quite simply, false.

I have just spoken of the modern project. For those who carefully study the authors mentioned above, the modern political world, whatever else it may be, is also the result of a project founded on a program. Charles Péguy, in a famous text in which he extols Descartes's greatness, describes the *Discourse on Method* as "a program, alas, and it is almost an electoral program."[4] What is so striking in the *Discourse on Method* is just as present in each of the major works of the first modern political philosophy that developed from Machiavelli to Montesquieu.[5]

Greek philosophy was the dialectical meditation on the Greek experience; of it one can truly say that "the owl of Minerva flew at dusk." The modern experience—in particular, the political consequences of the Catholic religion—certainly provided motives for modern philosophy. But they were motives that oriented the will toward the future instead of directing human intelligence toward the eternal and unconditional. One knew that the old world was uninhabitable; but before the nineteenth century there is still no actual experience with living in a new one. Nonetheless, this new world that we now inhabit was already built, in words and thought, by the end of the eighteenth century. Modern political development therefore maintains an essential relationship with the development of modern political philosophy. And observation of this fact led modern thought to elaborate explicit philosophies of history.[6] What was implicit with Montesquieu became explicit, and emphatic, with Hegel.

Hegel teaches us that a philosophy of history is possible only if history is essentially complete, that is, if the inhabitants of the modern state are satisfied—if we are satisfied. Aristotle would not have accepted such a criterion; satisfaction is not happiness. But even if we accept the modest Hegelian criterion, we are not certain of being satisfied. Therefore we have the job of thinking philosophically about political history, a history we hardly dare to pronounce finished.

Yes, we hardly dare to say it. But how difficult it is not to think it! Not thinking it actually amounts to admitting that radically new political principles can still legitimately spring up, or that the liberal-democratic principles of the modern state are not eternally rational and beneficial. Certainly the totalitarian experiences of the century have powerfully convinced us that we have exceedingly good reasons for contenting ourselves with liberal and democratic principles. But contenting oneself is not synonymous with being satisfied. It seems to me that a kind of diluted Hegelianism prevails today. One does not explicitly maintain that the modern state that guarantees human rights is the ultimate form of human order, but the rare authors who dare suggest a genuine alternative are severely reprimanded. It is asserted that for a serious person, only the modern liberal-democratic state can really be conceivable today. But the essence of diluted Hegelianism is pure Hegelianism. And if one is loath to support pure Hegelianism, why not try to think about modern political development without depending on Hegel at all—that is, without seeking any support from a philosophy of history, whether explicit or implicit?

To say that the modern state is the result of a long project directed by a radical program is to suggest that it has the character of a construction, of an artifact. The proposition on its own is often accepted. Authors are quite willing to speak of "modern artificiality." If the intention is critical, then the word is supposedly condemnatory. If it is used descriptively, then it is assumed to convey an important but trivial fact; history textbooks are quite likely to speak of the "construction of the modern state." But the idea of construction, in this context, is not trivial. Far from a banal if convenient and evocative metaphor, it is profoundly enigmatic.

It can be said that the philosophical character of the modern state is entirely contained in its artificiality. For the founders of modern politics, Hobbes and Locke to begin with, man creates the political and even the human order. No metaphor is involved here, since the actual articulation of the modern political order expresses exactly this basic fact. The division between society and the state, between the represented and the representative, expresses and institutionalizes this act of continuous creation of man by himself, which was presupposed by the modern plan.

I have just used the words "continuous creation." Actually, from the moment that the idea of modern representation emerged, it implied and set in motion an indeterminate history. I am not claiming that Hobbes or Locke wanted to set this history in motion. On the contrary, they wanted human nature to be effectively preserved in a habitable and comfortable political order, to be effectively shielded from the disorders induced by religion's political power. But the means of this limited end was an unlimited artifice: the absolute sovereignty of the body politic over itself. Realizing this sovereignty is necessarily an endless task.

Hobbes remarked sarcastically that the medieval theory of the two swords (religious and secular) had been invented so that men would "see double" and not recognize their legitimate sovereign. It can be said that in the modern construction, whose blueprint Hobbes provided, man continues to "see double." By nature he is in society, by sovereignty he is in the state. But since he wants to be a whole, he also wants to be in the state naturally and wants his sovereignty to be present in society through his action. Only exceptional, "unnatural" circumstances could have led modern man to form such a contradictory plan.

I have given elsewhere a schematic explanation of how I see the "theologico-political" origins of the modern state.[7] In my view, the conflict of loyalty between obedience to the natural (or secular) prince and obedience to the supernatural (or spiritual) prince is the key motive for constructing the new prince, who will be neither natural nor supernatural, neither secular nor spiritual, but artificial. Having done this, I felt that I was being strictly faithful both to the factual history of the first modern centuries and to the principal authors of that period, who from Machiavelli to Rousseau repeat that this conflict was the primary problem of "modern," that is "Christian," peoples.[8]

Such an interpretation is anything but original. Who can be unaware that modernity has an essential relationship with Europe's religious history, and that European liberty ultimately results from the conflict between the "two swords"? But the difficulty is to limit oneself as rigorously as possible to the real terms of actual political, religious, and intellectual history. The difficulty is to be as unoriginal as possible and to take absolutely seriously the problems that the men we are studying took absolutely seriously—and rightly so, since for them it was literally a matter of life or death. Above all, one must take absolutely seriously the question of legitimate obedience, to conceive and formulate it in the terms in which it was posed. And the obedience in question did not concern "Christianity" (which never existed as such), but above all the Catholic Church, as a religious "republic" of a new form, and later other churches and religious groupings that sprang up from this initial critique of the Catholic Church.

The men whose thoughts and actions we have to interpret were men like us. They faced real problems. They belonged to political and religious institutions that were fighting other political and religious institutions. In all camps they had convictions and passions, they confronted necessities, they deliberated on the best, the tolerable, and the worst. They were not, unconsciously and involuntarily, simply a passageway for an "anthropological history" or a "history of values" elevated above their trivial preoccupations with the Pope and his bishops. History was not unfolding behind their backs. It will be reasonably argued that these men, the first moderns, could not foresee all the consequences of their actions, and that we are obliged to think about both what they wanted to do and what they actually produced. It will perhaps be added that I myself have pointed out that the founders of modern development set in motion a history that was unintended. And the conclusion will be that our interpretation of modernity must necessarily go beyond what the first moderns explicitly said and did.

This is true. But are we certain we know what they actually produced—that is, do we really know what we are, what our society is? Only if we are strict Hegelians. But since no one really claims to be Hegelian in the strict sense, it must be admitted that we do not know, completely and satisfactorily, what we are. What help then is the frequently heard assertion that we are henceforth doomed to confront our "autonomy without transcendent foundation"? What meaning can be given to this pathetic and vague assertion, which exhorts us to liberty by depriving us of every motive for it?

Moreover, how can it be claimed that this diagnosis arises from the authentic experience—made by us alone, understood by us alone—of modern life, when the wise Locke said precisely the same thing more than three centuries ago and devoted enormous effort to establishing that man is a "self" who is the sovereign author of his "laws" and "moral ideas"?[9] We claim to interpret these men in terms of our unique experience, but in fact the concepts we employ to define ourselves are the same concepts that they themselves invented. We would be obliged to develop a philosophy of history only if our political situation could not be interpreted using concepts provided by these founders of the original modern project. It seems to me that such an interpretation is possible, although it certainly does not give us a complete or ultimate understanding of our situation. But at the very least it "saves the phenomena" with more exactitude than any available philosophy of history, and without claiming to recreate the "anthropogenic" act that anthropological history describes with so much assurance.

In suggesting what this "real history" might be, I would like to draw attention to the following fact: never, for three centuries, has our political situation, the body politic we inhabit, been as realistically close to the working drawing traced by those first architects in the seventeenth century. They constructed in thought that unlimited instrument of sovereignty, that "empty seat" for power, where society administers, represents, and gets to know itself. But this empty seat was for a long time occupied by others, not by Hobbes's geese of the Capitol, those "simple and unpartial creatures."[10] These occupiers included the absolute king, then the sovereign people or the sovereign nation. If the occupant was totalitarian it gave itself an ideological definition and claimed that the empty seat should be occupied by a class or race. In all Western countries today these occupants have lost their prestige. I could say that class as well as nation, not to mention race, are today *in statu evanescendi* as far as their political importance, their representation by or on the seat of power, are concerned. That seat is empty at last, and its occupants take great pride in no longer really occupying it, no longer cluttering it up with "ideologies" or archaic passions, in having finally become truly "modern."

The "class struggle," which evolved roughly between 1848 and 1936, convinced many people that the "abstract," "bourgeois" ideology of human rights and representative government was a temporary device destined to give way to the real agent of history, and that the abstraction of the state, its "religion" as Marx said, would be seized again in a new social and human unity, in a new man whose citizenship would be based on labor. We can see today that the abstraction is still present, and still more abstract; even its national color grows more blurred each day as we approach the working plan drawn up by Hobbes, Locke, and Montesquieu. Why pretend that history's impetuosity is leading us toward uncharted seas when we are actually simply marking time or even retracing our steps? When the historical movement itself leads us to observe as temporarily definitive what we had thought could only be absolutely temporary?

But it will be asked whether the modern state today is the abstraction I describe. Perhaps we have really come back to the beginning; but in that case the return has the freshness of a new beginning. What was in times past an abstract proposition, and not so long ago an ideological illusion, now animates the whole of society. This abstraction is "human rights."

Only a glance at history is needed to recapture the original meaning of the notion of human rights. For its inventors, Hobbes and Locke, the conflict between the incompatible ideas that men have of the supreme good (*summum bonum*) leads to the war of all against all, which endangers everyone's life and thus proves death to be the supreme evil (*summum malum*). Disagreeing about the supreme good, most men recognize death as the supreme evil. It is therefore on this basis, on the fear of death, that the body politic can and must be constructed. It will henceforth devote itself to the modest goal of maintaining the peace among citizens and no longer to making them virtuous or leading them to salvation. The good revealed by this evil is self-preservation, a purely animal impulse and consequently independent of all human opinions. Preserving one's life, then, is the first human right; it is the matrix of human rights. A poor wretch trembling with fear who does not want to die—that is man, and that is his right. And politics is about protecting the basic minimum possessed by all humanity—life, purely and simply. The first impulse leading to the formulation of human rights was defensive. As circumstances were altered, the original tone also changed. As domestic peace in European nations increased, that basic minimum soon appeared far too modest, and the right of self-preservation became the right to comfortable self-preservation. But comfort presupposes property, property presupposes labor, and labor's productivity presupposes the free use of one's talents and what those talents produce. Therefore as Locke saw, self-preservation implies the preservation of one's property and liberty. Soon the man expressing his right is no longer the poor wretch mentioned above but the competent proprietor who intends to obey no one but himself or his freely chosen representative. And little by little, the man who proclaims his rights will discover that he is entitled not just to life but to all desirable human goods, from health to "culture." But these various human goods, to which human rights entitle us, are no longer those whose conflict gave rise to the war of all against all. They have undergone the ordeal of the fear of death and have emerged transformed. In spite of the rapid growth and diversity of the "new rights," the right to self-preservation remains their subterranean and sovereign source.

Before the first moderns, the *good* was equated with man's *ends*, which to be realized or approached had to be inscribed in *law*. The first moderns note that this inscription of man's ends in law is no longer possible because men's ideas about them are incompatible. Furthermore, such inscription is not even desirable because a good cannot be a good for a man who has not freely sought and found it but rather has had it imposed on him by the magistrate. Instead of leading him toward the good in an authoritarian way, the law must allow him to seek his good freely, by prohibiting anyone from hindering this liberty.

Seeking his own good, the modern man of human rights will feel intensely that no one has the right to keep him from it. But simultaneously he will agree that he has no right to constrain his neighbor in the name of the good—that is, that the good he seeks has no claim on his neighbor because the constraint of others, even for the good, leads to the greatest of evils, war. But if my good cannot become law for my neighbor, can it be a very serious law for me? Why would I not abandon, or at least treat lightly, something that my neighbor has the right to do without? The fear of war between ultimate goods soon intervenes between each person and the search for his own good, or at least it colors that search by reducing its urgency. The poor wretch trembling with fear whispers in everyone's ear, "War is the greatest of evils, peace is the greatest of goods." And every person's right to seek his good eventually becomes the right not to seek the good at all.

It will be argued that this sketch of the dynamic of human rights concentrates on its negative side—fear—and slights its positive side—respect. This is not the place to examine the meaning of this noble idea or the role that it has played in our moral and social life since Kant. I shall only note that respect is not far removed from fear, that it is, shall we say, only a refined and superior form of fear; a person is intimidated by what he respects. This respectful fear before another's liberty is certainly one of the most elevated of human feelings. But it becomes such only when it is combined with the desire for another person's good. When, on the contrary, it reduces all social morality, it is nothing more than a spiritual point of honor in a civilized state of nature. At that stage, liberties communicate only through mutual renunciation.

Perhaps it will also be objected that, underestimating the role of respect, I am overestimating that of fear. After all, the memory of the war of all against all, of the wars of religion and the great ideological conflicts that followed, has tended to fade away. In future, it will have progressively less influence on each person's passionate search for his own good and for truth. Men will increasingly do what they recognize they have a right to do. And the eternal human quest for the good and the truth will continue undiminished, the memory of war having been replaced by spontaneous respect, both attentive and cordial, for the neighbor's person and right, without damaging the respect due to the good and the truth. All this is plausible, and it is undoubtedly the hope and wish of those who see in human rights the new spiritual determination of citizens of the modern state. But in my view, experience does not justify this hope. On the contrary, it seems to me that the more remote war becomes in memory, the more fear grows; an imperious assertion becomes bellicose, a confident assertion intolerant, a calm assertion dogmatic. In a word, the spontaneous expression of human nature, which seeks the good or the truth and announces what it believes it has found, now seems threatening and evokes the specter of war—of the state of nature that we have had so much difficulty overcoming.

These are some of the meanings and effects of the new form of law in modern states founded on human rights. The ancient law, whether pagan or Christian, was a commandment, an authoritarian injunction; the law of the modern state is an authoritarian authorization. Its effects force us to note that when authorization occupies the law's place, far from letting nature be what it is and liberty be what it wants to be (as the first moderns hoped), it transforms nature and reorients liberty no less (though differently) than ancient law did. By subtle, indirect but infallible means, authorization comes ever more to resemble an injunction and has the same effects. The law permits the citizen to be indifferent to all the goods that have been the object of the human pursuit; and little by little it orders that indifference. How is it possible to believe that what the law, which is naturally awe-inspiring, allows is truly wrong?

The ancients had recognized that law modifies, transforms, or orients nature; they then used this power to direct human nature toward its good, whether well or poorly conceived. The moderns wanted to construct a law that would be so detached from human nature, so artificial, that it would leave nature completely free to be itself. The result did not meet their expectations. From the moment law's place is occupied, its effect is the same: it modifies nature. Authorization itself becomes authoritarian.

Thus, for understanding the development of the modern state, there is no need to suppose that humanity changed "anthropological" regimes, going from "heteronomy" to "autonomy," for example. The human condition is continuously determined by the relationship maintained between nature and law—and humanity still obeys the law. Whatever the respective advantages and disadvantages of the Greek city-state and the modern state, the modern experience testifies that the Greek understanding of law was superior to the modern understanding. In the political order, at least, law cannot be separated from nature, nor nature from law.

I hope to have suggested this much at least. For appropriately interpreting the modern state, nothing is more necessary than a dialogue with the Greek city-state and Greek philosophy, a dialogue focused on the relationship between nature and law. Only in this way can we both grant the absolutely novel character of modern development and understand the ancient and the new as two versions of the same human order. I am not saying that by so doing we shall obtain the satisfactory knowledge that I am denying to philosophies of history. But the ignorance that remains will not be due essentially to the fact that history is unfinished. Rather it will result from the fact that the human problem, that of the relationship between nature and law, remains intrinsically, naturally, and therefore perpetually insoluble.

—Translated by Rebecca Balinski

Notes

1. The most important author in this context is Montesquieu, and his decisive analysis is found in chap. 20 of book 21 of *The Spirit of the Laws*: "How Commerce in Europe Emerged from Barbarism."

2. See Louis Dumont, *Homo hierarchicus*, 2d ed. (Chicago, 1980), *From Mandeville to Marx: The Genesis and Triumph of Economic Ideology* (Chicago, 1977), *Essays on Individualism* (Chicago, 1986); and Marcel Gauchet, *Le désenchantement du monde* (Paris, 1985).

3. Moreover, the self-interpretations of these societies do not conform to what appears to us to be the fundamental requisites of rationality and philosophy. Dumont subsumes Indian social organization and "conception of the world" under the term "holism"; Gauchet subsumes the political and spiritual regimes of primitive societies under the terms "heteronomy," "dependence," or "debt." In this sort of dialogue, in which one interlocutor (the modern) has the *logos*, there is a great risk of an essential arbitrariness stemming from the insurmountable distance between *mythos* and *logos*, especially when the latter refuses to claim its superiority to the former. One fears that what has been posed as the antitype of the modern has only been constructed. Both Gauchet and Dumont have a very keen sense of the specificity, the radicalness, the absolutely new character of the modern; they also sense that the modern regime is, in some essential way, the opposite of the ancient regime or regimes. Therefore they audaciously and geometrically reconstruct the ancient regime as the contrary of what they see before them. They do it with even greater freedom because their ancient "pole" can raise no objection, since it ignores the philosophical register they are using. In a word, their "ancient" risks being only the shadow cast by their experience of the "new."

4. See "Note sur M. Bergson et la philosophie bergsonienne," in *Oeuvres en prose, 1909–1914* (Paris, 1927).

5. See, for example, Machiavelli, *Proemio* to book 1 of the *Discourses on the First Ten Books of Titus Livius*; Hobbes, "A Review, and Conclusion" in *Leviathan*; Montesquieu, "Invocation to the Muses," at the beginning of book 20.

6. There is no contradiction between the two motives I have suggested, between the retrospective observation of the unwanted but fortunate effects and the prospective will to construct a rational order. The effects of commerce could appear truly fortunate only in light of the plan.

7. See my *An Intellectual History of Liberalism* (Princeton, N.J., 1994).

8. See, for example, Machiavelli, *Discourses on the First Ten Books of Titus Livius*, 2.2, and 3.1; and Rousseau, *The Social Contract*, 4.8.

9. *An Essay Concerning Human Understanding* (1689). But Locke was speaking out against the onto-theology invoked by the traditional authoritarian order, so as to divert us from sublime ends and thus deliver us from their political effects (which are less sublime). He was not claiming to create a new motive from the absence of all motive.

10. Hobbes, "To Mr. Francis Godolphin," dedicatory letter, *Leviathan*.

CHAPTER 9

Ancient, Modern, and Contemporary

JEAN-MARC FERRY

PAST WORLDS enter ours, serving as mirrors in which we see ourselves reflected, and through their mediation we arrive at our own identity. For our world, which has become a thoroughly historical world, is the medium in which the clash of different cultures and past epochs is internalized and appears to us as a conflict of values. Today we gain access to ourselves through others who are doubtless what we once were yet remain autonomous of what we think we now are. Even when we refer to the still-recent past that we call the "birth of the modern," we consider it alien. By contrasting the "modern" with the "ancient," we contrast it with ourselves as well. The "contemporary" world takes its identity from this contrast.

I wish to take up this question of identity from a systematic point of view. I shall begin with the contrast between two principles that are explicitly structured by religion: the *cosmocentric* (or cosmological) principle and the *theocentric* (or theological) principle. I shall then analyze the contemporary understanding of the world as seen through a third principle, which I call *logocentric*. In all these, what is in question is a system of background attitudes by which each member of a given culture establishes relations with objects, other subjects, and himself. Each system in turn might be compared to parts of a sentence: to a religion of the *cosmos*, I see a corresponding ontological primacy of the object; to a religion of the *theos*, an ontological primacy of the subject; and to a religion of the *logos*, an ontological primacy of the "verb." I find this grammatical image useful for distinguishing the meanings of the organizing principles expressed in the worldviews of the ancients, the moderns, and our contemporaries, respectively.

The cosmocentric principle. The idea of the *cosmos* is that of the objective universality of a unitary world that connects all beings according to a principle of order, and with a harmony that inheres in the teleological nature of things, in their purpose. The abode of living creatures—animals, men, and gods—is ordered under the immanent rule of justice; and the harmonious, beautiful order of the cosmos remains for all eternity. Though it is watched over by the gods, it was not created. The cosmos does not presuppose in its principle the activity of a transcendent Subject, nor the power of an original *theos*.

As Kostas Papaioannou once put it, the cosmos is the "history-less world in which the Greeks housed their gods."[1] This was a world "without history," not because ancient Greece objectively had no history but because Greek thought was "entirely focused on the idea of nature and the geometrical cosmos, and had never been able, or rather willing, to work out a *philosophy* of history in the modern sense of the term." Here the cosmos is to be contrasted with the theos the way "nature" is contrasted with "history," or as "objective" is contrasted with "subjective." Thus the Greeks saw the universe as "an order, a *cosmos*, that in a perfect and harmonious totality ordered the infinity of possible forms that are made real by the *phusis*, the eternal movement of procreation." As a cosmos, the objective world is deeply permeated by mind. Objective reality may thus be asserted, and to this extent the external world is not objectivized.

For Papaioannou, this view is quite different from that of modernity. It is also different from that of Christianity, which prior to modernity "internalized the mind in the depths of subjectivity." For if the mind is assigned to a subject that is contrasted with a shadowy world, the universe is not visible like an object for contemplation; external nature can only be reified, which is one way of denying it. But if the universe is the locus of meaning, if it is the cosmos that "no god has created" and that "is the same for all" (as Plato and Sophocles said), then it is impossible to objectivize it by reifying it. It is also impossible to deny it as fallen, as a "matter" to be redeemed by the "mind." Among the ancient Greeks, the classical natural law expressed an objective conception of norms, which did not originate in a subjectivity—for example, the will of God or the plans of men—but rather was inscribed in the immutable nature of things. Norms were objective while history remained ahistorical, as it were; it was conceived on the model of nature and moved like the regular course of the planets, biological cycles on earth, and the unvarying return of the seasons. There is no subject constituting this world—and therefore no historical plan, in either the messianic or the modern sense.

In the conception of the world centered on the cosmos, the subject is thus not *constitutive*. This does not mean, however, that it was not *constituted*. For the human subject, to be constituted is to be conscious of itself as an autonomous example of reflection and decision. And we know that the Greeks were this kind of "free" people before others. Nevertheless, the idea of the cosmos implies that the same universal principles must structure a totality that includes both the objective order of the world and the self's subjective identity. We think it a contradiction to postulate a "constituted subject" that is still guided by a normative system of cosmological references that presents itself as thoroughly objective. So how could (Greek) man set himself up as an autonomous authority for reflection and decision while dealing with an objective world whose normativity preexists him? How can a subject be constituted without being constitutive? In other words, how is the Greek subject possible?

On a practical level, the purpose of what the ancient Greeks called *theoria*, contemplation of the world, was to edify the self through *mimesis*. Mimesis, in turn, was the activity by which the wise man educates himself by communicating with the objective order of things for the purpose of reproducing this order within himself. This mimesis presupposed both a theoretical relation to the world and a practical relation to the self. The theory was thoroughly practical and directed to the self, not to the world; yet in it the subject confronted the universal determinations of being as an ought-to-be. For us, this is barely conceivable. But for the Greeks, this tension responded to the problem of reconciling the self and the world—and it is a tension that points to the advent of reflexive subjectivity.

But the Greek advent of reflexive subjectivity is not the Judeo-Christian advent of constitutive subjectivity. And it is the latter that represents the principle of the modern era. At the outset, this position was not necessarily more "critical" than the cosmocentric one and did not represent a kind of "progress" beyond it. It was simply different. It pertained to another view of the world whose principle could not be found in the Greek representation of the cosmos that "no god created" and that "is the same for all." This other principle had its origin in the Jewish representation of the *theos*, the creator of the sky, the earth, and man. Another constellation was formed on the basis of this principle and soon integrated the cosmological one as well. And it was this integration, first made by the thirteenth-century Christians, that takes us to the threshold of the modern era and the ontological constellation of the subject.

The theocentric principle. In this second configuration, the world is said to be constituted by an active subjectivity who is referred to as God. God is the Subject. It is God who ensures that the world is a determinable creature, an object; it is he who sets the norms through his commandments; it is he who orders human history on a plan actualized by a covenant. And, finally, it is he whom man will have to overcome if man wishes to become the author of his own history. This structure of subjectivity, alien to the Greeks, is present in ancient Judaism and is also essential to the birth of the modern idea of history. The Jews broke with the ahistoricity of the cosmic religion; they did not seek to contain the gods within the disciplinary frameworks of tragedy, nor did they mobilize the restorative powers of memory to struggle against destructive time. Rather they made a pact with time, turning its destructive power into a creative one. Time contains the promise; its horizon is redemption. Potentially now, time takes on the nature of a plan to be actualized. It has none of the ahistorical character of cyclical history, which is modeled on nature and makes no room for distinctively human time. Even if man was not a full-fledged subject, in this view he was at least conceived in the image and likeness of the true subject, God. This is where the specifically modern subjectivity has, if not its starting point, at least its prehistory.

Christian thought was first concerned solely with the relation of the soul to God. In its dialogue with itself, Christian subjectivity as depicted by Saint Augustine wished to know only God and the soul, nothing more. Subjectivity resolutely ignored the relation to the objective world—which Christians pejoratively called "the world"—until the thirteenth century, when the Greek philosophers were revived and, with them, the idea of the cosmos. Unlike the Greek philosophical idea of memory, Christian mystical asceticism did not seek to educate itself by the "recollection" of perfect ideal forms of which the objective world was the paradigm; rather, its task was to intuit in God the ideal of a self-subject, an activity that the human soul could recognize as the paradigm of its own. Through this other mimesis, which was very different from the Greek mimesis, the Christian did not learn to recognize the structure of an inner objective order but rather the activity of a subjective power. This relationship, established by the self to itself through the representative "soul" and "God," paved the way for the discovery of a freedom that was very different from Greek freedom. Greek freedom was political, discursive, and exercised in public debate; Christian freedom represented the subversive power of the individual who must find the principles of legitimacy and truth within. This only fully developed, however, when the Christians took up the task of harmonizing the laws of the cosmos with the Ten Commandments. This onto-theological synthesis put an end to the earlier devalorization of the objective world, thus working out the relation between the subject and the object on an almost modern basis; the object became the restored cosmos, and the subject of the cosmos became the theos. And this meant that for the first time, the laws objectively structuring the universe had their origin in a subjectivity.

It is significant that the birth of the modern corresponds rather precisely to a period of crisis in which, after the collapse of Thomistic onto-theology, no order of the world was symbolically guaranteed. The Machiavellian moment was not, however, the Kantian moment—that distinctively "contemporary" moment that, several centuries later, provided new philosophical foundations of science and morality to replace ancient ones. The distinctively modern moment was rather a moment of crisis and transition, a critical moment in which the primacy of the human subject had to be affirmed in order to escape the world's intrinsic absurdity.

In this respect Hobbes's position is representative; only the subjectivity of a distinctively human project could endow the unintelligible world with meaning and purpose. Hobbes could not accept an objective teleology, and he found the mechanistic philosophy of his time absurd; as Kant said, he only offered a "distressing indeterminacy." And as Leo Strauss put it, Hobbes needed "an island" from which to determine external reality.[2] That island is the subject whose activity determines the knowable—that is, a subject knows it on the basis of the subject's own ends, will, and self-interest. To the challenge of the absurd, Hobbes appeals to a subjective teleology by which man posits his ends and in doing this posits himself as a constitutive subjectivity. But on this new basis a completely new problematic took form for other thinkers: that of synthesis. God's veracity does not guarantee agreement between the subject of knowledge and the object known. The edifice of a "metaphysics of subjectivity" in the strict sense collapses with the obsolescence of the Spinozistic principle equating God and nature.

This principle also underlay the metaphysical project of deducing nature a priori on the basis of the understanding. Spinoza declared that the universal laws of nature "are nothing other than the eternal decrees of God"; human understanding could then reconstruct these same laws solely through intellectual intuition, provided that God made human understanding the (finite) analogy of divine understanding. But the divine guarantee of an *adaequatio rei et intellectu* cannot work as long as the human mind remains autonomous relative to the laws of nature in God. At the same time, nature cannot be interpreted by reference to what it would be for God. Nature changes its nature, so to speak, with the abandonment of an intellectual intuition that communicates between the three poles of the metaphysical triangle: soul, world, and God. "Sensory intuition" took the place of "intellectual intuition" to ensure the objectivity of knowledge. Man could now know the physical world only by following the course of things as produced externally, independently of the thinking substance in us. It was no longer the definition of essences that provided access to the real but the description of phenomena. Physics was no longer reducible to geometry; instead, arithmetic became the means of connecting observed phenomena according to the relations of the theory of numbers and the general logic of relations.

This Hume-inspired criticism pointed the way to a postmetaphysical era. Without eliminating the constitutive role of human subjectivity—rather, by radicalizing it through a conception of human finitude free from comparison with God's infinite understanding—the eighteenth century explicitly recognized in this subject an *other*. This other was in objective nature, the object as such, but also in the intersubjective relation itself, the alter ego of the other subject. For the old problematic of deduction, it substituted the analytic faculty; and for the problematic of connection, it turned to a new problematic of seeing the world under the sign of synthetic operations. Let us call this the principle of the "verb."

The logocentric principle. The logic of the verb does not lie in the terms of a relation, either the term "object" or the term "subject," but in the relation itself or, so to speak, in the principle of connection. This third determination seems to us less obvious than the two preceding ones, however, because many contemporary thinkers have accustomed us to thinking of the history of modernity as a process of the radicalization of subjectivism. This interpretation is quite simply untrue. It began when Heidegger and some of his followers treated the whole period running from Descartes to Nietzsche as partaking of a "metaphysics of subjectivity." This view has almost become the dominant ideology within philosophy, as far as the historical understanding of its own identity is concerned. However, ontological criteria such as the "forgetfulness of Being" (Heidegger), the "loss of common sense" (Arendt), and the "lowering of the standard" (Strauss) do not permit us to understand Machiavelli, More, Bacon, and Hobbes in the same way that we understand Kant, Fichte, Schelling, and Hegel.

It is important, therefore, to describe the emergence of a new problem, as crucial for us today as was the subjective appropriation of the world for the first moderns or the objective consolidation of the self for the ancients. And what distinguishes the "contemporary" is its turn toward a logos that is secularized in everyday communication: it is the problem of the reciprocal recognition of individuals and cultures within an apparently "empty" space. The images of the world inherited from religion have lost their normative power for regulating common life and by themselves can no longer ensure the stability of social bonds. In this "disenchanted" world, as Max Weber called it, in which even the ethical core of religion has ceased to be the ground for collective practices and the reference point of common identity, the fundamental questions to be asked are these: How can individuals enter into a reciprocal relation and so constitute the community they need in order to constitute themselves? How can the ego recognize in the "alter" the one who can recognize the ego as an Alter-ego? In other words, how can two subjects reciprocally constitute themselves as such, thus constituting the community that constitutes them?

At the outset, the logical problem is that of a society both established and establishing; if society thus presupposes an original "social contract," the contracting parties can have no existence prior to the more profound community assumed in the contract. This vicious circle made its appearance with the overthrow of Hobbes's absolutist formula: "Authority, not truth, sets the law." The fact that "truth" and not "authority" was henceforth to set the law might certainly lead to a dictatorship of reason, as when the spirit of the Enlightenment was perverted into that of the Terror. The idea behind the reference to the "verities of reason," however, was aimed more at the common sense of "enlightened minds," a consensus of "reasonable beings." Philosophically, the principle of the Enlightenment must be interpreted in the light of Kant and not of Descartes. Kant did not simply say that legitimacy is founded in truth; he meant that the objectivity to which this truth could aspire is ultimately grounded in the idea of a possible intersubjectivity, and not in the monological certitude of the *cogito.* Truth is not despotic. The first moderns did not believe in this difference between certitude and truth; truth presupposes getting beyond the subjectivity of an "I" to the intersubjectivity of a "we." Sociologically, we can connect this philosophical intuition with the historical changeover from "community" to "society," the affirmation of individualism, the formation of systems of competing values, the "social question," as well as the recognition of a lingering division within developed societies.

When the problem of a chronic structural conflict between the interests of individuals or groups clearly arises within a community, and when the transition from "community" to "society" is perceived as an affirmation of individualism, the problem of social pacification becomes less important than that of social harmonization. The Hobbesian model of a univocal subject with a vital interest common to all humanity must in turn be rethought. We must put an end to any preconceived idea of the empirically homogeneous subject and take up the problematic of the coordination of social interests and the connection between particular subjects. Historically, these problems were first resolved in new conceptions of the social order, which corresponded to what has sometimes been called the "bourgeois" vision of the world. This was the model of the market in Adam Smith's economic philosophy, and also the model of the social contract in Rousseau's political philosophy. But it was also evident in Leibniz's monadology, which as a model of preordained harmony did not lose its metaphysical credibility until the mid-nineteenth century and still retains its power as a paradigm for science.

Thus, even before the advent of the great "philosophies of reason" with German idealism, the real was considered from the viewpoint of the rational outcome of a competition between elementary subjective and objective forces. On the basis of these, a social entity was thought to be constituted, whose logic or "reason" was not reducible to that of its individual components. Norms were then determined on the basis of a universality that is not that of the subject's common nature but the objective result of the interaction of all the subjective purposes of the agents. This vision of the social order was also found in the conception of history. History is indeed constituted by the interplay of individual activities, particular passions, and subjective interests. But the rationality that emerges from it is of a quite different order from the one that is valid for each agent taken separately, even when the agents all behave in a rational or reasonable way. Following this dialectical structure, the integration of the singular subjective activities reflects the logic of an interaction that may be strategic or communicational. This is the core of the scheme that was presented in the rationalist tradition.

Among the "contemporaries," we have as a foundation a more complex scheme of synthesis explaining the social and historical process in terms of a rationalization of the real. The model remains valid today, even if we judge ideologically outmoded a belief in human progress through the dissemination of the Enlightenment, the eschatology of societal emancipation through the rule of law, or the ideal of unifying mankind under laws of freedom. But a crisis affecting the European consciousness began in the second half of the nineteenth century and has lasted a long time. It culminated in the first half of the twentieth century and is only now ending with the death of the leading thinkers who dominated German culture up to the end of the 1960s. It brought forth new models, both opposed and complementary, of technocratism and decisionism, scientism and historicism, positivism and existentialism. And since, under Nietzsche's influence, people ceased to believe in reason understood as the principle of connecting the particular and the general within a universal, Western culture today gives the impression of permanently wavering between blind adherence to the achievements of science and technology, and the reactive invocation of the nonaligned forces of desire, violence, and madness. Despite these theoretical blows, however, nothing could dislodge the contemporary understanding of the world from its rational moorings. From the start of German idealism around 1800, this contemporary understanding overturned the schema of a subject that can be contrasted with the object as a thing in itself. What I have called the logic of the "verb" comes out notably in the idea of a medium in which we find the reciprocal determination of the objective and the subjective. This medium is that of *differentiated relations*: the subject's relation to the object (I–it), its relation to another subject (I–you), and its relation to itself (I–I). Thus the "verb" is explicitly "conjugated" in the grammatical ontology of the three personal pronouns: I, you, it. By granting primacy to these sorts of relations, we can arrive at a pragmatic view of truth that does not need to be hypostatized in a metaphysical idea but becomes only a question of method.

For example, take the three statements: (a) "This is"; (b) "This ought to be"; and (c) "Assertions A and B are true." For every domain of validity, the constitution of knowledge presupposes a permanent interplay of iterations between the questioning "subject" and the questioned "object." For the constitution of what is objective, legitimate, or true, the *experiments* in the first domain, the *negotiations* in the second, and the *discussions* in the third express a logic in which validity is established at the conclusion of exchanges that are methodologically ordered and systematically organized. The question of truth is addressed here in terms that are unlikely to be disputed by the contemporary models of disillusioned thought. The "truth" becomes a pragmatic question that can be taken up without dramatic entreaties to "overcome metaphysics." It is enough to pay attention to the meaning involved in the performative dimension of language acts when they refer either to states of things and events that occur in the objective world, or to situations and acts that are expected in the social world, or to emotions and opinions that are experienced in the subjective world.

Descriptive *observations*, normative *prescriptions*, and expressive *evaluations* give rise to those elementary language acts by which socialized subjects make reference to the world in general and seek to understand each other concerning what is, what ought to be, and what is felt in relation to what is or what ought to be. Any process of understanding presupposes a proposer and an opposer, each affirming something that is, that ought to be, or that is experienced. Even when such assertions are put forward in the hypothetical mode by the one who proposes, and are seen from a problematic viewpoint by the one who opposes, they are still connected with a claim to validity. In saying that "this is," or "this ought to be," or "I am having this experience," I am not merely making a claim about the correctness of a fact, the rightness of a norm, or the authenticity of an expression. I also making a claim about the truth of the proposition. It is unimportant what the nuances and hypothetical restrictions are to which we subject both our own assertions and those addressed to us. They have the propositional structure of human knowledge in general, without which no community of language, representations, and background knowledge—and consequently no *world*—could be constituted.

Just as there is no assertion without a claim to truth—including, of course, the case of the assertion that there is no truth—there is no world in the absence of a propositional form of assertions. So that the "propositional text" presented in language acts may be socially accepted as a symbolic component of the world experienced in common, this text must be considered from the viewpoint of a "communicational act" whose claim to validity demands to be recognized. While the propositional structure of the text forms the theoretical element of reason embodied in the symbols of a culture, the communicational procedure of the act that is linked to illocutions forms the *practical* element of reason. This element is designed to perpetuate or renew the knowledge stored up in these symbols by ensuring the relation between the agents and their world. The hermeneutic intuition of a world that is historically conditioned by a structure of linguistic precomprehension is not enough to establish the social bond as a product of language. To this must be added the pragmatic intuition of a world historically actualized in the process of linguistic intercomprehension, in the intersubjectivity of reciprocal conversation.

In the twentieth century, the postmetaphysical streams of phenomenology and existential ontology have highlighted the hermeneutic aspect of a structure of linguistic precomprehension that "speaks us" and "possesses us." In the tradition of Heidegger, the attempts of Hans-Georg Gadamer are exemplary in this regard. The linguistic logos becomes the "verb" that no subject can appropriate. To affirm the religion of the logos, however, one does not need to cut the "verb" off from its intimate relations to the object and the subject; we need not treat it as a metahistorical event, a "destiny" or "miracle of Being," that "throws" meaning down to human beings from the height of ontological "difference." The pragmatic element in language shows not only the locus of the "verb," the creator of meaning, but also the activity of the subjects communicating among themselves and the diversity of the objects they refer to. Without hiding behind the veil of a theos, this logos uncovers the rational core of religion as such: the daily performance of the reason that connects us.

A glance at Anglo-Saxon analytic philosophy or German hermeneutic philosophy suffices to show how important the themes of language and communication have become. These "turns" do not necessarily betray the powerlessness of philosophy. Rather, they represent an innovative activation of age-old ontological preoccupations: those concerning the constitution of the world and the nature of our relations in it—which are organized by religion. But this religion no longer designates the reason of a cosmos ensuring the harmony of objective relations in nature; nor is it the religion of a theos governing the order of the world through the subjectivity of a free will. Rather, it is connected with the idea of a logos that mediates the communication by which the subjects assure themselves of both the objectivity of the external world and the intersubjectivity of their internal world. What is at stake is a reappropriation of objectivized meaning in our institutions. The representations that orient actions socially according to culturally differentiated "spheres of values," as Max Weber called them, can be thematized in the reflexive form of arguments that respect the diversity of "language games" and reflect the heterogeneity of "forms of life."

—Translated by Franklin Philip

Notes

1. Kostas Papaioannou, *La consécration de l'histoire* (Paris, 1983).
2. Leo Strauss, *Natural Right and History* (Chicago, 1953).

PART FOUR

What Are Human Rights?

NOWHERE HAS the break with postwar modes of French thought been more apparent than in the new interest, both theoretical and political, in human rights. Whereas the "philosophies of suspicion" ignored such "discourse" or tried to delegitimize it as ideological, more recent writers have sought to provide a foundation for rights and liberal law. In contrast to the Anglo-American tradition, however, their theoretical writings begin in a critical analysis of the philosophical tradition on these questions. In "How to Think about Rights," Luc Ferry and Alain Renaut argue that no philosophy of rights is compatible with the Hegelian and Heideggerian historicims that recently dominated French philosophy, and that the latter must therefore be abandoned. As an alternative they propose a revision of Kant's and Fichte's theory of subjectivity as a possible foundation for modern ethics and politics. Blandine Kriegel vigorously criticizes this modern subjectivist approach, tracing its lineage back to Pufendorf and Descartes. There is, she insists, a superior tradition of modern natural law beginning in Spinoza and Locke that offers a more realistic picture of man's natural sociability. Stéphane Rials raises a slightly different problem, that of the radical voluntarism of certain modern theories of rights. Rials sees the roots of this voluntarism in medieval nominalism, and its flowering in Rousseau's depiction of the "general will." He believes that this conception of rights as willed and created by political society made it difficult (especially in France) to conceive of modern rights as limits to the exercise of political power.

CHAPTER 10

How to Think about Rights

LUC FERRY AND ALAIN RENAUT

THE RECENT return to the idea of rights is historically paradoxical. Marxist analysis, continuing in the vein of *On the Jewish Question*, has traditionally portrayed human rights as those of the self-interested person isolated from the collectivity—in short, as the rights of particular interests in bourgeois society and not as a universal model. While still significant, Marxism has been so undermined recently that Marx's supposedly "demystifying" readings no longer preclude other understandings of human rights. Rather, the paradox is to be found in the establishment of *man as such* as a value: in defending man as such against his negation by totalitarianisms, the present call for human rights presupposes the idea of a human nature or essence and makes this idea the foundation of juridical values. In this sense, a reference to human rights today clearly entails what must be called "humanism."[1]

There are two reasons why the simultaneous return to human rights and to humanism is paradoxical. The first is that this concept of "man" whose rights are now being recalled has been considered old hat by many for more than two decades now.[2] Under these circumstances, how are we to understand such a "return"? Second, in the political spheres where the discourse of human rights now reigns, the dominant mode of thought is still largely historicist even if the Marxist component is less important than it once was. Leo Strauss defined historicism as a kind of relativism, the refusal to admit a standard that is not a pure convention validated by history.[3] How can such a rejection of essences, the wish to historicize and "dialecticalize" everything, square with a discourse that makes man and his rights a kind of atemporal universal, a suprahistorical value implying a limit to the systematic historicization of all notions?

To summarize the paradox, how can we speak of human rights against a background of antihumanism and historicism? Highlighting this paradox enables us to set out a possible philosophical investigation into the contemporary return to rights. For if philosophizing consists in thinking one's own thought, in clarifying the theoretical conditions of possibility of one's utterances (as Fichte believed), the "philosophy of right" will consist primarily in clarifying the theoretical conditions of possibility for particular juridical discourses. In this regard, the present renewal of a certain juridical discourse in politics ("rights talk") would gain in clarifying its transcendental conditions of possibility, thus subjecting itself to philosophical interrogation. This is especially true if these are questions about the compatibility of this discourse with some of the most salient components of contemporary thought, particularly antihumanism and historicism.

To sketch out such a philosophy of human rights, we must first proceed by identifying (without analyzing) the ontologies with which juridical humanism is clearly incompatible. This would call for an outline of the theoretical frameworks within which any idea of human rights would be incoherent. From this vantage point two ontological models seem necessarily to be excluded.

The first, which found its fullest historical presentation in Hegel, can be called the theory of the "cunning of reason." It was Hegel's well-known thesis that everything in history has unfolded rationally, including what may seem to be irrational or senseless (passion, wars, evil); indeed, the rationality of the historical process is even said to be actualized through them. But if we conceive of history as governed by laws such that nothing in it happens without a reason, if we subject the historical to the principle of reason, how is this *historicism* incompatible with the juridical humanism of human rights?[4] Without rigorously analyzing the way in which the incompatibility can be seen in the Hegelian idea of right, we shall stress the necessarily *antijuridical* meaning of this conception of history. For if a rationality is at work in the historical process, the course of history is clearly necessary, and thus what happened had to happen when it happened and as it happened. In other words, the "cunning of reason" rules out any discrepancy between the "is" and the "ought to be," thus ruling out any distinction between the domain of facts and the domain of values. As we read in Hegel, the Ideal is actualized for all eternity through the historical process; this process is also the Good actualizing itself.[5]

In this sense, just as the "cunning of reason" implies a criticism of the moral view of the world, it involves a criticism of what could be called a juridical view of the world. That is, it rules out the possibility of coherently disputing fact in the name of right, of condemning a political reality in the name of juridical values thought to be transcendent relative to that reality—particularly relative to the historical reality of the state.[6] (And here historicism necessarily goes together with juridical positivism.) In short, we clearly see what meaning the idea of natural right—that of modern jusnaturalism—could have in a theoretical context where the idea of the "ought to be" makes no sense. In the celebrated formula that Hegel took from Schiller, the history of the world becomes the world's tribunal ("Weltgeschichte ist Weltgericht"): the standard of justice becomes success or effectiveness in history. The inevitable result is that, for any historicism or theory of the "cunning of reason," the conception of the social as the locus of rights tends to be merely a moment in a process that culminates beyond right. As in Hegel, the changeover from right to state—which, actualizing the aspirations of individuals, embodies right—becomes what Michel Villey called "the supreme right against individuals."[7] It becomes an *Aufhebung* of the traditional idea of right, by which the individual could be defended against the state. This is just as clear in Marx and in the Marxist tradition, which treats communism as the supersession of right.[8]

This connection between the "cunning of reason" and the negation of right is well known. But there is a danger in drawing hasty conclusions from it for developing a consistent juridical humanism. If the historicist subjection of destiny to the powerful principle of reason implies a negation of rights, one easily arrives at the conviction—a correct one, moreover—that a philosophically grounded return to rights must involve a criticism of the rationalist philosophies of history. But here there is a risk of falling into a second theoretical model that also seems incompatible with a nonpositivistic conception of right. In fleeing the necessity of the "cunning of reason," one could be led to an idea of history that abandons the principle of reason altogether: from the rejection of the thesis that everything in history has unfolded rationally to the pronouncement that in history the event, like the rose, "is without a why." We would then find ourselves in Heidegger's company. If criticizing "reason in history" means excluding history from the metaphysical tyranny of reason, the Heideggerian notion of the "history of being" offers a model antithetical to that of the "cunning of reason."[9]

The model of the "history of Being," however, seems no more compatible with the discourse of human rights than the Hegelian one. One reason is Heidegger's calling into question of humanism, which he believed to originate in the metaphysics of subjectivity as a valorization of man—or simply as a valorization, for as he wrote, "every valuing . . . is a subjectivizing."[10] Another is that the Heideggerian model seems to represent simply a new form of historicism.[11] In his *Principle of Reason*, for example, Heidegger stresses that every era of history has "its own necessity." Certainly, this is a nondialectical necessity and does not imply any possible deduction of an era on the basis of preceding eras; rather, it is a "historial" or "destinal" necessity wherein each era can be thought of as an aspect or "opening" of Being.[12]

The clearest sign of historicism here, however, is the fact that Heidegger's deconstruction of metaphysics (like Nietzsche's) involves a criticism of the split between the real and the ideal, between the "is" and the "ought to be." We can see this clearly in the *Introduction to Metaphysics*, in which, from the Platonic meditation on the idea of the good to the modern idea of "values," the distinction between the "is" and the "ought to be" is presented as one of the faces of that "limitation of Being" by which Being found itself progressively emptied of everything contrasted with it: being and becoming, being and appearing, being and thought, being and ought-to-be. This distinction lowers the question of Being, taking part in the history of the forgetting of Being, hence of the "decline of thought." Through it, Being is distinguished from the "beyond being" that is "thus attributed to being itself as a reference," and "Being is no longer what gives the measure."[13]

Consequently, if the distinction between the real and the ideal is inscribed in the logic of the metaphysical forgetting of being, it is clear that the thinking that tries to be faithful to its "fundamental question" must also steer clear of this obstacle to the recollection of Being. But if that is the case, if no mention can be made of the distinction between the real and the ideal, one certainly finds oneself within the space of *historicism*. The disappearance of all measure "beyond Being" to judge "Being" strongly risks draining the idea of right of all meaning. This explains the severity with which Strauss, in his effort to restore the dimension of right against the different forms of historicism, discusses Heidegger's thought (though on many points his deconstruction of modern thought is comparable to the Heideggerian analyses).

Nonetheless, if the two Hegelian and Heideggerian models whose historicist implications we have just sketched are incompatible with an authentic idea of right, a critique of the "rationalist philosophies of history" is not enough to give the discourse of human rights the philosophy that it deserves. This discourse must also be philosophically rooted in a *critique of reason*. But not just any critique of reason is suitable for theoretically grounding such discourse, since the Heideggerian denunciation of reason as "the enemy of thought" threatens to rob this discourse too of any meaning. Philosophical thinking about human rights therefore requires a critique of reason that does not obviate the possibility of referring to "man taken uniquely as such" or condemn the establishment, beyond being, of a measure of being. In other words, a philosophy of human rights must be a humanism that does not lapse into a naive metaphysics of subjectivity. For as Heidegger correctly showed, such metaphysics culminates in the Hegelian model of a system in which the self is all reality, a system that by identifying the real with the rational also prohibits any idea of the "ought to be"—and consequently any idea of right.

These formulations of the philosophical "requisites" of a discourse of human rights define, negatively as it were, a place for philosophical *criticism*. A radical criticism of reason, as a reading of the *Critique of Judg-*

ment shows, allows reference to "values" (aesthetic and ethical) around which "common meaning" or "intersubjectivity" may be conceived.[14] It is no coincidence that even before Kant published his own *Doctrine of Right* in 1797 his earliest disciples indicated the fruitfulness of criticism in this domain in a proliferation of juridical writings. Someday it will be necessary to trace the stages in this extraordinary history of the Kantian juridical school through the works of Hufeland, Schmid, Maimon, Reinhard, Ehrard, Schelling, Feuerbach—and of course Fichte, whose *Principles of Natural Right* (1796) is surely the greatest expression of the power of a certain critique of reason in grounding a "non-naive" idea of juridical values (without lapsing into a naive metaphysics of subjectivity).

The existence of such a school cannot by itself establish that philosophical criticism can fulfill the theoretical conditions required for giving a coherent foundation to the discourse of human rights. For this, it would be necessary to show how the criticist critique of reason preserves the notion of value after the criticism of metaphysics. Here we shall merely say provisionally that if reference to values is still possible within the framework of such a critique of reason, it is precisely insofar as Kant's critique is incomplete. If indeed the valorization of the Beautiful (hence of the Good) is thinkable through the *Critique of Judgment*, it is because the metaphysical ideas, once deconstructed and deobjectivized (that is, concerning their ontological claims), preserve a form of legitimacy after that critique. Although criticized as to their possible truth value, as to their illusory capacity for constituting the real, their meaning is still preserved by virtue of purely subjective exigencies distinctive of every human subject, and consequently in their ideas' capacity for regulating the theoretical or practical functioning subjectivity.[15]

We are in no way claiming that these necessarily allusive and incomplete suggestions are sufficient to guarantee the possibility of establishing criticism as the "philosophy of human rights." For this, it would have to be shown that Kant's or Fichte's doctrines of right can legitimately also refer to a non-naive notion of humanity, to that notion of "man as such" which, as we have seen, the discourse of human rights needs to exist. Such an exercise would have to show, first, that in his *On Education* Kant dismisses any "naive" concept of "man," since he clearly explains that there can be no question of "human nature" and hence of a conceptual essence of humanity.[16] Second, it would have to show that, despite this "deconceptualization" of man, the notion of humanity is retained as a regulative idea, with a value of meaning, or as Kant also says, as a symbolic value. Still, registering this symbolic status of the idea of "humanity" in criticist discourse cannot resolve all the problems. For that would mean going into the details (and difficulties) of Kant's general theory of the schematism, of which symbolism is only a special case. Above all, it would be necessary to determine the real impact of this shift from the level of *truth* or *concept* to that of *meaning* or *symbol*. Is this shift enough to guarantee a theoretical "escape" from metaphysical discourse about "man as such"? And, practically, does it sufficiently preserve the possibility of a reference to a "man" whose rights could be concretely defended?

These are surely the main questions that make this labor necessary and can drive the search beyond a simple return to the letter of the Kantian or Fichtean texts. It seems to us, however, that if one is not inspired by the criticist critique of reason, by its preservation of what remains of metaphysics after criticism, one is liable to fail to ground references to values and to the idea of "man." Without these, the appeal to human rights remains eternally ungrounded and literally meaningless.

—Translated by Franklin Philip

Notes

1. We refer to Heidegger's definition of humanism. In his "Letter on Humanism" he calls it the conception of the real, for it takes man as such to matter and, by making human ego the foundation, implies the metaphysics of subjectivity.

2. See, for example, Marcel Gauchet, "Les droits de l'homme ne sont pas une politique," *Le Débat* (July–August 1980), and Claude Lefort, "Droits de l'homme en politique," *Libre*, no. 7 (1980).

3. Leo Strauss, *Natural Right and History* (Chicago, 1953).

4. This time the term "historicism" is used in Popper's sense (See Karl R. Popper, *The Open Society and Its Enemies* (London, 1945). But it is clear that the historicism criticized by Popper also implies historicism in the sense attacked by Strauss. If everything in history has unfolded rationally, everything is necessary as a moment in the historical process, and thus there can be no transcendent norm for judging the real; consequently, all norms are themselves to be thought of as historical, and their emergence is a mere moment in the process. Thus we arrive at the Straussian concept of historicism as relativism.

5. Leo Strauss analyzed the successive waves by which the "ought to be" was eliminated in modern political thought. See his "The Three Waves of Modernity," in *Political Philosophy: Six Essays by Leo Strauss* (Indianapolis, 1975).

6. We are of course aware of the recent works that have tried—often successfully—to "revalorize" Hegelianism (such as those of Joachim Ritter or Eric Weil), in which Hegel is presented as attacking the injustices of some particular political or juridical model, for example, that of Roman law or the Terror. We are also aware of the passages in his work criticizing the Historical School's juridical positivism. It is well known that Hegel did not see himself as either a jusnaturalist or a positivist. Nevertheless, as Habermas has shown in his *Theory and Practice* (Boston, 1973), it is still true that the denunciation of injustice is the very stuff of history, that it is history itself that plays the role of critical authority with regard

to positivity in Hegel. In other words, it is history that criticizes history, and not right that criticizes right.

7. Michel Villey, *Philosophie du droit* (Paris, 1975), vol. 1, 177.

8. See Philippe Raynaud's excellent article, "Bourdieu," in the present collection.

9. On this antithesis between Hegel and Heidegger as to the idea of history, see Martin Heidegger, *The Principle of Reason*, trans. Reginald Lilly (Bloomington, Ind., 1991), 84–92.

10. See his "Letter on Humanism," trans. Frank A. Capuzzi and J. Glenn Gray, in David Farrell Krell, ed., *Martin Heidegger: Basic Writings* (New York, 1977), 229. See also Luc Ferry and Alain Renaut, "La dimension éthique dans la pensée de Heidegger (de Heidegger à Kant)," in *Nachdenken über Heidegger* (Hildesheim, 1980), 36–54; "La question de l'éthique après Heidegger," in *Les fins de l'homme* (Paris, 1981).

11. On this "existentialist historicism," see Luc Ferry, "De la critique de l'historicisme à la question du droit," in *Rejouer le politique* (Paris, 1982).

12. On *Geschichte*, *Geschick* and *Schicksal*, see for example Heidegger, *Principle of Reason*, trans. Reginald Lilly (Bloomington Ind., 1991). The statement, "Each era has its own necessity," comes from Heidegger, *Nietzsche*, vol. 2, trans. David Farrell Krell (San Francisco, 1979), part 1.

13. Martin Heidegger, *Introduction to Metaphysics*, trans. Ralph Manheim (New Haven, 1959), 165.

14. On the articulation to be worked out between esthetics and dialectics, see Luc Ferry and Alain Renaut, "D'un retour à Kant," *Ornicar* (1980), reprinted in our *Système et critique* (Brussels, 1985).

15. See the appendix to the *Transcendental Dialectic*. For a somewhat less sketchy outline of this argument, see the conclusion of our "La question de l'éthique après Heidegger."

16. Fichte repeats this theme in his *Principles of Natural Right*: "Every animal *is* what it is, man alone is originally nothing." On this point, see the introduction by Alexis Philonenko to the French edition of Kant's *On Education* (*Réflexions sur l'éducation* [Paris, 1970]).

CHAPTER 11

Rights and Natural Law

BLANDINE KRIEGEL

WHAT LED French thought to drift away from natural law? Attempting to answer such a question leads one to confront the enigma of natural right, about which both ancient and modern thinkers had their theories. *Natural law* and *natural right* are not simple expressions, nor do they mean the same thing. The idea of natural law implies the existence of an immutable justice inscribed in the universe. In their relations men must conform to this standard of justice, independently of positive laws and prior to or along with civil conventions. The law of nature presupposes an order in the world, in external nature as well as in human consciousness. What makes modern natural right such an enigma is its connection with the two distinct ideas of law and nature. Defining natural right depends on how one defines both of these terms.

Let us take the idea of law first. When modern natural right made its appearance, it did so under the direct influence of the Bible, at the hands of theologians such as Vitorio, De Soto, Las Casas, and Suarez. These writers, whose thought bore the influence of the Marrano experience, were the leading figures of the new wave of Spanish scholasticism that emerged in the sixteenth century. The founder of modern international law, Francisco de Vitorio, who read and admired Erasmus, pointed out that civil society rests on a natural foundation and that human law has its roots in divine law. In his *De Indis* of 1539, Vitorio maintained that Indians had the same right to liberty and property as all other human beings and that a number of rights can be deduced logically from human nature itself. Not long after, in his *De legibus ac Deo legislatore*, Suarez grounded his rights doctrine in the moral law commanded by a higher authority, which the theologians were charged to interpret.

As for the idea of nature, modern natural-right theory came into its own in the sixteenth century, thanks to Grotius, Pufendorf, Burlamaqui, Barbeyrac, and other thinkers of the so-called school of natural right and the law of nations. Their clean break with classical and scholastic natural right in turn had its origins in the revolution in the concept of nature brought about by Galileo, Descartes, and Newton. Galileo introduced a Euclidean perspective into physics and formulated the principle that the book of nature is written in the language of mathematics. That principle expanded the bubble of what Alexander Koyré called the "closed world" until it burst into the "infinite universe." More than that, it destroyed the concept of a heterogeneous and inegalitarian universe of beings with greater or lesser intensity depending on their value. Finally, it contradicted the idea of a convoluted labyrinth of formal, material, efficient, and final causes in a purposive cosmos running the range from contingency to necessity, possibility to reality, potency to act. It then replaced that cosmos with the uniform leveling of necessary causal connections. The idea of infinity formerly associated with *ens realissimum*, the most perfect being (that is, God) now became ensconced in material nature. In one move, Galileo's new account of nature as infinite and isotropic destroyed the natural scheme of a hierarchical society firmly rooted in Aristotle's cosmology and gave modern political philosophy a new set of problems to handle. Once this decisive shift had occurred in thinking about the nature of things, human nature also had to be rethought.

It is widely held that the achievement of this modern school was to transfer natural right totally to the nature of the human being. Faced with having to distinguish the state of civil society from the state of nature, the moderns are thought to have designed a solution rooted in juridical subjectivism. As they saw it, right could no longer be thought of within a cosmological perspective now that nature itself no longer contained obligation, quality, or purpose. The moderns (so we are told) were thus led to adopt an antinaturalist and subjective view wherein law could be assigned a place within human reason alone, crimped into the *ego cogito*. It is also held that out of this subjectification of legal theory there arose the idea of human rights. The modern ring to the late eighteenth-century Declarations of the Rights of Man is thereby connected to earlier modern theories of consciousness and subjectivity. These theories are then taken reciprocally as signs of an irreversible turn in the history of philosophy, the transformation of the concept of nature and the emergence of the modern subject.

But is this what actually happened? To answer this question we must turn back to the birth of modern philosophy, back to Descartes.

Descartes's success in achieving canonical status in European philosophy was tied to his epistemological theory that linked mechanics, theology, and psychology. Descartes forged an acceptable compromise among diverse realms of being—nature, God, and man—that the explosion of "natural philosophy" had recently put out of joint. It was Descartes's genius to have re-established a coexistence between the new physics and the old theology which the Galileo-Bellarmine dispute had rendered irreconcilable. The collapse of Aristotelian philosophy, so it seemed, had undermined realism, destroyed rationalism, and given rise to a consciousness whose conceptualizations bore no connection to reality. But in the wake of Aristotle's demise, it was also Descartes's genius to have reconstructed the foundations of thinking solely on the strength of the *ego cogito*: "I think solely by virtue of the power to judge residing in my mind."

Such success was not achieved without great cost. It was paid for in the concept of a real division between mind and body that sunders the universe in two absolutely distinct parts: *res extensa*, the realm of matter organized in a geometric, mathematical scheme devoid of all quality and form; and *res cogitans*, the realm of thought and its relations to values and to God, a realm rooted in the human subject.

This separation of nature and man had significant consequences for understanding human nature and man's relations to nature and to God. The subject was now "decentered," set apart from objects, expelled so to speak from the external world as a thinking subject. It becomes a prey to solitude and the doubt that any concern with metaphysics threatens modern method. Existence itself seems weak, unsure; people appear to be mere phantoms rather than flesh-and-blood individuals. Descartes's heirs had to slam their fists on the table to remind themselves that existence precedes essence, that consciousness possesses intentionality, and that subjectivity is intersubjectivity.

The dualisms of mind and body, will and understanding, are the guiding forces behind the modern project to make man "master and possessor of nature." From this point onward, nature is delivered up to the brute force of "animal machines" and to the eternal silence of the infinite spaces that filled Pascal with dread. Nature is dispossessed of values and qualities. Man's only remaining connection to nature is quantitative and lies in the clear and distinct mathematical ideas of number, figure, extension, and time that make up his *ratio*. Viewed in this light, nature is the object of finite knowledge but it cannot be the object of infinite moral engagement. Man is still seen as the image of God by virtue of his infinite will, but this will is linked to the force of desire and severed from understanding and from the objects of nature. In Descartes's divisions of mind and world, thought and reality, subject and object, something has fallen by the wayside, and something else has come to the fore. On the one hand, the concept of natural law is gone. Man and the world are no longer bound together in harmony like twins playing together. On the other hand, the order of human nature is now conceived in terms of art and making, as a product of convention and intellection. Man is now set on the path to discover Being anew through a hard and complicated quest. With the *cogito* as phenomenological backdrop, the adventures of modern subjectivity begin as man sets himself to inventing new possible worlds.

This is the conception of human nature held by a good many thinkers of the modern natural-right school. Grotius, for example, explicitly formulated the idea that law is founded above all else on reason: "The law of nature is a dictate of right reason."[1] Echoing Gregory of Rimini's hypothesis, he adds that this would still be true even if there were no God, or if God had no concern for human affairs.[2] For Grotius, in other words, legal acts are to be measured not by a standard of external natural law or the will of God but by the rational nature of man—by what human consciousness holds to be reasonable. The force of law has ceased to be natural and objective; it has become rational and subjective. Natural right now receives rational foundations that are autonomous and secular, severed from natural law.

A similar view of nature devoid of values and spirit is at the root of Pufendorf's hostile, almost horrifying account of the state of nature: "In one [the natural state] there is the rule of passion, war, fear, poverty, ugliness, solitude, barbarism, ignorance, savagery; in the other [the community], the rule of reason, peace, security, riches, beauty, society, refinement, knowledge, good will."[3] For both Grotius and Pufendorf, civil society is founded on man's natural inclination to sociability, and the commonweal is only a human invention. If God no longer exists or has no concern for human affairs, if the state of nature is a state of war where lawless passions are unleashed, then one must imagine a conventional foundation for legitimate power. Civil right must stem from a contract of submission or association promulgated by an act of free will, and civility must be reconstituted through the will of the human subject. For Pufendorf in particular, contract theory is founded on an account of individual subjective right. In terms that differ little from Descartes's "seed of truth implanted in us by God," Pufendorf maintains that each individual possesses the "seeds of supreme sovereignty."[4] Sovereignty, then, issues from an individual right that is potentially present in every human being. By a free act of alienation individuals forsake their natural freedom and transfer it to a power that may be one individual, an assembly, or a group.

It is not at all unreasonable to observe that the fundamental inspiration at work in this theory's juridical subjectivism is the essential division in Cartesian psychology between the nature of things and the nature of man. It is just as pertinent to note that this theory's conception of the equality and natural freedom of individuals also reinforces the part played by consent and contract in the establishment of political society, and thereby finds a place for particular civil rights. But the fact remains that the voluntarism in the school of natural right is simply too weak to provide a juridical basis for human rights. In the end, Grotius and Pufendorf are nothing more than theorists of voluntary servitude and absolute monarchy.

There is an alternate path, suggested by both Spinoza and Locke. Despite the widespread confusion about juridical subjectivism, the rights of man, and the school of natural right, I would like to suggest that a distinction be made. There are, it seems to me, significant divisions that must be examined within the school of natural right, which is far from a homogeneous entity.

The school's divisions can be seen quite clearly in the different conception of the state of nature held by natural-right thinkers from Hobbes to Rousseau. To one thinker, the state of nature is sociability; to another, solitude; to others, either instinct, morality, war, or peace. There is a more fundamental disagreement among them, however, regarding their recognition or rejection of natural law. Everyone in the school recognizes natural right, but natural law is another matter. The difference in viewpoints here is linked to different conceptions of human nature and the relation of man to the world. Indeed, not all the natural-right thinkers are Cartesian; neither Spinoza nor Locke hold the views about nature, man, natural right, and natural law that were sketched above. In his *Ethics*, Spinoza writes explicitly of the problematic alienating of individual natural right in the process of constituting civil society: "In order, then, that men may be able to live in harmony and be a help to one another, it is necessary for them to cede their natural right, and beget confidence one in the other that they will do nothing by which one can injure the other."[5]

Even though Spinoza accepted Descartes's mechanics, his conception of nature was quite different. Convinced that the doctrine of final causality turned nature on its head, Spinoza did not take up the idea of a geometrical expanse devoid of immanent law.[6] Instead, he showed the following: that at the heart of nature essence and existence have equal value; that all is necessity and there is no contingency; that nature is immanent; that there is but one world, since God could not have fashioned things other than they were made nor in any other order; and that there is thus no free creation.[7]

In book 2 of the *Ethics*, Spinoza adds that there is no real distinction of mind and body because thought and extension are equal attributes of nature, and that there is no distinction between concept and nature because "the order and connection of ideas are the same as the order and connection of things."[8]

In book 4, Spinoza then maintains that there are no insurmountable contradictions or unbridgeable gaps among nature, man, and the city: "Reason demands nothing which is opposed to nature, it demands . . . that every person should love himself, should seek his own profit—what is truly profitable to him—should desire everything that really leads man to greater perfection, and absolutely that every one should endeavor, as far as in him lies, to preserve his own being."[9] Reason is rooted in the natural law, which seeks our conservation and utility in the affirmation and full blossoming of life. It is natural for man to live by reason and to live with other men; indeed, they are the same. By living under the guidance of reason, men get along naturally and desire nothing for themselves that they do not desire for other men.[10] In the same way, the rational association of men is founded on natural law, "For that is most profitable to man which most agrees with his own nature, that is to say, man (as is self-evident). But a man acts absolutely from the laws of his own nature when he lives according to the guidance of reason, and so far only does he always necessarily agree with the nature of another man."[11]

Did Spinoza abandon natural right? In one sense he did, inasmuch as the natural right of the state of nature does not provide a sufficient foundation for rational civil right, since that natural right is only the combined manifestation of each body's individual force. But natural law has not been eliminated since the realm of nature has not been left behind. As Spinoza suggests, one cannot escape nature; it encapsulates society and culture. The full range of sentiments suited to civil life can be deduced from within the natural order itself. What is more natural than a sentiment? Instead of opposing the natural right of individual force with the conventional and voluntarist character of civil legislation, Spinoza speaks of civil laws finding their roots in natural law. A natural movement governs the progress achieved in establishing the body politic and civil society. Nature's movement does not consist in an exercise of the will but in attaining the knowledge that man needs nature and other individuals, and that nothing more affirms and preserves his life than other men who have made the same discovery. Unlike other modern natural-right theorists, Spinoza does not ground legal theory in the subjectivity of the will. He writes that "a man who is guided by reason is freer in a state where he lives according to the common laws than he is in solitude, where he obeys himself alone."[12] Civil society for Spinoza does not rest on subjective individualism. Instead, he kept a place for the idea of a legal standard that is both natural and rational, an idea of a rational right in harmony with man's natural need as a natural being. In this sense, Spinoza anticipated Kant's philosophy of right.[13] More than anything, Spinoza gave man's right to security a natural foundation by making the individual right to self-preservation and self-determination the immanent law of civil association.

Locke's foundations are no more Cartesian than Spinoza's. Of course, along with everyone else in the natural-right school, Locke recognizes the existence of a state of nature distinct from the state of civil society. As he says in the *Second Treatise on Civil Government*, "All men are naturally in that state and remain so till by their own consents they make themselves members of some politic society."[14] The natural state is a state of perfect freedom and equality but in no way is a state of license because it is subject to natural law.[15] As it is for Spinoza, natural law for Locke is first and foremost the right to life: "Being all equal and independent, no one ought to harm another in his life, health, liberty, or possessions."[16]

Man may freely dispose of his person and his property, but he must not destroy himself since life itself does not belong to him. Likewise, the possibility of seeking compensation against aggression is founded on the right to self-preservation, the "right of preservation of the human race." Matters of natural law—life, the body, security—cannot be the object of despotic determination because they are divine gifts flowing from man's membership in the human race. For Locke, the state of nature is in no way a state of war, wherein life is laid bare to enmity and destruction.[17] On the contrary, the state of war is the opposite of the state of nature, since natural law and justice are lacking in war. As Locke puts it, "He who attempts to get another man into his absolute power does thereby put himself into a state of war with him."[18]

The state of war only forges a bond of servitude and domination. It was precisely to bring an end to that state and to rediscover order and natural justice that "men formed societies and left the state of nature." The establishment of political society does not appear to Locke, any more than to Spinoza, as an escape from the rule of natural law. It is rather an attempt to fulfill natural law by other means and so to overcome the state of bondage and war that disrupted the state of nature. Locke similarly denies that the bond of paternity is a model for society. The beginning of political society is the union of man and wife in their procreative destiny to continue the species.[19] The law of nature is still binding in society, "as an eternal rule to all men, legislators as well as others."[20]

Political society is established wherever people associate in a body politic and appoint for themselves judges to settle their differences in accord with explicitly declared laws.[21] But in doing this, civil society does not abolish the natural law. What men abjure, what individuals give over in civil society, is only "the executive power of the laws of nature," that is, the natural right of justice. Natural law itself never disappears. When legislators make laws, "the rules that they make for other men's actions must, as well as their own and other men's actions, be conformable to the law of nature—i.e., to the will of God, of which that is a declaration—and the fundamental law of nature being the preservation of mankind, no human sanction can be good or valid against it."[22] A text such as this, stipulating that legislation is not above the law that it is bound to declare, is at the very roots of the American Declaration of Independence of 1776.

In short, the natural-right school is a house divided. Some of its members followed Descartes's concept of nature and subjectivity. For them, nature is remote and separated from the subject, right resides within reason alone, and society is founded on an act of calculating will. The entire legal structure is reconstructed on the basis of individuals who make up its indivisible elements, while the civil order is reconstituted on the basis of geometry, as if human beings were lines and points. At times, these natural-right thinkers see men forming associations based on conventions and rights granted to individuals, at times they see them agreeing to voluntary servitude. Real human rights, however, are consigned to oblivion, obliterated by the civil rights they give way to.

Other natural-right thinkers opposed Descartes's imaginary division between man and the world. When an individual renounces his natural right, he does not thereby remove himself from the natural law. When he surrenders his right to act alone and to seek revenge, he delegates his initiative to a larger body and thereby establishes a more complete form of justice. This preserves his life and perpetuates his species, for the sake of life itself. As a being created by God and existing in nature, man preserves his own life, but he can neither sever himself from life nor seize complete control of it. The sole foundation of society and the only legitimation of the political order do not lie in an act of free choice made by the individual consciousness. They lie in delegating the executive power of the natural law that founds sovereignty and justice, so as to guarantee the conservation of life and to assure human rights to security, freedom, and equality. Human rights determine civil rights, but natural law remains an abiding principle.

This brief investigation teaches us an important lesson about the development of human rights. If these rights have their origin not in subjective idealism and legal voluntarism but rather in those works of modern legal theory which preserve a link with natural law, then it is essential for those who believe in human rights that they be rooted in the idea of natural law. We must, quite simply, return to natural law and further enlarge the clearing it has already carved out for itself in the texts of our tradition. The fate of human rights depends on the future of natural law theory and, today as in the past, on a critique of subjectivity.

—Translated by Marc A. LePain

Notes

1. Hugo Grotius, *On the Law of War and Peace*, trans. F. W. Kelsey et al. (Oxford, 1925), book 1, chap. 1.10.1.

2. Grotius, *On the Law of War and Peace*, Prolegomena 11.

3. Samuel von Pufendorf, *On the Duty of Man and Citizen*, trans. Frank Gardner Moore (Oxford, 1927), book 2, chap. 1, par. 9.

4. "Since sovereignty results from the non-resistance of subjects, and their willingness for the sovereign to dispose of their strength and property, it is easily seen that seeds, as it were, of supreme sovereignty, lie scattered in individuals, and that it germinates and grows by the pacts which bring sovereign and subjects together" (Samuel von Pufendorf, *The Law of Nature and Nations*, trans. C. H. Oldfather and W. A. Oldfather [Oxford, 1925], book 7, chap. 3, par. 4).

5. Benedict de Spinoza, *Ethics*, ed. James Gutmann (New York, 1949), book 4, proposition 37, scholia 2.

6. "Nature has set no end before herself, and (that) all final causes are nothing but human fictions" (Spinoza, *Ethics*, book 1, Appendix).

7. Spinoza, *Ethics*, book 1, propositions 20, 24, 15, 32.

8. Spinoza, *Ethics*, book 2, propositions 1, 7.

9. Spinoza, *Ethics*, book 4, proposition 18 (scholia).

10. Spinoza, *Ethics*, book 4, propositions 35, 18 (scholia).

11. Spinoza, *Ethics*, book 4, proposition 35.

12. Spinoza, *Ethics*, book 4, proposition 73.

13. See the fine book by Simone Goyard-Fabre, *Kant et le problème du droit* (Paris, 1975).

14. "All men are naturally in that state and remain so till by their own consents they make themselves members of some politic society" (John Locke, *The Second Treatise of Civil Government*, chap. 2, par. 15).

15. Ibid., chap. 2, par. 4.

16. Ibid., chap. 2, par. 6.

17. Ibid., chap. 3, par. 16.

18. Ibid., chap. 3, par. 17.

19. Ibid., chap. 7, par. 79.

20. Ibid., chap. 11, par. 135.

21. Ibid., chap. 7, par. 89.

22. Ibid., chap. 11, par. 135.

CHAPTER 12

Rights and Modern Law

STÉPHANE RIALS

THE MODERN IDEA of human rights is taken for granted today, but this idea is the outcome of a tremendous shift in the understanding of rights that people once had. This shift raises a number of questions. How is it that the most solemn proclamation of modern human rights, in France in 1789, was so soon followed by terrible abuses of human will, which have been repeated in worse forms since? How could the securing of these rights be forgotten in practice so soon after their exaltation in theory? At the heart of this paradox, as with other paradoxes, there lies a rigorous logic. In this case, it is the paradoxical metamorphosis of modern natural right into revolutionary voluntarism, whose wellspring can be traced back to the late Middle Ages.

The germ of this fantastic shift within modern times can be isolated in the early fourteenth-century nominalism of William of Ockham. Without getting into the complexities of his thought, one can say that Ockham saw the idea of a natural order as contrary to the divine freedom understood as the absolute power of God (*potentia Dei absoluta*). Divine freedom, so conceived, implies that whatever order one claims to discover at a given moment is, along with everything else outside God, contingent. Furthermore, no such order constitutes a norm for God's activity. Ockham thereby arrives at what Paul Vignaux called a "metaphysics of the individual," which gives primacy to the singular over the universal. The universe is no longer a cosmos (etymologically, an order or ordered system) but merely an aggregate of isolated individuals. The only realities are this particular man, this tree, this stone—all of which can be known intuitively and immediately. Notions of things in general do not exist. "Universals" such as man, tree, or mineral are merely signs or names.

The legal and political consequences of this nominalism can be seen quite readily. Society is but an agglomeration of individuals who are free by virtue of being created in the image of God. As such, they are invested in their own way with a *potestas absoluta*, without the mediation of natural order and without objective and necessary relations among themselves, that is, without natural right in its classical sense. Social and political "universals," such as the family and the city, have no other reality than an instrumental or verbal one.

Ockham's nominalism anticipated many distinctive traits of the modern natural-right school. It, too, is individualistic, subjectivistic, mechanistic, and in the final analysis voluntarist as well. In the absence of any natural order, legislation has no other grounding than the force of irreducible individual wills. The slide from nominalist individualism to legal positivism seems clear. Ockham's own thought, of course, was limited by the supremacy of "divine positive right" or "divine law." But this limitation carried no great force, given the radical rupture between faith and reason that Ockham brought to the Augustinian view of reality. The ultimate paradox of his project is that it paved the way for the laicization of thought.

The sixteenth and seventeenth centuries saw a revival of Thomism under the Dominicans (Vitoria) and Jesuits (Suarez) of the brilliant Salamanca school. This revival was not a restoration of classical natural right, however. On the contrary, some of them (such as Molina) got carried away and exaggerated the implications of the secularization of legal theory. Suarez in particular broke with classic natural right when he glorified law as an act of will and encouraged the rigorous logic of systematic and deductive thinking. Of greater significance is that in their development of the concept of domain or property, and without being individualists as such, these thinkers endowed man with prerogatives previously attributed only to God. The Franciscan theologians had already championed God's *potestas absoluta*, or unmediated rule over the world, and a number of late medieval theologians came to see the divine *dominium* over the world as a right, a *jus*. That right then became the model for every other kind of right. Human dominion henceforth was to be conceived following the example of divine dominion, in which it participates and which it extends as an unlimited and universal power-right.

The next step was to see this right as inherent in human nature. Although the scholastics understood human dominion as both empowered and limited by divine dominion, they provided decidedly modern answers to the contemporary questions they faced. Around 1540, for example, Vitoria argued that Indians were human beings endowed with rights (notably the right to property) that are inherent to their human nature. Given the circumstances, Vitoria's judgment is praiseworthy. However, it clearly anticipated the true father of the modern natural-right school, Hugo Grotius, whose thought is permeated with Spanish scholasticism.

Grotius's thought is in fact no more than the condensation of this long evolution, which was continued by successors such as Pufendorf. To state matters very simply, the main themes of the modern natural-right school that would later develop can be summed up in a few key ideas. Against a backdrop of the law's laicization and the entrenchment of individualism, the school abandoned the idea that right can be discerned in the nature of *things* and favored an abstract notion of *human* nature from which all right is to be deduced. What henceforth would be called the rights of man, particularly the right to property, were no longer viewed as the image of divine right. Rights were now severed from the source that originally bound and sacralized them, and only those rights grounded exclusively in human nature were exalted as being prior to society. Civil society was henceforth not to be conceived as naturally given but as rationally established, with a starting point in an act of human will. The old idea of a social contract now came to occupy center stage in political theory.

It is important to understand clearly how these modern natural-right thinkers dealt with the matter of maintaining man's natural rights in society. This issue takes us back to what these thinkers understood by the idea of "natural law." And what they meant is perfectly clear: the law inscribed in human nature is actualized in the state of nature and remains above any expression of the will that is subsequently grounded in the social contract. Pufendorf articulates this principle forcefully in *The Law of Nature and Nations*, as does Locke in his *Treatise on Civil Government*, although their formulations do not go so far as to provide an effective guarantee of natural law's superiority. Pufendorf's wording is revealing on this score: "A civil law could, of course, be passed which is opposed to natural law; yet none but an insane man, and one who had in mind the destruction of the state, would wish to pass legislation of that kind."[1] Modern naturalists allow only for the refusal to obey a command contrary to natural law, prudently reserving such insubordination (Pufendorf here is particularly cautious) for exceptional instances of manifest violation of the natural law.

Locke is particularly important for our considerations, since it is through him that the propositions discussed above were adopted by the United States. He can be viewed as associated with the modern natural-right school, provided that the specific character of his thought is not forgotten. In the *Second Treatise on Government* (1690), Locke explains why "mankind, notwithstanding all the privileges of the state of nature . . . are quickly driven into society," to unite in a social compact and to invest their power in governors, not by a compact of submission but through a fiduciary trust. People "take sanctuary under the established laws of government and therein seek the preservation of their property." Locke goes on to say that "in this we have the original right of both the legislative and executive power, as well as of the governments and societies themselves."[2]

Locke thus clearly identifies the basis of the body politic's organization with securing the twofold dimension of freedom: safety and property. Consequently, the legislative power, without doubt "the supreme power of the commonwealth," cannot be "absolutely arbitrary over the lives and fortunes of the people," for the people cannot transfer to the legislature any power that they themselves did not hold in the state of nature.[3] Nor could they do so in the fiduciary trust, since the motive for leaving the state of nature was the desire to protect liberty and property. And so Locke logically ends up affirming the legitimacy of resistance to oppression whenever public powers overstep the limits of their authority.

Locke's emphasis on law influenced the French, but it was only elsewhere (notably in the United States) that his insistence on the limits of the will produced serious limits on legislative power. His influence on this score can be seen in some of the American colonial declarations at the time of independence. These declarations did not merely enumerate endless rights and freedoms but resolved once and for all the question of the supremacy of rights over laws. To cite but one example, the "Declaration of Rights made by the . . . people of Virginia . . . as the basis and foundation of government" states in section 1 that "all men are by nature equally free and independent and have certain inherent rights, of which, when they enter into a state of society, they cannot, by any compact, deprive or divest their posterity; namely, the enjoyment of life and liberty, with the means of acquiring and possessing property, and pursuing and obtaining happiness and safety."[4] It is easy to understand how such a step—based on the actual experience the oppressive laws that England imposed on the colonists—led America to seek and formulate a sure guarantee of these rights and freedoms that could not be subject to legislative prescription. In his great speech before the House of Representatives (8 June 1789), Madison stated clearly that the amendments that later were to constitute the Bill of Rights had as their great object "to limit and qualify the powers of government," and especially to guard against abuse in the legislative department, "for it is the most powerful and most likely to be abused . . . by the majority against the minority."[5] The First Amendment's opening words, "Congress shall make no law respecting . . . ," must have sounded strange to the members of France's Constituent Assembly who knew them. Only a few among the framers of the American Constitution foresaw the possible development of a judicial check on the constitutionality of laws. The Supreme Court took that critical step in 1803, and after a few decades of prudent practice gave the procedure its full weight in the years after the Civil War.

There is an element of objectivism in the Lockean tradition that holds that there exists a right prior to the legislative will, which the latter secures but does not create. The state of civil society restores rather than supersedes the state of nature in the wake of whatever turbulence has beset it.

The juridical tradition that passes through Hobbes and Rousseau took a different direction, which led to what might be called the triumph of the will. Hobbes saw men as isolated from one another, without any social ties, in his hypothetical state of human origins. He writes that "the right of nature, which writers commonly call *jus naturale*, is the liberty each man hath, to use his own power, as he will himself, for the preservation of his own nature; that is to say, of his own life; and consequently, of doing any thing, which in his own judgment, and reason, he shall conceive to be the aptest means thereto."[6] At first glance, this passage seems to contain the modern definition of "subjective right" as an individual "power." But the matter is in fact more complex. Hobbes does not think that the "right of nature" dissolves, despite his ambiguous phrasing, into the "natural rights" of individuals. Right is constituted only once the individual "powers" or "forces" come together to constitute a societal machine, the "artificial man" (Leviathan) whose strength is the sum of all prior individual forces that have made him sovereign. This is the difference between Hobbes and the teachers of the modern natural-right school. If there are no "natural rights" while the social contract is in the making, there surely are none once it is made. In the contract, the "right of nature" gives way entirely to the "civil right," which is the fruit of law's exaltation. With Hobbes one already has voluntarist positivism.

Rousseau proceeds by a different route than does Hobbes, but they both arrive at the same point. Rousseau's general will, whose specific elements are often misunderstood, might lead one to believe that he was a pure voluntarist and a positivist. Some of his formulations about law being "prior to justice" only reinforce that impression. The matter is not that simple, however. One has only to recall that, notwithstanding the fundamental and inalienable character of human freedom in Rousseau's scheme, he recognized three authorities above the sovereign in a letter written in 1758: "First, God; next, the natural law derived from man's make-up; and lastly, honor." In his sixth *Lettre écrite de la montagne*, he says that "the social contract must not violate the natural laws." He is most explicit in *The Social Contract*:

> In addition to the public person, we have to consider the private persons who compose it and whose life and freedom are naturally independent of it. It is a matter, then, of making a clear distinction between the respective rights of the citizens and the sovereign, and between the duties that the former have to fulfill as subjects and the natural rights to which they are entitled as men.[7]

Is there a contradiction between the exaggerated prominence assigned to the general will and Rousseau's recognition here of some transcendent principles? Rousseau must have thought there was not, since for him, given that the general will came "from all to hold for all," it was "impossible that the body should will to harm all its members," and that "since all were bound in the same condition, it would benefit no one to burden the others."[8] Under such conditions, it was out of the question that the general will would ever conflict with natural right. Rousseau sought to reconcile, or rather transcend, voluntarism and naturalism by turning "the idea of right that the natural right school took to be transcendent" into an "immanent" idea, as Giovanni Sartori said so well.[9] And as Leo Strauss wrote earlier,

> By surrendering all his rights to society, man loses the right to appeal from the verdicts of society, i.e., from the positive law, to natural right: all rights have become social rights. Free society rests and depends upon the absorption of natural right by positive law. Natural right is legitimately absorbed by the positive law of a society which is constructed in accordance with natural right.[10]

Together with Hobbes, Rousseau maintained that natural rights as such disappear in the state of civil society. Yet natural right reappears in the form of the positive laws, since "in the sate of civil society . . . all rights are *fixed* by the law."[11] Natural standards are viable only as they are sanctioned by law. There is a movement from "natural right properly so called," as Rousseau wrote in the Geneva manuscript, to "rational natural right."[12]

These propositions shed an important light on certain aspects of the French Declaration of the Rights of Man of 1789. Article 16 reads as follows: "Every society which has no assured guarantee of rights, nor a separation of powers, does not possess a constitution."[13] The article is logically grounded in two transcendent principles determining the conditions under which a document bearing the title of constitution is to be considered valid. In the terms of article 16, there is no constitution unless two such conditions are met: on the one hand, limitations are set on the "powers" (an *organizing* constitution, so to speak) and on the other, the overall power of the various powers is limited (a *limiting* constitution).[14]

At the onset of the revolution, the idea of a limiting constitution appears not simply as a dominant theme but as fundamental to the whole discussion. There were, of course, lively debates over whether there also ought to be a declaration of the duties of man and citizen, though in the end this was rejected. It is important to note, however, that in all the speeches and lampoons supporting the Declaration, the same idea recurs: the Declaration is the foundation of the constitution, and therefore its limit, since the constitution is properly founded only to the degree that it respects the Declaration. This idea is echoed in the preamble to the Declaration, which states that rights are declared "in order that acts of legislative and executive power can be frequently compared with the purpose of every political institution."

This idea seems a commonplace today, but it played little role in the French tradition until quite recently. Instead, from the summer of 1789 onward the idea of an organizing constitution prevailed. Why was the limiting dimension of the constitution, which carried the day in the long run, omitted in the earliest French deliberations? The answer lies in the combined influence of Montesquieu and Rousseau.

Montesquieu referred only hypothetically to the state of nature. But, as Goyard-Fabre appropriately put it, he reduced the natural laws to a few "elementary psychic laws" regarding the individual's awareness of human fragility, the need for food, the sexual impulse, the "desire to live in society."[15] This is far from the modern meaning of "natural rights." Indeed, in reading Montesquieu, one often senses the spirit of Aristotle beneath the veneer of modern Enlightenment. Elsewhere the great lawgiver refers to "human reason" as the foundation of laws or to "relations of possible justice" before laws were made.[16] Nevertheless, Montesquieu's system as a whole is governed by a radical relativism, so much so that one is not quite sure what to make of the enigmatic book 12 of *The Spirit of the Laws*.

In book 11, Montesquieu deals with "political liberty with regard to the constitution."[17] In this best-known (but not necessarily best understood) passage of the whole work, Montesquieu argues for the "distribution" of duties sufficiently independent of agencies (and not for the "separation" of whatever unspecified "powers"). All the claims in favor of an ordering constitution that have been made over the past two centuries are rooted in this formulation. Montesquieu's lesser-known book 12 deals with "political liberty in relation to the subject." From this perspective, freedom "consists in security." The notion of "political freedom" does not appear well fitted to the topic at hand here. In this poorly constructed passage, Montesquieu basically concerns himself with the full range of penal law guarantees and sketches a defense of what Benjamin Constant later called the "freedom of the moderns." For Montesquieu himself, the origin of this freedom, broadly understood as security, is not some higher legal principle but rather the "customs, manners, received examples" as well as "particular civil laws."[18]

If one considers that by different avenues, and consistent with their respective teachings, Montesquieu and Rousseau both end up giving such prominence to law, one can then better understand the tensions in the Declaration of 1789. These tensions arise from what might be characterized as a logical slippery slope. In conceiving of political society as a rational construct in which every individual deemed rational surrenders the power with which he was born, law-centered voluntarism gave to political society an authority that is indisputable by virtue of its rationality, and irresistible because of its sovereignty. If law fails to be the undefiled expression of reason, this can only be due to an error at the founding of a particular society. But to admit this is to destroy the edifice of all political society!

The secularization of law was also important. Once law is no longer the reflection of divine law it becomes the inscription of human nature in consciousness. The lawgiver's task then is the rational examination of consciousness in order to make positive laws compatible with natural law. Almost inevitably, then, *natural right* will be transmuted into *positive rights* and then into *civil rights*, *nature* into *will*, *human rights* into *laws* of citizens. As Patrick Wachsmann recently put it, "Any reference to natural right in the domain of positive law carries no force whatever. . . . Positive or civil right is a closed system with no opening whatever to a transcendent natural right. . . . The lawgiver holds a monopoly on decreeing rights."[19]

Some members of the French Constituent Assembly could feel themselves slipping down this slope, but they were unable to stop their movement. The result is clearly seen in the Declaration itself. On the one hand, article 2 forcefully declares the existence of "the natural and imprescriptible rights of man. These rights are liberty, property, security and resistance to oppression." On the other hand, most of the articles call for the lawgiver to set the terms for the exercise of these rights. The Declaration itself speaks only of "limits . . . determined . . . by the law," of the suppression of disturbances in the "public order established by law," of sanctions on the "abuses of . . . liberty in cases determined by law," and of "public interest, legally defined" having priority over a "sacred and inviolable right." Article 5 is a charter of positivism of markedly liberal inspiration: "What is not prohibited by law cannot be forbidden and nobody can be forced to do what the law does not require." The definition of law in article 6 is clearly marked by Rousseau's thought, even though its consequences are not fully articulated: "The law is the expression of the general will."

This very incomplete and intentionally summary account must have a nuanced conclusion, even though the shift it has sketched is clear enough. The logic of modern natural-right theory leads, paradoxically, to the establishment of a law-centered voluntarism. The apparent contradictions in the 1789 Declaration owe a great deal to Rousseau, who laid out this logic. Still, the Declaration (at least the 1789 text), does not entirely abolish the tension that remains between naturalism and voluntarism. The Declaration specifically mandates a general respect for a few great principles. Its demand is not sanctioned by any legal control, however, only by the principle of resistance to oppression. Still, human rights are not entirely absorbed into civil rights, natural rights cannot be prescribed, and the law remains only their servant. This is the loophole through which the idea of controlling the constitutionality of laws in France eventually, and belatedly, slipped. The constitutional judges still appear to be up against the will of the constituting legislator. Nonetheless, it is still possible to speak of a return to Locke in France today—or, if one prefers, of the victory of the American tradition of guaranteeing rights over the French.*

—Translated by Marc A. Lepain

Notes

1. Samuel von Pufendorf, *The Law of Nature and Nations*, trans. C. H. Oldfather and W. A. Oldfather (Oxford, 1934), book 8, chap. 1, par. 2.

2. John Locke, *Second Treatise on Government*, chap. 9, par. 127. On Locke, see the classic work by Raymond Polin, *La politique morale de John Locke* (Paris, 1960), and the recent and stimulating book by James Tully, *A Discourse on Property: John Locke and His Adversaries* (Cambridge, 1980).

3. Locke, *Second Treatise*, chap. 11, par. 135.

4. "Virginia Declaration of Rights," in *The Annals of America* (Chicago, 1968), 2:432.

5. "James Madison: A Bill of Rights Proposed," in *The Annals of America* 3:360.

6. Thomas Hobbes, *Leviathan*, book 1, chap. 14.

7. Jean-Jacques Rousseau, *On the Social Contract*, ed. Roger D. Masters, trans. Judith R. Masters (New York, 1978), book 2, chap. 4.

8. Rousseau, *Social Contract*, respectively, book 2, chap. 4; book 1, chap. 7; and book 1, chap. 6.

9. Giovanni Sartori, *Théorie de la démocratie* (Paris, 1973), 234.

10. Leo Strauss, *Natural Right and History* (Chicago, 1953), 286.

11. Rousseau, *Social Contract*, book 2, chap. 4.

12. Rousseau, "Geneva Manuscript," *Social Contract*, book 2, chap. 4.

13. "The Declaration of the Rights of Man and the Citizen, 1789," in D. G. Wright, *Revolution and Terror in France 1789–1795* (New York, 1990), 118–20.

14. I am fully aware that this distinction will elicit formalist critiques in part based on sound considerations. I attempt to show that this not quite the case in my forthcoming handbook, *Droit constitutionnel et institutions politiques*, in the collection "Droit fondamental," published by Presses Universitaires de France.

15. See Simone Goyard-Fabre, *La philosophie du droit de Montesquieu* (Paris, 1973).

16. One can even consider that by a process akin to classical naturalism Montesquieu's uniform conception of law as relationship—whether juridical or physi-

* Since publishing this article in 1986 I have modified some of the views expressed here. For a reformulation, readers may consult my volume *La Déclaration des droits de l'homme et du citoyen* (Paris, 1989) and my article "Sieyès ou la déliberation sans la prudence" in *Une prudence moderne?* (Paris, 1992), edited by Philippe Raynaud and myself.

cal law—eliminates the breach between what later was called the worlds of nature and culture.

17. Baron de Montesquieu, *The Spirit of the Laws*, trans. Thomas Nugent (New York, 1949), book 11, chap. 1.

18. Montesquieu, *The Spirit of the Laws*, book 12, chap. 1.

19. Patrick Wachsmann, "Naturalisme et volontarisme dans la Déclaration des droits de l'homme de 1789," *Droits. Revue française de théorie juridique* (1985): 2.

PART FIVE

The Liberal Political Order

A RECURRENT concern in French thought from Rousseau to the present has been that of reconciling modern individualism with social consensus and public order. This question has once again become central in the wake of the progressive liberalization of French political life over the past half century. Pierre Manent gives a historical account of this society's genesis out of the theological-political struggles in early modern Europe. As in *An Intellectual History of Liberalism*, Manent portrays liberalism as an attempt to escape the contest for command between absolute monarchy and the semipolitical church. The power of all direct commands was weakened by liberalism and replaced by those of the anonymous market order and the representative state, with mixed results. Bernard Manin sees a different problem in reconciling the unanimity of individual wills needed to establish liberal legitimacy and the rule of majorities needed for action. Departing from the standard liberal responses from Sieyès to John Rawls, Manin proposes a strong theory of deliberation that sees it transforming the wills of those deliberating, thereby legitimizing majoritarian decisions. Jean-Marc Ferry is also concerned with deliberation, though within the framework of a "rationalized" modern society as described by Max Weber. Ferry, however, distinguishes different spheres and modes of modern reason, focusing on communicative rationality as a modern means of achieving social consensus without appealing to scientific or legal rationalism.

CHAPTER 13

The Contest for Command

PIERRE MANENT

THE SIGNIFICANCE of the present liberal revival, whatever its extent or duration, goes beyond the political and economic measures it now inspires. Today liberalism provides the terms and sets the tone in which Europeans and Americans express the problems of their societies. In continental Europe, at least, this situation is new. For two centuries, in fact, liberalism in Europe had a continuously precarious political and ideological existence, caught between the Ancien Régime it claimed to succeed and the revolutionary or socialist radicalism that contested this succession.

Liberalism was born as critique, a critique of political and religious powers under the Ancien Régime. The organization of these powers retrospectively referred to as the Ancien Régime is difficult to define since it was utterly heterogeneous. Two of its elements in particular must be distinguished: royal absolutism and the semipolitical power of an exclusive or dominant church. In one sense these two elements were contradictory because absolutism also needed to pacify religious conflicts. For the prince to raise himself "sovereignly" above them, the political order had to reign supreme over religion. But this reign was never completely realized. Absolutism stopped midway, contenting itself with backing a dominant church and in return demanding its support. Whatever role the prince took in defining authorized religious opinion—it was important in England under Henry VIII and Elizabeth, nonexistent in France—its content and therefore its internal dynamism essentially eluded him. Instead of neutralizing religion, he compromised it and was compromised by it. All things considered, political power imposed on its subjects an opinion not strictly its own, while the dominant church made the faithful obey by means of power that was not strictly its own. The more uncertain the motive for obedience became, the more imperious the order. This was why the need to refound legitimate obedience became so urgent. And to refound it, power and opinion had to be radically separated.

This was liberalism's original task, the one on which it cut its teeth and from which it acquired its historical features. On the one hand, it sought to establish that religious opinions were of no interest to political authority, since men's actions in this world are independent of their opinions about the next one. A person can fail to believe in salvation through faith alone, or even in the existence of God, and still be a good citizen. Therefore, all opinions must be tolerated, as long as members of society do not use them as arguments for violating civil laws or the rights of their fellow citizens.

On the other hand, liberalism reinterpreted the meaning of men's political existence. The traditional conception of politics closely linked it to the superior ends of human life; the law of the body politic was an expression or refraction of that ultimate law whose observance defines humanity, the "human law" of the "divine law." Liberalism challenged the sublimity of this law and deliberately lowered its status. Precisely because men disagree on the superior law's content and still must live together, the foundation of political laws must be sought on earth, not in heaven. Prior to any law or any opinion about himself and the whole, this weak, wretched animal called man wants to survive. This natural necessity is his *natural right*: who would dare say that he has no right to what he urgently needs? It is on the lowly but sound foundation of animal need that liberalism erected its ingenious constructions.

The individual's right to life has three inseparable and yet distinct aspects: the right to security, that is, to the body's integrity; the right to property, that is, to means allowing him to live; the right to liberty, that is, to the free determination of means for self-preservation, of which each person can best judge for himself. The raison d'être of liberal institutions is to guarantee these three rights, which without they would be continuously precarious. These political institutions are an indispensable artifice and are legitimate only if they fulfill this end. They accomplish this if the laws they promulgate regulating relationships among citizens express the desire for the proprietors' preservation. Since each person is the best judge of what is good for him, the laws faithfully express this desire only if everyone has agreed to obey them, on his own or through his representative. Since unanimity is impossible to obtain, and the vote of the totality of the people is unrealizable in large states like ours, legitimate laws in practice are those which have been voted by the majority of the people's representatives.

However simplified this summary of a long and complex development may be, it suffices to characterize the liberal political system. Since society is defined by the aggregation of rights of individuals, with these rights belonging equally to every man as man, irrespective of his opinions, those opinions should be separate from power; they should also be free. Although liberal political institutions are supposed to guarantee these rights, they are to be neutral regarding opinions: legitimate power has no opinion; it is "neutral and agnostic." Powerless opinions, opinionless power: the link formed by the Ancien Régime between power and opinion has now been severed.

Once liberalism has elaborated the idea of a rigorously "neutral power," it is able to represent society while respecting and protecting its autonomy. But from the moment that the ruling power ceases to be responsible for the safeguarding of the nation's traditions or religion, or for extending the boundaries of its domination, it is affected by a new indetermination. It is no longer independent and self-ruling but depends on the society it represents or whose instrument it is.

The former opinion, to which ruling power was attached and which deemed itself responsible for imposing that opinion on the nation by authoritarian means, marked out its sphere of action. It also regulated it. The very independence of that power led it to consider society as somewhat independent of itself, at least as long as it obeyed. Absolutism was often "benign neglect," tempered by a heavy hand. Once its motivation was no longer drawn from itself, the ruling power implicitly had only as many occasions and reasons for acting as society had "problems." In the end this also meant that society might eventually hand over all its problems to the ruling political power, since it wants to be represented by that power.

Certainly the French Ancien Régime in its absolutist phase did not recognize the principle of social autonomy. Everything was done "in the name of the king." In fact, after assuring the unity of the faith by authoritarian means and bringing social anarchy under control by exercising the monopoly of legitimate violence, it agreed to go no further. It flattered its *chère noblesse*, gratified the Church, and dealt tactfully with the bodies making up the body politic. The long-term tendency of its action surely suggested a radical transformation of social life, which would render all members of society equal under the prince's law. But absolutism did not acknowledge this idea and thus never achieved it. This was because the primary object of its attention was not society but itself as supporter of the true religion and bearer of dynastic French glory. At the same time, it had already gone too far: while leaving the "bodies" their influence, it took from them the power to command and the legitimacy of commanding. The subjects, ever more equal, no longer found the motives for their actions in a particular "body" but only in an order administered by the prince through general rules. They were more and more left to the power of their own dictates and became individuals.

However, the autonomy produced by absolutism was contradicted by its own principle of legitimacy, the prince as the image of God on earth.

The new individual felt assured of his new liberty only if he could transform the cause of his autonomy into its effect: the central power must now represent man as an individual. Originally the absolute prince forbade any member of civil society to be ruled by another and reserved for himself the right to command. The idea of representation now forbade the central power to rule the individual without his consent. The representative regime inherited from absolutism the "seat of power," that is, a command post in principle equidistant from each subject. But now, under liberalism, that seat was empty, and each person was potentially its occupant.

The inhabitant of liberal regimes escaped the personal commands of the prince and was assured that natural equality would be respected by the body politic in two ways. As a member of civil society today, as worker or entrepreneur, he derives his motivation from a general situation that he freely assesses; as a potential occupant of the seat of power, he prohibits any individual or group from violating equality through personal commands or monopolies. Thus the representative state and the market each imply the other. The individual gains his liberty, and is freed from personal powers, only by dividing his faith between these two impersonal authorities. In the two roles, he obeys orders from no one. Market indicators do not result from any single individual's wishes but from the combined actions of individuals; the state's laws are also general and are written through representation by the individuals subject to them. Through the state, others are forbidden to rule the individual, who instead finds his motives for action in the market.

A major difficulty persists, however; civil society remains in fact bristling with personal commands, even if they no longer have the legitimacy that they once had under the Ancien Régime. These commands are of three kinds: those maintaining small subpolitical societies such as the family; the commands of opinion, formulated primarily by the churches; and finally, those involved with the management of the economy and the professions.

As for the first two, the logics of the market and of the representative state work together. The family provides an example. The new principle of legitimacy required that this small hierarchical society be broken up, that it become an association of strictly equal individuals (the only restriction being that an age of majority be fixed). The logic and attraction of the market induces everyone to act as autonomous individuals and to profit from the "opportunities" offered by the new situation. As for children and adolescents, who cannot yet be producers, they are consumers: a specific segment of the market is reserved just for them. The same logic affects the church. The neutral state must work toward the church's complete disestablishment, transforming it into a strictly private association and reducing as much as possible its means of influence. In short, it must secularize society. The market's logic points in the same direction. It is not that the church can "go on the market," like the family. It is simply that its commands place its faithful in a particularly awkward position in the new situation. The market is, just like the state, neutral and agnostic as to opinions. But this neutrality does not mean that authoritarian opinion no longer reigns; from now on it is neutrality itself that becomes the authority. Thus each of the faithful is offered every means for action while the bells of authoritarian agnosticism resound: "One principle alone is sacred, that nothing is sacred. The only command is to choose freely." How could religion retain power over morals when what used to be considered sin now becomes sacred?

Now we must consider the commands internal to civil society, those of the market and the professions. Liberal authors have a tendency to explain them away by using the term *function*. Professional or functional commands are not real ones, we are told; they are strictly limited to the job to be done. Jobs require the subordination of functions, not of persons, and the equality of persons is not contradicted by the subordination of functions. Certainly, here or there an individual can profit from his functional superiority to exercise arbitrary power. But such behavior, always deplorable, will be progressively eliminated by the natural play of competition, which requires "rational" behavior.

These liberals forget, however, that a market command can be perfectly "rational" and yet be terribly onerous for the person to whom it is addressed. They also forget that the rational analysis of a situation rarely leads to the conclusion that only one decision is possible. They forget especially that liberalism came into the world to establish representative institutions so that no one would be compelled to do anything without having consented to it. If a person refuses to obey the prince and the priest, why then should he have to obey the boss or the "decision maker"? After all, liberalism said that he was sovereign. Why would man in civil society not be tempted to use that sovereignty to lighten his burden? Man prefers commanding to being commanded: why should the one who is commanded by the market not desire to command it through the state? Liberal authors often portray this desire as abusive, as envy gripping those who are not, or do not feel themselves, capable of "pulling themselves up by their bootstraps." But the envy to which they point is rooted in the political system itself, which considers great differences in conditions among men to be unjust and inscribes the refusal to accept such differences in its central institutions. Since each free individual has two roles, as actor in the market and elector in the state, it is natural that he appeal to the state's resources when faced with failure, or the fear of failure, in the market.

All the same, the liberals are right, even if their arguments are not always the best. For although market logic can be influenced to a certain extent, it can only be hindered, not replaced. The representative nature of the state, which makes its intervention inevitable and legitimate, is also what deprives it of definite rules. Since it does not have its own ends, since no single opinion orients it, how can it know what to do once it has freed the individual from the powers of the Ancien Régime? The only thing left is to react against the real or supposed defects of the market and to correct them. The state will sometimes be tempted to take an idea to the market and develop it (though that idea will most likely have been superseded by the time these investments produce results). And so it will go from "industrial policy" to "industrial policy," always running, always late. Most often, it will limit itself to freezing an economic situation formed by the market. What the market had done and was getting ready to undo, the state keeps alive with interventions and subsidies.

No one of good sense will deny that such interventions are sometimes necessary, and therefore legitimate. Certainly, the desire to stop the perpetual motion of the market is legitimate, since it is inscribed in human nature. All men seek to live in lasting proximity with the goods found in human society. It is to recover this closeness to things, delivered at last from the unpredictable changes of supply and demand and the abstract mediation of money, that people with the best intentions want to substitute "another logic" for that of the market. Alas, they only produce the contrary of what they hope to accomplish. By suppressing the real exchange value of goods, they cut their production off from human needs and pleasures. The most singular trait of "existing socialism" is that whereas it can control highly developed technologies, it does not know how to produce simple goods for everyday use—goods that all societies, even the most archaic, have always known how to produce. It is true that human societies can live under rules other than that of exchange value, that they are not obliged to produce for the market. But such societies must then be founded on an authoritarian opinion. If the rule for the production of goods is not exchange among equals, it must find its source in a power or an idea that is not neutral. From the moment that power has to be neutral among equal men, their various activities and capacities must find a common measure and space where they can collaborate without commanding each other. The division of labor and the exchange of services through the mediation of money are the sole substitutes for this domination.

I have conceded to liberalism's critics that personal commands are practiced on the market, and to its partisans that the market's logic excludes domination. The former are correct in the short term, the latter over the long term. If it is true that every profession presupposes a functional hierarchy, and that this functional hierarchy is in fact inseparable from a personal one, it is simultaneously true that the market's logic tends to abolish, asymptotically so to speak, the distance between the commander and the commanded. The fact that social positions are no longer institutionally linked to birth, that they are much more mobile than in preliberal regimes, plays a central role in reducing social distance. Professional commands are also toned down by their multiplication, and social commands are toned down through their professionalization. What was once commanded becomes a market service; where once there was command, now there are several professions. In short, although each profession has its functional hierarchy, the professionalization of human life tends to efface commands from the social landscape. But, it will be argued, they survive in masked and perverse form. That may be, but I doubt it. Insofar as commands become less visible, social life comes more to resemble the idea that extreme liberals have of it: a general situation defined by an increasingly complex group of "objective indicators," behind which it is impossible to discover anybody's will. Every person must choose for himself, prey to a growing uncertainty. For how can a person's will be exercised in a world where the will never appears? It is still possible to point to a few impetuous "decision makers," a few "press lords" who seem to control the situation. But in fact, most of them share the good-natured and distressed perplexity of Woody Allen characters.

With social commands being continuously eroded by the market, it would seem that the directing capacity of the representative state would be bound to grow incessantly, since it alone possesses legitimacy through consent. And it is true, as I have already noted, that appeal to the state against the market's commands is inscribed in the liberal political system. But as the state's leeway for possible intervention increases, so does its uncertainty. The fear of commanding that affects civil society also affects the state, or at least those who administer it. Now as before, liberals lay great stress on the incompetent and costly character of the state-controlled administration. But even if they are right, I am not sure that they conceive of its present function correctly. It is untrue that the administration imposes a norm that is essentially external to civil society. The administration is separated or functionally distinct from civil society, but it is not foreign to it. It too is "representative." Its role is not only to transmit the government's orders, it also collects the most complete and discriminating information possible about how society functions and then inscribes that data in the public registers where the government, and members of society as well, can peruse it. Of course, in carrying out its task, the administration necessarily always lags behind civil society's actual evolution; in this sense, it is never up to the job, regardless of the competence of its officials. One of the liberals' strongest arguments is that only the market is in a position to deal with the vast amount of information produced by civil society. But if in Western countries the administration is encumbered and restricting, this is less because it has made itself the docile instrument of arbitrary government than because it is structurally induced to "freeze" society, so as to guarantee its hold on information. In our time, the administration is less a machine for giving commands than one for producing social knowledge—statistics.

This is why relations between the market and the administration are not solely conflictual. No one can say exactly to what extent the market's functioning is dependent on administrative regulations and information. Conversely, it is certain that the administration's gathering of information is all the easier and more complete because civil society acts more in conformity with market rationality, now that silent orders and clandestine exchanges have been replaced by public exchanges. We are not dealing here with a zero-sum game, in which what is gained by the administration is necessarily lost by civil society or the market. The market's effort to satisfy consumers' needs and desires, and the administration's effort to inform itself of individuals' situations and incomes (and also their needs and desires), are only two aspects of the obsessive labor of introspection practiced by contemporary societies. To this should be added, of course, the activity of journalists, pollsters, and sociologists busy tracking down the variations and infinitesimal modifications of the behavior and opinions of the citizenry. The administration and the market are jointly writing the private diaries of our societies.

Liberalism eroded social commands and individual will. But it also has a remedy for that erosion. Amid the discrediting of every norm, it retains one: competitiveness. This is one of the principal reasons that liberalism has come back into favor. Everyone in liberal society shrinks at the prospect of giving or receiving a genuine order, since nothing seems to justify commands or obedience. Competition therefore remains the only acceptable candidate for social regulation, since the norm it offers is immanent to social activity. It is imposed on no one, it implies no dogmatism. This motive for the return to liberalism also establishes its probable limits: an increased attention to market indicators, a keener sense of international competition, a trimming down of the welfare state—but that is about all. Going beyond this would necessitate giving liberal politics traits that would immediately be labeled authoritarian. And that is precisely how most liberals would view them.

—Translated by Rebecca Balinski

CHAPTER 14

On Legitimacy and Political Deliberation

BERNARD MANIN

LIBERAL THEORIES of justice try to answer the question: How can we establish a political and social order based on the will of individuals? From its inception, modern democratic thought has been confronted by the same problem because, like literalism, it is based on the principles of individualism. This is so regardless of the differences between the liberal and the democratic points of view. Both arrive at an identical conclusion: in the political sphere, it is unanimity that provides the principles of legitimacy. Most democratic theories, however, are concerned not only with legitimacy, but also with efficiency. Thus they must bring into play a more realistic principle of decision making than that of unanimity, namely the majority principle. Yet the means they use to reconcile the principle of decision making (by majority) with the principle of legitimacy (by unanimity) underlines even more strongly the requirement for unanimity in any political thought that is based on individualism.

The thought of Sieyès presents a remarkable example of this process. Sieyès states that men are by nature free. When they form an association or a society, "only relations based on the free act of will of each individual can be established among them."[1] Only an individual's will can give his agreement the character of a moral obligation. Consequently, "laws can only rest upon the will of individuals."[2] In order for a society to exist and to act, it must have a common will. "This will must of course be the sum of *all* individual wills, as was doubtless the case when a group of men joined in a political society, and the common will represented exactly the *sum of all* individual wills.[3] "This sum of all individual wills is what is meant by unanimity. Elsewhere Sieyès writes: "A political association represents the achievement of the unanimous will of its members."[4] Yet he continues as follows:

> Its public institution [that is, its government] is the result of the will of the plurality [that is, of the majority] of its members. Unanimity being a very difficult objective to attain even among a rather small group of people, it becomes impossible in a society of several million individuals. Since civil association has certain goals, reasonable means must be used to attain them. We must be satisfied with plurality. . . . Thus, with good reason, plurality becomes legitimately a substitute for unanimity.[5]

To require that the common will always equals the exact sum of all individual wills would lead to the "dissolution of the social union. It therefore becomes absolutely necessary *to recognize all the characteristics of the common will* in whatever plurality a community sets as decisive."[6]

Sieyès's argument indicates how the requirement for unanimity follows from the original postulate (that the individual will is the sole source of legitimate obligation); but it also stresses the extreme difficulty of reconciling this principle of legitimacy with the practical necessities of political life, which make it essential to settle for a majority. This solution, in a way, transsubstantiates *majority* into *unanimity*: majority is not identical to unanimity, but we must resolve to find "all the characteristics" of the latter in the former. Majority *must* be considered as equivalent to unanimity.

Unanimity thus remains the true source of legitimacy. Majority will becomes legitimate when one has conferred upon it all the attributes of unanimous will. It is obviously possible to object that the difference between the will of the majority and the will of all is an incontrovertible empirical fact. The ingeniousness of Sieyès's argument cannot mask this fact. Sieyès simply presents the transfiguration of majority will into unanimous will as a practical necessity, whose unique justification is the need for a realistic principle of decision making. Yet this move remains completely unrelated to the rest of the argument; the majority principle is a simple necessity of fact with no reasonable link to the principle of legitimacy. It is merely a convenient convention.

Rousseau, too, trusts unanimity as the only true source of legitimacy although the theory stated in the *Social Contract* differs in several essential aspects from that of Sieyès. This is particularly true with respect to the question of representation, which Rousseau rejects and Sieyès justifies. Furthermore, Rousseau offers a different solution to the problem presented by the requirement of unanimity. But the terms of the problem are the same. The only legitimate source of political obligation is the will of individuals. In obeying the common will, each person is in fact merely obeying himself. Therefore, the general will must equal unanimous will as a matter of principle.

As is well known, Rousseau distinguishes between the general will and the will of all. But the difference between the two is merely the distinction between principle and practice. It is empirically possible for all individuals not to have agreed with what came to be the general will, but in principle, they are necessarily in agreement. "The more agreement prevails in the assemblies, that is to say the more closely opinions approach unanimity, the more the general will prevails."[7] The general will is, in principle, the will of all the members of society; otherwise, it would be impossible to understand how they could remain free, and obey only themselves, while still submitting to it. If disagreements arise, and certain people do not agree with what has been decided, it is because those who disagree had in fact misunderstood the question put to them.

> The firm will of all the members of the state equals the general will. By its exercise they are citizens, and free. When a law is proposed in the people's assembly, what is asked to them is not exactly whether they approve of or reject the proposition, but rather whether it conforms to the general will, which is also theirs. Each person in voting, gives his opinion in this matter, and the general will is then deduced by counting the votes. Therefore, when an opinion contrary to my own prevails, it merely proves that I was mistaken, and that what I had taken to be the general will, was not.[8]

A minority opinion is, therefore, nothing but a mistaken *opinion* about the general will. But we must then also acknowledge that people were not really asked what they *wanted*, but only what they *believed to be the general will*. Unanimity is no longer required, but this result has been obtained at the cost of an obvious contradiction with the principles presented at the outset of the *Social Contract*.

The remarks of both Sieyès and Rousseau show that it is impossible coherently to reconcile the majority principle with the requirement for unanimity that seems to derive from a rigorous form of individualism. But these theories make it possible to understand the particular interpretation of individualism on which the requirement for unanimity is based. These theories do not merely affirm that legitimate collective decision making must proceed from individuals; they also state more precisely that political obligation flows from individual *wills*, that is to say, from choices arrived at by individuals. Thus it is not only the free individual who makes legitimacy possible, it is his *already determined will*.

This appears with great clarity in Rousseau and becomes particularly apparent in the meaning he gives to the term *deliberation*. Following a usage that goes back to Aristotle, philosophic tradition generally takes deliberation to mean the process of the formation of the will, the particular moment that precedes choice, and in which the individual ponders different solutions before settling for one of them. Rousseau uses the term *deliberation* in a different sense, one that is accepted in common language, and uses it to mean "decision." We can see the difference that separates these two definitions: in the vocabulary of philosophy, deliberation describes the process that precedes decision; in Rousseau's writings, it signifies decision itself.[9] He writes as follows:

> It follows from the preceding that the general will is always right, and always tends toward the public good. But it does not follow that the people's deliberations have always the same righteousness [rectitude]. One always wishes for one's own good, but one cannot always see it. The people cannot be corrupted, but they are often deceived, and it is only then that they seem to wish for what is bad.[10]

In this passage, the "deliberations of the people" obviously refers to the choices the people make, and not to the process that leads to the choice. There would be no sense in saying that a process is morally right or not. In the *Discourse on Political Economy*, the term is used in the same fashion. Rousseau shows how the existence of "partial associations" harms the general will. He says, "Such deliberation may be to the advantage of a small community, but very harmful to the larger one."[11] Here again, deliberation clearly means decision: it is the decision made by a group that can be both beneficial for the small group and harmful for society at large.

The term *deliberation* taken in this particular sense comes up precisely in those passages where Rousseau condemns those groups that normally constitute the mainstay of public discussion: the groups or parties who face each other in an exchange of argument. "If citizens had no communication between each other while a sufficiently well-informed public deliberated, the general will would always become apparent, in spite of a great number of small differences, and the deliberation would always be good."[12] This formulation is remarkable because we can simultaneously see the reduction of deliberation to decision (in this context, only a decision can be either good or bad, but not the process of the formation of the will) and the rigorous exclusion of communication between the citizens. The remainder of the chapter develops the famous critique of "partial associations," and/or parties. The interests of groups or parties corrupt the general will:

> When special interests begin to make themselves felt, and when smaller societies influence the larger one, the common interest changes, and finds opponents. Unanimity no longer reigns, the general will is no longer the will of all, contradictions and debates arise, and the best point of view is no longer accepted without disputes.[13]

The existence of parties is not the only cause for alarm; the mere communication between citizens is considered dangerous. What danger does

Rousseau wish to ward off? The answer is to be found in the passage of the *Discourse on Political Economy*, which I have quoted above. Rousseau wants to show that the public will is always right, except if the people are

> seduced by special interests, which certain shrewd people, by means of influence and *eloquence* manage to substitute for the general will. Then public deliberation will differ from the general will. Athenian democracy ought not to be brought up against me, because Athens was not in fact a democracy, but rather a very tyrannical aristocracy, governed by *scholars* and *orators*.[14]

What we must exclude from a democracy are the effects of rhetoric and the powers of persuasion that some individuals might exercise over others.

A careful examination of Rousseau's texts shows the real reason for his desire to exclude parties, a desire often noted by commentators. Contrary to what is wrongly supposed, this desire does not result from a sort of pretotalitarian point of view but rather in a much deeper way from the fact that Rousseau's individuals are already supposed to know what they want when they come to a public assembly to decide in common. They have already determined their will, so that any act of persuasion attempted by others could only taint their will and oppress it. One could object that instead of deliberating collectively, Rousseau's citizens have only deliberated within themselves, in the secret of their hearts. Certain texts might lead one to such an interpretation. That interpretation would nevertheless be false because, strictly speaking, when all decide for all, the choice becomes absolutely simple, and there is nothing uncertain.

> Whenever men who have gathered together, consider themselves as one single body, they will have only one will, dedicated to the preservation of the community, and the general well-being. Then all the actions of the state would be vigorous and simple, its maxims *clear* and *luminous*. There will be no tangled, contradictory interests, the public good would be *evident* everywhere, and would only need common sense to be apprehended. Peace, unity, and equality are the enemies of political subtleties.[15]

What is evident, simple, and luminous does not need to be *deliberated* in the strong sense of that term. On the contrary, deliberation is necessary for what is uncertain, when there may be reasons to decide one way but also reasons to decide another way. "The subjects of our deliberation are such as seem to present us with alternative possibilities; about things that could not have been and cannot now or in the future be other than they are, nobody who takes them to be of this nature wastes his time in deliberation."[16] The citizens of Rousseau's democracy do not deliberate, not even within themselves, because Rousseau considers politics to be essentially a simple matter. That is why the process of the formation of the will, individual as well as collective, does not concern him. He is thus able to identify deliberation with decision making and decision with self-evidence.

But aside from the objections that such a concept of deliberation gives rise to, it is important to note that, for Rousseau, the basis for legitimacy lies not in the free individual capable of making up his mind by weighing reasons, but rather in the individual whose will is already entirely determined, one who has made his choice. This insight allows us to understand the grounds of the requirement of unanimity in Rousseau's thought: the individualistic and democratic principle requires that collective decision emanate from all individuals; but as they are seen from the start as bearers of a completely determined will, it follows that if a collective decision does not conform to the sum of individual decisions, democratic individualism will no longer be respected. Furthermore, as the terms of reference (the individual choices) are supposed to be completely determined, the collective decision either does or does not conform to the sum of individual decisions. There is no other solution. The requirement of unanimity does not spring from individualism, but from the manner in which the individual is perceived: namely, as the possessor of a completely determined will. The lack of *deliberation* in the strong sense of the term is only a consequence of this fundamental presupposition.

We find the three elements of Rousseau's conception (the requirement for unanimity, the absence of deliberation, the predetermined will of individuals) in the work of John Rawls. One cannot avoid being struck by the close resemblance between the situation of Rousseau's citizen and that of the individuals in the original position that we find in the work of Rawls. Rawls, as Rousseau, uses the term *deliberation*: individuals behind the veil of ignorance are supposed to deliberate in order to know what principles of justice they are to adopt. But what does deliberation mean in this situation?

> To begin with, it is clear that since differences among the parties [i.e., the individuals] are unknown to them, and everyone is equally rational and similarly situated, each is convinced by the same arguments. Therefore we can view the choice in the original position from the standpoint of one person selected at random.[17]

Therefore, there can be no arguments among individuals because, by definition, they all have the same point of view. It is true that Rawls imagines individuals communicating between each other through a referee, "and that he is to announce which alternatives have been suggested and the reasons offered in their support," but he adds immediately, "but such a referee is actually superfluous, assuming that the deliberations of the parties must be similar."[18] Public deliberation is, therefore, excluded, and

Rawls adds a precise point that cannot but recall Rousseau: the formation of coalitions is forbidden. This point is in fact also superfluous because the hypothesis states that only one point of view exists, which is the same for all. Must one, however, add that the representative individual deliberates within himself? It does not seem so. This is how Rawls defines the rational individual: he is exclusively concerned with finding the solution, that is, those principles of justice, that most clearly advance his own interests. He is the classic "homo oeconomicus."

> A rational person is thought to have a coherent set of preferences between the options open to him. He ranks these options according to how well they further his purposes; he follows the plan which will satisfy more of his desires rather than less, and which have the greater chance of being successfully executed.[19]

This means that what Rawls calls deliberation is nothing but the calculation of the classic economic agent: he is provided with a coherent set of preferences (that is, A may not be preferred over B, while B is simultaneously preferred to A), certain given constraints restrict his actions, and he chooses the optimal solution, taking these constraints into account. He is assumed to have criteria for evaluation that permit taking *all* possible solutions into account, and ranking them so that he can select the best one. One might be tempted to say that the individual does not know a priori which solution he will prefer and will discover it while applying his criteria of evaluation to the propositions put to him. Such an implication is in fact incorrect: the criterion for evaluation is given, as is the set of solutions, so that the procedure of forming the will loses its importance. The result is already contained in the premises and is only separated from them, one might say, by the time needed for calculation. Reflection and the calculations necessary for obtaining a solution teach the individual nothing new; in particular, he learns nothing about his own preferences.[20] There is, therefore, no *deliberation*, in the full sense of the term, to be found here. The process of forming a decision is reduced to calculation. As with Rousseau, the individual is already supposed to know exactly what he wants, or more precisely, he already possesses the criteria for evaluation that will permit him to appraise all possible alternatives.

Rawls is currently reproached for what is taken to be an excessive individualism. He has been criticized for reducing the citizen to an economic man who calculates his own advantage in a solitary and egoistical manner. Some critics contend that the Rawlsian theory does not give sufficient weight to the fact that man is also a social and political being, belonging to a community and attached to it. Such criticism misses the point. Neither Rawls nor Rousseau denies the collective dimension of human existence.

The real problem for a society that claims to be based on the liberty of individuals is to find a way to reconcile each individual's free pursuit of his own objectives with the common good. As Rousseau understood, it is a matter of reconciling the interests of each individual (the good as he sees it) with justice. Reproaching Rawls with neglecting the "collective" dimension of life and the importance of the sense of community does not advance the philosophical debate at all, because the problem consists precisely in finding out how it is possible to constitute a collective entity that does not violate the freedom of individuals. When one confines oneself to commending the virtues of collective existence and of community, one assumes that the crucial problem is already solved, or rather one throws it into the darkness of incomprehensibility. Critics such as these invariably find their conclusion in the pathos of "community" and its unfathomable mystery.

In fact, what must be criticized in Rawls's and Rousseau's theories is not their neglect of the collective dimension, but the assumption that individuals in society, in particular, those having to make a political decision, possess an already formed will, already know exactly what they want, and at most only need to apply their criteria of evaluation to the proposed solutions. This criticism can be conducted in accordance with the principles of individualism. We need not argue that individuals, when they begin to deliberate political matters, know nothing of what they want. They know what they want in part: they have certain preferences and some information, but these are unsure, incomplete, often confused, and opposed to one another. The process of deliberation, the confrontation of various points of view, helps to clarify information and to sharpen their own preferences. They may even modify their initial objectives, should that prove necessary.

It is, therefore, necessary to alter radically the perspective common to both liberal theories and democratic thought: the source of legitimacy is not the predetermined will of individuals, but rather the process of its formation, that is, deliberation itself. An individual's liberty consists first of all in being able to arrive at a decision by a process of research and comparison among various solutions. As political decisions are characteristically imposed on *all*, it seems reasonable to seek, as an essential condition for legitimacy, the deliberation of *all* or, more precisely, the right of all to participate in deliberation. We must, therefore, challenge the fundamental conclusion of Rousseau, Sieyès, and Rawls: a legitimate decision does not represent the *will* of all, but is one that results from the *deliberation of all*. It is the process by which everyone's will is formed that confers its legitimacy on the outcome, rather than the sum of already formed wills.

The deliberative principle is both individualistic and democratic. It implies that *all* participate in the deliberation, and in this sense the decision made can reasonably be considered as emanating from the people (democratic principle). The decision also proceeds from the liberty of individuals: those individuals deliberate together, form their opinions through deliberation, and at the close of the process each opts freely for one solution or another (individualistic and liberal principle). We must affirm, at the risk of contradicting a long tradition, that legitimate law is the *result of general deliberation*, and not the *expression of the general will*.

There is a double dimension to the process of deliberation; it is simultaneously collective and individual. It is individual in the sense that everyone reasons for himself, finding arguments and weighing them. Because the aim of the deliberative process is to broaden the participants' information and enable them to discover their own preferences, that process requires a multiplicity of points of view and/or arguments. As the individual listens to arguments formulated by others, he broadens his own point of view and becomes aware of things he had not perceived at the outset. Deliberation requires not only multiple but conflicting points of view because conflict of some sort is the essence of politics. The parties in deliberation will not be content to defend their own positions, but will try to refute the arguments of the positions of which they disapprove. New information emerges as each uncovers the potentially harmful consequences of the other parties' proposals.

Thus deliberation tends to increase information and to pinpoint individuals' preferences. It helps them to discover aspects both of proposed solutions and of their own objectives that they had not perceived earlier.[21] But deliberation is not only a process of discovery: the parties are not satisfied with presenting various and conflicting theses; they also try to persuade each other. They argue. Argumentation is a sequence of propositions aiming to produce or reinforce agreement in the listener. In this sense, it is a discursive and rational process. Yet, in contrast to logical proof, argumentation does not result in a necessary conclusion that the listener cannot reject. A conclusion developed from argumentation is not a necessary proposition. The listener remains free to give his agreement or to withhold it. The listener is free because argumentation does not start from evident premises or from conventional ones. Rather, one starts by taking propositions one assumes are generally accepted by the audience being addressed. In politics, one would argue by assuming certain common values as held by the public at a given moment. Argumentation is, therefore, always relative to its audience. Someone who does not share these values will not be convinced by the arguments presented. Nor are the procedures of linking the propositions logically binding. One may use, for example, arguments by analogy and a fortiori arguments. These do not make the passage from one proposition to another strictly necessary. It is, therefore, not said of a conclusion developed from arguments that it is either true or false, but that it simply generates more or less support depending on whether the argument was more or less convincing. Nor is an argument either true or false; it is stronger or weaker. Whatever the force of an argumentation, its conclusion is never strictly necessary. The listener may withhold his approval, and it must even be acknowledged that his refusal to approve a conclusion may have reasons as well. The force of an argumentation is always relative.[22]

One argues in order to try to persuade others. But one tries only to persuade, that is, to produce or reinforce agreement to a proposition, in cases where no proposition imposes itself with unimpeachable and universally recognized force. People need not be persuaded of the truth. In this sense, argumentation differs from a logical demonstration. On the negative side, it differs also from refutation. One piles up several arguments against a thesis, one tries to weaken it because one lacks the refutation that would incontestably destroy it.

Thus argumentation is particularly suited to the nature of political debate, which most frequently consists of a confrontation between opposing norms or values. We must admit, with Weber, that no science can resolve this conflict in a rigorous and necessary manner. However, contrary to Weber's thesis, it does not follow that the choice of values remains ineluctably arbitrary. Some values are more likely than others to win the approval of an audience of reasonable people. It is impossible to *demonstrate* their soundness; they can only be *justified*. A decision or a norm is not either true or false. But we are nevertheless not reduced to pure arbitrariness because a norm can be more or less *justified*. The relative force of its justification can only be measured by the amplitude and the intensity of the approval it arouses in an audience of reasonable people.

Political deliberation and argumentation certainly presuppose a relatively reasonable audience. They also require a certain degree of instruction and culture on the part of the public. But they constitute processes of education and of training in themselves. They broaden the viewpoints of citizens beyond the limited outlook of their private affairs. They spread light. Such a concept of deliberation implies that the majority of citizens should be educated, but it is not the kind of pedagogic model in which an enlightened elite is intended to bring the light of science down from its pulpit to a backward people. Rather, the people educate themselves. Certainly, knowledge is not distributed equally, and all speeches will not have the same weight, but because those who are more knowledgeable tend not to be in agreement among themselves, their exchange of opinions, refereed by the public, offers an education without a unique and eminent teacher. J. S. Mill has analyzed this educational function of arguments remarkably well.

In the political sphere, deliberation does not permit us to arrive at necessary and universally admitted truths,[23] but it also does not permit the absolute and incontestable refutation of a norm or a value. It is doubtless possible to show that a policy that was based on given normative principles failed, but most of the time, this failure is not sufficient to refute either the policy in question or the normative principle from which it was derived. This is so because first of all it is extremely difficult, if not impossible, to discover exactly what in a given policy caused the failure. In order to find that out, it would be necessary to isolate exactly what derived from the initial conditions in which the policy was adopted and what derived from the normative principles themselves. Even supposing that one succeeds in isolating the normative principles that caused the failure, the unhappy outcome does not necessarily prove that this principle should be rejected. One can always argue that it should have been put into practice in another form or to a lesser degree. The planned economy is surely a failure with respect to its own objectives, but for all that, economic planning as a normative principle is not absolutely refuted. A limited nonbinding form of planning may be defended. Ascertaining a failure does not refute a political principle; it merely creates a *presumption* against it. Despite a certain closeness, political deliberation and scientific argumentation remain separated by an irreducible difference. One does not really say that the scientific community *deliberates* when it exchanges conjectures and refutations.

The failure of unanimistic theories of justice or legitimacy leads us to note, once more, that the definition of what is just remains the subject of constant debate, and on the theoretical level, an attitude of constant questioning is surely the only warranted one. But a society cannot live and maintain itself solely on the basis of principles and institutions that reflect only an ultimately indeterminate justice. For a society to continue to exist, decisions must be made and conflicts resolved; power also must be exercised and in the last resort must be sufficient to restore some unity to the multiplicity of actions and desires that make up social life. To make room simultaneously for the indeterminacy of justice and the necessity for decision, those in power and their idea of the common good must be questioned, if not constantly, then at regular intervals. Between those intervals, societies need to keep in place some power of ultimate decision making, even if it does not constantly interfere everywhere. Therefore, unless we believe that this power of decision making may be constituted simply in any manner, as long as it somehow exercises the function of making a decision, we must try to uncover the procedures most likely to make those decisions reasonable. If such procedures cannot be found, the indeterminacy of justice and the practical necessity of decision making will in reality simply result in arbitrariness. But between the *rational* object of universal agreement and the *arbitrary* lies the domain of the *reasonable* and the *justifiable*, that is, the domain of propositions that are likely to convince, by means of arguments whose conclusion is not incontestable, the greater part of an audience made up of all the citizens.

The theory of deliberation offers only an imperfect method for making the decision process as reasonable as possible. We cannot guarantee that a deliberation consonant with the stated rules will always be rational, or even as rational as possible. But this process makes the realization of reasonable results more likely, especially if one takes into account the dimension of time and the educative effect of repeated deliberation. The weakness of universalist theories of justice lies not in their lack of realism (indeed, they often explicitly concede their nonrealistic character). Rather, those who propose these universalist theories present them as models that simultaneously permit the evaluation of actual societies (making it possible to determine whether society approaches the model more or less closely) and at the same time set a standard: a goal that must be pursued with the knowledge that it can never be attained. This is where the inadequacy lies. We want not only to know whether a society is more or less just, and what the ideal society should be like, but we also want concrete means to make real societies as reasonable as possible. The idea of setting standards that are explicitly unrealistic is unsatisfactory because it leaves totally open the question of the means necessary to approach this state.

As long as we accept the predetermined will of individuals as the unique basis for legitimacy, we must inevitably conclude that only the object of unanimous agreement is legitimate. The requirement for unanimity is justified in a pure theory of justice because a *pure* theory does not encompass the practical conditions for its realization nor the means necessary for attaining it. Yet unanimity is an inadequate requisite for a theory of political decision making; a theory of decision making cannot, without falling into pure empiricism and relativism, avoid concerning itself with legitimacy. It is unrealistic, and more important, unjustified, to assume that individuals faced with the necessity of having to make a political decision already know exactly what they want. The free individual is not one who already knows absolutely what he wants, but one who has incomplete preferences and is trying by means of interior deliberation and dialogue with others to determine precisely what he does want. When individuals approach political decision making, they only partially know what they want. We are justified in taking as a basis for legitimacy not their predetermined will but the process by which they determine their will. This is the process of deliberation. This perspective is strictly compatible with the principles of individualism. It in no way implies that someone who possesses knowledge should teach other individuals what their wishes are, but rather that they find them out for themselves. Without renouncing a concern for legitimacy, which in the modern world can only be based on the individual, deliberation makes it possible to avoid the exorbitant requirements of universality and unanimity.

—TRANSLATED BY ELLY STEIN AND JANE MANSBRIDGE

Notes

1. Emmanuel Sieyès, *Vues sur les moyens d'exécution dont les représentants de la France pourront disposer en 1789* (Paris, 1789), 15. Sieyès is mostly known as the author of the pamphlet *Qu'est-ce que le tiers état?* and as a leader of the French Revolution; his importance as a political thinker is often underestimated. In fact, he is probably one of the first and most important theoreticians of representative government; his influence on French and German constitutional thought has been considerable. Because most of his writings have not been published since the French Revolution, they must be consulted in their original editions.

2. Sieyès, *Vues sur les moyens d'exécution.*

3. Sieyès, *Vues sur les moyens d'exécution.*

4. Emmanuel Sieyès, *Préliminaire de la Constitution Française* (Paris, 1791), 38.

5. Sieyès, *Préliminaire*, 38.

6. Sieyès, *Vues sur les moyens d'exécution.*

7. Jean-Jacques Rousseau, *Du contrat social*, book 4, chap.2, *Oeuvres Complètes*, ed. by B. Gagnebin and M. Raymond (Paris: Gallimard), 3:439.

8. Rousseau, *Du contrat social*, book 4, chap. 2, 441.

9. The term has in fact two meanings in French. This ambiguity surely justifies Rousseau's usage but in no way lessens the importance of his choice in favor of one and only one of the two meanings.

10. Rousseau, *Du contrat social*, book 2, chap. 3, 371. The term *rectitude* in French has the meaning of both "rightness" and "righteousness"; however, the context makes it clear that Rousseau wants to stress here the moral character of the decision.

11. Jean-Jacques Rousseau, *Discours sur l'économie politique, Oeuvres complètes*, 3:246.

12. Rousseau, *Du contrat social*, book 4, chap. 3, 371.

13. Rousseau, *Du contrat social*, book 4, chap. 1, 438.

14. Rousseau, *Discours sur l'économie politique*, 246, emphasis added.

15. Rousseau, *Du contrat social*, book 4, chap. 1, 437, emphasis added.

16. Aristotle, *Rhetorica*, 1. 2. 1357a.3–6, vol 9, *The Works of Aristotle Translated into English*, ed. by W. D. Ross (Oxford: Clarendon Press, 1910–52).

17. Rawls, *A Theory of Justice*, 139.

18. Rawls, *A Theory of Justice*, 139.

19. Rawls, *A Theory of Justice*, 143.

20. The nondeliberative aspect of the classic conception of economic rationality is especially highlighted in the work of H. Simon. He has constructed a model of "procedural" or "limited rationality" to take into account a certain number of empirical situations with which the classic model of optimization (or maximization) did not seem to be able to deal. In this conception, "the conditions for choice, for the ends as well as for the means, are not given to the decider, but are the object of the search," whereas the classic conception "regards the conditions for choice as fixed, and therefore identifies decision-making with the mere application of criteria of evaluation given to a set of possible actions, as equally given" (Philippe Mongin, "Modèle Rationnel ou Modèle Economique de la Rationalité?" *Revue Economique* 35, no. 1 [January 1984], 26, 27). The most recent formulation of Simon's theses can be found in Herbert A. Simon's *Models of Bounded Rationality*, 2 vols. (Cambridge: MIT Press, 1983), and H. A. Simon's *Reason in Human Affairs* (Stanford: Stanford University Press, 1983). For a sociological application of this model of limited rationality, see Michel Crozier and E. Friedberg. *L'acteur et le système* (Paris: Seuil, 1977).

21. Individuals deliberate because at the start they are relatively uncertain as to the solution they should adopt. The concept of deliberation used here is, therefore, in a sense, close to that of Aristotle, for whom deliberation bears on that which is neither absolutely certain (that is, the domain of "science") nor completely contingent (in this case, deliberation could serve no purpose). See Aristotle, *Ethica Nicomachea* 3.e.1112A18 1112B31, *The Works of Aristotle*, vol. 9. However, in Aristotle's thought, this relative indeterminacy results from the nature of things and the order of the world. It is a cosmological and ontological indeterminacy. In the theory of deliberation outlined here, I make no assumptions about the order of the world. Individuals are assumed to be relatively uncertain, not because of the intrinsic nature of the subjects they deliberate but because they lack complete information, and their preferences are not entirely determined. This relative uncertainty is related to the deliberating subjects themselves, and not to the nature of the objects of their deliberation. Aristotle furthermore assumes that people deliberate only the means and never the ends. The ends are given by nature. Such a vision is too closely linked to the teleological conception of the world for the theory presented here.

22. With reference to the conception of argumentation sketched here, see Chaim Perelman and Lucie Olbrechts-Tyteca, *The New Rhetoric: A Treatise on Argumentation*, trans. by John Wilkinson and Purcell Weaver (Notre Dame, Ind.: University of Notre Dame Press, 1969); and also Chaim Perelman, L'empire rhétorique: rhétorique et argumentation (Paris: J. Vrin, 1977).

23. The conception defended here differs, therefore, from that of Habermas. For him, deliberation plays the central role in "practical questions," that is, questions about the validity of norms, whether they are moral or political; furthermore, the validity of a norm is neither, in Habermas's conception, susceptible of proof (reducible to deductive argument) nor is it decided only by an arbitrary act of will, as is affirmed by decisionist theories; as a result, for Habermas, the recognition of the validity claim of a norm can be rationally motivated. On all these accounts, I

find myself in agreement with Habermas's conception. However, when Habermas deals with this rationally motivated agreement about norms, he apparently means the consensus of *all*, at least in principle. "Since," he writes, "all those affected have, in principle, at least the chance to participate in the practical deliberation, the 'rationality' of the discursively formed will consists in the fact that the reciprocal behavioral expectations raised to normative status afford validity to a *common* interest. . . . The interest is common because the constraint free consensus permits only what *all* can want" (Jürgen Habermas, *Legitimation Crisis*, trans. by T. McCarthy [Boston: Beacon Press, 1975], 108, emphasis in the original). Thus Habermas maintains, in my view, the requirement for unanimous consensus, at least in principle. He fails to recognize that there are various degrees of agreement, which if the appropriate rules for deliberation are respected, reflect in turn the respective strengths of the arguments put forward in the defense of the conflicting norms. Given the appropriate procedural rules for deliberation, the better argument is simply the one that generates more support and not the one that is able to convince all participants.

CHAPTER 15

Modernization and Consensus

JEAN-MARC FERRY

To MAKE a broadened concept of modernization possible today, we must return to one of the great philosophers of modernity, Max Weber. The central theme of Weber's theory of society is modernization as rationalization. This rationalization, according to Weber, takes place through systems of socially organized activities: essentially, the modern economy and modern bureaucracy. These systems or spheres are, as it were, the loci of the practical agent's material incorporation of the rationality that is elaborated theoretically in modern science and individualist ethics. Weber spoke of spheres of "rational activities relative to an end" that are progressively extended to the whole of society. He thus saw in modernization a process that subjects actions, relations, and social institutions to the criteria of a formal rationality oriented to the strategic effectiveness and technical success of economic and political undertakings.

Correspondingly, Weber thought that this mode of development, which was tied to Western rationalism, inevitably endangered the traditional spheres of society that pre-existed the capitalist economy, formal law, and modern bureaucracy. These traditional spheres form what has since been called the "experienced world" or the life-world, where beliefs, images of the world, traditional values and norms, sociocosmic representations, and cultural symbols are handed down. Weber believed that we now live in a "disenchanted world" produced by the typically modern destruction of the prejudices accumulated and enshrined by these traditional spheres. Consequently, the very principle of modernization has undermined the cultural bases of consensus resting on the pure and simple authority of tradition. Under modern conditions, consensus can no longer be formed on the basis of a common cultural identity.

After Weber, many philosophers worried about the propensity of "rationality" to dominate social reality. Their verdicts on modernity were only one-dimensional, however, whether they were articulated as critiques of technology as an extension of metaphysics, the "will to will," and the total mastery of being (Heidegger); critiques of instrumental rationality's "purposefulness without a purpose" (Horkheimer); critiques of the "unreason of reason" and the "end of the individual" (Adorno); or critiques of rationality itself as structured to manipulate both things and men (Marcuse). It is these one-dimensional verdicts that I would like to call into question.

In order to do this, however, I must return to an older modern tradition, that of philosophers like Kant and the young Hegel, who were able to rethink modernization along various autonomous dimensions of rationalization. Among our contemporaries, Jürgen Habermas now judges a thoughtful renewal of this idealist tradition to be indispensable. But even Weber himself had also insisted that modernity is characterized by the formation of differentiated and autonomous spheres of validity: the domain of facts and scientific objectivity; the domain of norms and juridical legitimacy; the domain of values and symbolic meaning. In making these distinctions, Weber was asserting a certain vision of modernity that had already been established by Kant in his architectonics of pure reason and then indirectly reinterpreted by the young Hegel in his "Jena" philosophy of the spirit. In Kant, the three domains of validity and rationality were distinguished as science, ethics, and aesthetics; in the young Hegel, they were work, interaction, and representation.[1] One could say that Weber was better served by his predecessors than by his successors.

I believe that the logical analysis of these three domains can serve as a basis for re-establishing a broadened concept of modernization, a concept that takes account of the differentiation and logical autonomy of the directions that rationalization has followed. Let us take them up in order.

The first domain, that of *objectivity*, corresponds to a model of rationality conceived on that of modern science. From an ontological point of view, we may characterize it as the "objective world": the world of states of things, given in the spatiotemporal framework as observable and measurable material events. When the "states of things" are interpreted from the viewpoint of "what is," we have what are called "facts" (for example, "salt dissolves in water"). These facts are presented in judgments of existence with a claim to truth. The constitution of these facts presupposes a "synthesis of objectivity" for which the relevant constellation is formed by the relation between the subject and the object. Once constituted in experience and controlled in scientific experimentation, these facts must be established through argumentation; and once recognized as true, they assume a place in a universe of interpretation and explanation, the universe of scientific laws.

The second domain, that of *legitimacy*, corresponds to a model of rationality that is not that of modern science, but that of modern ethics. From an ontological point of view, this domain of validity forms the normative contours of another "world" that might be characterized as the "legitimate world." This is a social world of human interactions regulated by legitimate norms that are recognized as just. The primitive "given" is not that of the states of things observed but that of interests asserted. When interests are then interpreted, not from the viewpoint of what is, but from that of what ought to be, we are dealing not with "facts" but "rights" that are presented in normative or prescriptive utterances. The forming of these rights also presupposes a "synthesis," but one that should be distinguished from the first. For here, the relevant constellation is not the one formed by the subject-object relation, but that of the relation between the interest of the individual and the society as a whole. Specifically, the problem is one of reconciling the particular and the general with a view to a synthesis whose universality is legitimate rather than objective. Hence we can speak of a "synthesis of legitimacy." These formations of rights, however, because they are still only claims, remain problematic until they are publicly recognized as socially valid. This presupposes the test of public argumentation, or at least the possibility of such a test.[2] Only then can the subjectively claimed and intersubjectively recognized rights assume their place in an autonomous system of juridical norms.

The third domain, that of *meaning*, is the hardest to analyze logically, for it does not correspond to the "hard" rationality of modern science or formal ethics. For purposes of simplicity, let us say that this third domain corresponds to a model of rationality conceived on that of *aesthetics*. Etymologically, the word "aesthetics" refers to what one experiences subjectively. But to make a claim to universality, and hence to a certain rationality, lived experience must be communicable in a language. Hence, I shall characterize as a "symbolic world" the world of feelings experienced.

Like states of things, like interests, these events of our inner mental life must be connected with a universal. But if we consider them as not connected with what exists (the synthesis of objectivity), nor with what ought to be (the synthesis of legitimacy), they can only be connected with what has meaning for oneself and others. Thus we can speak of a "synthesis of communication." The expression of private experience represents what subjectivity experiences; this representation must in turn make that experience accessible to any subject of the relation; and this communication must be the possible object of an objective valuation.[3] Such valuation will not take place according to the scientific criterion of truth (accuracy), nor according to the ethical criterion of rightness (suitability), but according to the aesthetic criteria of comprehensible, well-formed, and authentic expression—in short, according to the criterion of meaning. Thus, this expression translates private experience, to which each individual in principle has privileged access, into a communicable and meaningful representation. The aesthetic (in this sense) is "synthesized" with the symbolic in the sense of language. And in this synthesis of communication, the relevant constellation is not formed by the relation between subject and object, nor by the connection between the particular and the general, but by the relation between experience and language. The analogies between these three worlds can now be established: just as the *states of things* interpreted from the viewpoint of *what is* take their place in the system of *scientific laws* as *facts*, and just as *interests* interpreted from the viewpoint of *what ought to be* take their place in the system of *juridical norms* as *rights*, so *experiences* take their place in the system of *symbolic forms* as *representations*.

This construction is primarily important for determining the status of aesthetics. It will be readily conceded that a fact is not a right, that theoretical reason is not practical reason, and that the objectivity of scientific laws is not the legitimacy of juridical norms. Less often conceded is that the universe of meaning, which is that of symbolic forms, is distinct both from the universe of objectivity and from the universe of legitimacy. Norms (second domain) are not values (third domain); institutions (second domain) are not representations (third domain); the elements of legality (second domain) are not the elements of legitimation (third domain). Not only is rationality not the same in these three domains; even rationalization understood as a process of modernization does not take place in the same sense. On the one hand, technological achievements have made it possible to orient modernization in the direction of economic progress by exercising the first form of rationality, that of the scientific realm. On the other hand, the extension of democratic institutions orients modernization in the direction of political progress by exercising the second form of rationality, that of the ethical-juridical order. We must logically assume a third dimension that works on the basis of aesthetics.

This third dimension is harder to grasp than the first two because we do not yet see a corresponding "revolution" in history. We can, however, at least postulate that this would involve neither an economic revolution corresponding to a change in science and technology, nor a political revolution corresponding to a change in law and morality. It would surely involve a "cultural revolution" corresponding to a transformation in relations to science, to politics, to tradition and culture, to the self, and to others as well. In my opinion, this cultural revolution would be more gradual than the economic and political revolutions precisely because it would be a prelude, a spiritual preamble, to them. In *The Philosophy of the Enlightenment*, Ernst Cassirer analyzed one such revolution in the ideals, attitudes, hopes, and utopias that transfigured for a time the relations to others and to the world—the same revolution that Habermas has described in his writings on the public sphere.[4] In eighteenth-century Europe, the ideal of new, authentic relations stimulated the public spheres formed by the bourgeois, landowners, and cultivated men, who claimed to meet together "as mere human beings" in the salons, cafes, and clubs of the prerevolutionary period. Before being politically oriented, these public spheres were aesthetic, in the sense that their discussions were about works of art, music, the theater, and literature but were not conducted as struggles for power. Their goal was mutual comprehension, accord, and communication, which were desired for their own sake.

Today this aesthetic element can be found in the emergence of "new needs" and "new social movements," all of which emphasize the quality of life, the authenticity of relations, the "rediscovery of the other," and the development of a new relation to nature. Some of the currents may seek to reappropriate a threatened cultural identity or express negative themes such as the rejection of an overtechnological, materialistic, and dehumanized society. Such themes are certainly seen as political today, but they are also a form of cultural protest that calls into question a certain type of civilization. The year 1789 may have been a political revolution, but 1968 was in its way such a cultural revolution.

It is difficult to speak of all these movements as part of the process of "modernization," if only because they are often ambiguous: sometimes they take "premodern" or "antimodern" form, as with Christian or Muslim fundamentalism; sometimes they seem "postmodern," as with environmentalism, pacifism, or certain aspects of feminism (the "radical difference," and the like). What seems clear, however, is that apart from the reactionary incantations and the aestheticizing ideologies of our day, there is a typically modern ideal that all these movements share. That is the ideal of securing the autonomy of the subject.

Here we run up against a difficulty for thinking through modernization on the basis of aesthetics. The difficulty is that we can imagine rationalizing society by applying scientific laws and juridical principles, but we do not have a clear idea of rationalization through the application of aesthetic, symbolic representations. Scientific laws and juridical principles can be worked out in theoretical systems and then practically implemented. But what sense does this have in the case of symbolic representations such as beliefs, meanings, legitimations, ideologies, cultural values, and living traditions?

In fact, there are three possible modalities of modernization conceivable on the basis of aesthetics. The first, connected to that of modern social movements, is that of the practical *application* of aesthetic criteria to construct communicational utopias. The cardinal values of imagination and creativity, expressivity and authenticity, intersubjectivity and publicness—the quintessence of aesthetic values—do in fact propose new forms of social life, new landscapes of community. The communicational and communitarian utopias are surely rooted in modern aesthetics, since they involve the application of aesthetic criteria to social relations (and, beyond, to the environment in general). These utopias, conceived by "aesthetic reason," play a decisive role in modernization. Today the demand for "the good life" means a life in which public housing projects, pollution, anarchical urbanism, and the degradation of the countryside are put behind us. In one sense, this is the futurist dream of a large-scale plan for integrating the environment. The difference is that it would not be carried out by the practical application of scientific or political knowledge but by the practical application of aesthetic knowledge. Such knowledge would not be limited to certain privileged objects in the world but rather would take the world itself as an object to be transformed through beauty. Only in this sense can we speak of the effective application of aesthetic criteria to social reality, in the same sense that we speak of applying technical or juridical rules. However, such an "aesthetic rationalization" of the environment does not take into account the reflexivity of hermeneutics and criticism, a reflexivity that expresses both the essence of aesthetics and the highest form of modern rationality. Aesthetics is fundamentally symbolic. And although we can speak of applying scientific laws or juridical principles, we cannot speak sensibly of applying symbolic forms. Here I mean "symbolic forms" in Cassirer's sense: the symbols of art, religion, beliefs, narrative history, and systems of philosophy—in short, the world of the culture transmitted by tradition and endlessly recreated.[5] One does not "apply," for example, the Pastoral Symphony or the *Phenomenology of the Spirit* as one applies the principles of thermodynamics or the rights of man. But modernization on the basis of aesthetics is also possible through a second modality, that of "dissemination," "transmission," and "communication." If we do not "apply" the *Phenomenology of the Spirit* the way we apply the principles of thermodynamics, it is interesting to note that we do "transmit" both through communication. In relation to modernization, "transmission"—whether the transmission of scientific and technical knowledge, the transmission of moral and political knowledge, or the transmission of cultural and aesthetic knowledge—is primarily a pedagogical project. This project can be deduced only on the basis of reflection about aesthetics, a reflection that brings to light its symbolic essence in communication.

A third modality of modernization, after those of the *pragmatic application* of autonomous knowledge and its pedagogical dissemination, is its *critical appropriation*. Like the second, this third modality can be justified only on the basis of aesthetics. Criticism of transmitted contents is indeed a work specific to reflection and a distinctive exercise of judgment. Nonetheless, criticism is practiced on realities that are already symbolized and interpreted by the reflexivity of cultural discourses. These discourses transmit the rational consistency of the physical, social, and historical world using criteria of objectivity, legitimacy, and meaning. Criticism defetishizes and desacralizes the symbolic by interrogating its rational content—in other words, by testing the claims to validity involved in each case. This may be a claim to the *truth* of the constative utterances inherent in scientific laws, a claim to the *rightness* of prescriptive utterances inherent in the juridical norms, or a claim to the *representativeness* of the expressive signifiers inherent in symbolic forms.

Rationalization through permanent criticism is perhaps the most typical aspect of modernity, appearing as philosophical criticism, ideological criticism (Marx, Nietzsche), and even psychoanalytic criticism in the broad sense (Freud, Bloch, Marcuse). It is a modern model of self-reflection that also constitutes the modern concept of *autonomy*: criticism as self-reflection aims to reappropriate for the subject its own objectified productions in science, politics, and culture. The metaphysical idea in Kant, the objective appearance in Hegel, the fetishized commodity in Marx, and the dream or the neurotic symptom in Freud: all point to the danger of objectifications becoming alien to the subject by acquiring an independent and autonomous existence. Everything produced in civilization has this potential for alienation. Autonomy is the reconquest of what has been externalized and made impenetrable, "alien" to the self. For modern thought, the means for achieving this autonomy is self-reflection.

The rationalization of the world through criticism, in which modernity continually reflects on and judges itself is the source of both modernity's glory and fragility. Modernization is both the theoretical accumulation and practical implementation of a fantastic product of rationality in the various domains of science and technology, law and politics, art and criticism. As a function of criticism, however, it is also a project of autonomy for the producer who is ever threatened with losing himself in his production, the "subject" ever threatened with being brought down in its "system." Furthermore, criticism presupposes the permanent and systematic destabilization of the traditions that in principle make it possible to establish a social consensus, whether on the basis of an identity of shared convictions, prejudices, or authority.

This brings us back to Weber, and to the question of whether a modern form of consensus is possible. By this I do not mean a consensus about modernist values, for modernity itself will not be spared from criticism. I mean rather a consensus formed under the conditions of modernization, which are those of rational criticism. In the logic of modernity, there cannot be a pregiven consensus on the basis of authority. Such a consensus can only be problematic, for it is constructed on the basis of a reference to truth, and the truth in the modern sense is perpetually on trial. To my mind, this problem of achieving social consensus under modern conditions logically calls for *the maximally generalized institutionalization of the public debate in the form of rational argumentation.* The question of the citizen's political autonomy would then be posed in terms of an essentially procedural ethics. Such an ethics would not, strictly speaking, impose any axiological content, only the principle of a *discursive formation of the will.* In my view, the conception of a "communicational ethics" as developed by Habermas best expresses this through the principle of the universalization of universalizable interests in discussion.

—Translated by Franklin Philip

Notes

1. For the young Hegel of the Jena period, work is the (instrumental) relation in which the technical consciousness is formed; interaction is the (strategic) relation in which the practical (moral) consciousness is formed; representation is the (reflexive) relation in which the theoretical consciousness is formed. The objectifications would be the technical rules, the social norms, and the symbolic forms, respectively.

2. Nevertheless, the access of modern consciousness to the universalist principles of law and morality has allowed for the establishment of a system of a priori coherent rational law. This potential of rationality must in principle make possible the discursive/interactive procedure classically required for the reconciliation of social interests.

3. This valuation is objective in that it thematizes the conditions of rationality to which a symbolic structure may be held to be valid in general. See Jürgen Habermas's introduction to volume 1 of his *The Theory of Communicative Action*, trans. Thomas McCarthy (Boston, 1984).

4. See Ernst Cassirer, *The Philosophy of the Enlightenment*, trans. Fritz C. A. Koelln and James P. Pettegrove (Princeton, N.J., 1951), and Jürgen Habermas, *The Structural Transformation of the Public Sphere: An Inquiry into a Category of Bourgeois Society*, trans. Thomas Burger and Frederick Lawrence (Cambridge, Mass., 1989).

5. Ernst Cassirer, *The Philosophy of Symbolic Forms*, 3 vols., trans. Ralph Manheim (New Haven, Conn., 1955–57), and *An Essay on Man: An Introduction to a Philosophy of Human Culture* (New Haven, Conn., 1962).

PART SIX

The New Individualism

THE ALMOST TOTAL disappearance of Marxism from recent French thought has not meant the end of critical sociological analysis of liberalism. Its intellectual reference point, however, is now more likely to be Tocqueville's *Democracy in America* than Marx's *1844 Manuscripts*. The lively writings of Gilles Lipovetsky (whose style reminds one of the Situationists and Jean Baudrillard) are exemplary in this regard and have inspired many others. In his collection of essays, *L'ère du vide* (The empty age), and in his later books, Lipovetsky has drawn a sharp picture of the new individualism he sees in postwar life and analyzed many of its problems. What distinguishes this individualism from that anxiously described by Tocqueville, he argues, are the personalization, diversity, and seduction made possible within a society dominated by consumption and leisure. The massification and tyranny of opinion that Tocqueville feared have not materialized, but in their stead we must now cope with a profound sense of psychological indifference and emptiness.

Lipovetsky's general approach is reflected in his hotly debated essay on May '68, where he maintains that the "events" were more self-referential than political, reflecting the personal and psychological concerns of the young generation. He calls it a "transpolitical" episode signaling the end of the revolutionary age and the birth of a new, more individualistic one. Anne Godignon and Jean-Louis Thiriet describe some other social transformations set off by this individualization in their two essays on modern consumption and work. Individual freedom is so great today, they assert, that consumption now drives production rather than the reverse. Alienation in the classical Marxist sense is therefore over, but it has been replaced by the inauthentic search for satisfaction in an endless stream of fleeting experiences. They then note that this modern freedom for consumption has been accompanied by a new slavery to jobs and careers, in which empty individuals seek self-definition. Even leisure has now been transformed into a kind of work, robbed of pleasure in the breathless search for identity in liberal society.

CHAPTER 16

May '68, or the Rise of Transpolitical Individualism

GILLES LIPOVETSKY

THIS ARTICLE does not offer a conventional analysis of May '68. The May revolution has usually been seen as a multidimensional crisis that shook the disparate worlds of students and workers and profoundly altered the structures of French politics and trade unionism. Instead, I want to examine the "spirit of May": that original ensemble of attitudes and actions so characteristic of the times, which was to be found wherever there were young people.

This spirit can only truly be understood in the context of the rise of modern individualism. The "spirit of May" was an example of a larger development in our modern societies, even if it appeared as merely a short-term, intermediate link between two ages in the history of democracy. Although young people did indeed rebel against the privatization of modern life as the product of capitalist bureaucracy and the "consumer society," their movement was as much about attributing moral value to individualism and laying claim to it. To be sure, it would be absurd to reduce the May movement to any single all-inclusive principle, given that it had multiple causes arising from circumstances unique to France in the 1960s. Still, no interpretation of May '68 has placed enough emphasis on the importance within the movement of certain moral values and symbols that strove to make sense of our individual and collective lives. The real historical significance of May '68 only becomes apparent when it is seen as part of the long-term dynamic of democratic individualism.

To speak of individualism in the context of May '68 seems somewhat paradoxical if one takes a traditional, Tocquevilleian view of the term. "Individualism" usually refers to a particular way of life, type of personality, or is seen to emerge when social hierarchies begin to disintegrate, the state becomes increasingly centralized, and the equality of conditions is established. Individualism in this sense can be identified by two interconnected characteristics that reflect the weakening social bond. On the one hand, it means withdrawal into private life: individuals turn in upon themselves, pursuing only their own, private interests. On the other, it indicates an indifference to public life: individualism is equated with "depoliticization," that is, with limited participation in communal activities and little interest in maintaining ties to the collectivity. Given this understanding of the term, it might be difficult to see May '68 as a movement promoting individualism. On the contrary, the May crisis appears marked by an intense though brief mobilization of youth toward collective public action. For several weeks, politics in its broadest sense stood at the center of public debate. It was no longer simply a question of university reforms, the crisis of capitalism, or social revolution; in the endless cascade of mass demonstrations people laid claim to public discourse in both the classrooms and the streets. Everywhere a new value was accorded to collective action as the days of May unfolded, as seen in the political commitment of students who occupied the universities; discussions became highly politicized in the various gatherings and committees, and participation became emotionally charged. May '68 seemed to represent the very opposite of egocentric individualism. It was animated by the ideals of solidarity—with imprisoned demonstrators, the people of Vietnam, and striking workers. Hence the slogan of the time, "We are all German Jews." The red flag reappeared, and the "Internationale" was sung again. The student movement did not remain enclosed within the universities; instead, it conformed to revolutionary tradition by reaching out to the working classes in hopes of detonating their anger. The spirit of May, or at least one of its components, conferred a new revolutionary faith in the proletariat by assigning it the mission of opening a new epoch in history. "This is only the beginning. Let us continue the struggle!" Even if there was no clear objective, even if the movement never had as its goal the total overthrow of power, even if it distinguished itself with its complete indifference to specifically political solutions, May '68 must take its place within a revolutionary tradition that sought to transform society from bottom to top. The intent was to exacerbate conflict and promote social agitation, to oppose the establishment, and to incite a permanent struggle that could mobilize young people and workers against the very structure of the "proprietary police state." The May movement wanted to create a break in history and fix a boundary between "before" and "after." If only for a few weeks, it opened up the revolutionary possibility that "anything is possible."

Nonetheless, May '68 also saw the explosion of explicitly individualist claims and aspirations. Undoubtedly this aspect of the May movement has greater historical significance, even though it is often overlooked by commentators who emphasize its revolutionary inspiration. If it is viewed in a comparatist, anthropological perspective, the individualism embodied by the May movement was but an extreme variation of the individualist ideology that Louis Dumont's work has clarified for us. This modern ideology is something unique in the history of societies. It simultaneously affirms the ideals of equality and of individual autonomy by placing the social atom first. Acknowledged as free and independent, the individual is the yardstick against which all other values are measured, and the collective is subordinate to him. The spirit of May was a perfect example of this new supremacy of the individual. The collective call to arms hardly stifled the principles of individual freedom and personal initiative—indeed, it accompanied a new and complete autonomy of the individual within the structure of collective action. "It is forbidden to forbid," said the often-copied grafitto. The exaggerated individualism of May was embodied in this call for unlimited, absolute freedom, indifferent to the inherent restrictions in collective life. The revolutionary enthusiasms of May glorified the supremacy of the subjective agent over the structures of society and the obligations it imposed.

Moreover, May '68 established a new, antiestablishment and utopian individualism. In the demands for an antibureaucratic, antihierarchical, and antiauthoritarian order we can immediately recognize the hallmarks of the May movement. The students organized themselves against the university hierarchy, the form and content of the curriculum, the repressive State and its political machine. It relentlessly denounced political parties and trade unionists for stifling the independence, creativity, and fighting spirit of the masses. In the same way, the students sanctified spontaneity, in both collective and individual imagination ("Power to the imagination!"), regardless of the activities of certain Trotskyist and Maoist factions that remained faithful to the disciplinarian ethos of orthodox revolutionary parties. In the occupied university buildings, mass meetings, and demonstrations, young people expressed the same hostility to large bureaucratic organizations, made the same demands for self-management on a permanent basis, expressed the same concerns for maintaining a grassroots initiative, and voiced the same claim for everyone to exercise his right to speak out and challenge authority.

What is important to remember here is that although May '68 was a revolution, at no time did anyone prevent the free expression of opinion. The May movement did not demand of anyone the sacrifices and self-criticisms of the old revolutionary tradition. However impassioned the debates and rhetoric of May, and no matter how violent the confrontations on the barricades with the forces of order, the movement was essentially tolerant and displayed more respect for individuals and their subjective opinions than thirst for social antagonism. In short, May '68 was a "soft" revolution, without deaths, traitors, orthodoxies, or purges. Indeed, it manifested the same gradual softening of social mores that Tocqueville first noticed in personal relations characteristic of an individualistic and democratic age. The fact that it permitted an exceptional degree of individual autonomy within its collective action, denounced authoritarianism and bureaucracy, and was conducted internally, in a tolerant and peaceful manner, confirms that May '68 was a highly individualistic movement. The black flag carried through the streets did not announce the return to anarchist action and ideology in its strictest sense. Instead it signified the glorification of a neolibertarian spirit, the self-evident ideal of individual sovereignty asserting itself beyond the sharp rifts in political persuasions.

Another defining trait of May '68 was a certain utopian spirit. There were no concrete plans for a society to be built, and a startling indifference to the political consequences of the crisis and to economic constraints. "Be realistic. Demand the impossible!" Much of the May graffiti expressed an entirely original utopian spirit without equivalent in the great philosophical utopias, where the government of the ideal city is described down to the smallest detail. The May movement had no actual plan for society. It challenged everything in the established order and proposed nothing in its place. It called for revolt without plans for the future and rose up against any form of organization in the name of spontaneity and the direct expression of the masses. May '68 put its utopian spirit into practice against capitalist and bureaucratic domination, but in the name of daydreams, vitality, and personal gratification. Signs of the irruption of this poetic and hedonist utopia could be found on walls everywhere. The revolution was no longer announced in impersonal, austere slogans; its mottos appealed to a new permissiveness that can be seen in the playful use of language itself: "I love you, Revolution!" "There's a beach under the pavement!" "Life is elsewhere!" The claims for free sexual expression and the struggle against the proprietary, police state were one and the same: "Come in the streets," "The more I make Revolution, the more I want to make love; the more I make love, the more I want to make Revolution." There was another dimension unique to May: here and there, the revolutionary slogans abandoned their historical solemnity and acquired an ironic distance. A new pleasure taken in humor and irreverence: "I am a Marxist . . . Groucho faction." The revolution relaxed and exchanged its previous tragic overtones and emphatic style for a playful freedom of expression. The prevailing mood of May was not a petit bourgeois individualism but an individualism that can be called *transpolitical*, in which the political and the existential, the public and the private, the ideological and the poetic, collective struggle and personal gratification, revolution and humor, all become inextricably intertwined. May '68 destabilized boundaries and reference points in politics; by advocating existential, poetic, and libidinal subjectivity, May '68 blurred the line between public and private, just as it scrambled the traditional codes of militancy. "Change life!"

meant to change society and one's own life all at the same time. What made May '68 unprecedented was this hybrid union of revolutionary intent and passionate individualism.

Let us come back to the revolutionary inducements to pleasure and play. The May movement certainly stigmatized the futility and alienation in the kind of life created by the consumer society, as evidenced in Situationist-inspired graffito: "Beat it, things!" Yet in its own way, the spirit of May recaptured what historically has been the central tenet of the consumer society: hedonism. The ideology of modern hedonism—a phenomenon inseparable from the rise of democratic individualistic society—was that consumer society made hedonism the universal goal by entirely redefining lifestyles and personal aspirations. From now on, no value carried greater legitimacy across all social classes than the demand for personal gratification and self-fulfillment. By emphasizing permissiveness, humor, and fun, the spirit of May was largely molded by the very thing whose damaging effects it denounced in politics. That was the paradox of the movement: it depended on the euphoria of the consumer age. Mass hedonism, leisure time, and increased choices made possible by economic abundance all played a role in reinforcing and legitimizing the need for personal happiness and personal autonomy. May '68 gave only the impression of opposing the capitalistic creation of needs. In reality, it was the dynamic of capitalism that multiplied cravings for independence and the emergence of the hedonist utopia, a cultural revolt demanding "everything right now." The sociological, political, and institutional factors responsible for unleashing the events of May have been analyzed many times: an outdated university system, unemployment, a centralizing, all-powerful state buttressed by ten years of Gaullism, and a generational crisis. All played their parts in May '68. Yet these combined factors alone, however important they may be, could not have produced the May movement had they not converged with the dominant values of modernity, the idea of revolution, and the recognition of individual autonomy. One must surely recognize the importance of revolutionary ideology in the highly politicized student groups of the late 1960s. But one must also insist on the significance of the social recognition of individual liberty and its ties to modern individualist ideology, which had recently been reinforced by psychoanalytic notions about the repression of desire (Freud and Reich) and by the hedonism of mass consumer culture. The characteristic features of the spirit of May were undoubtedly the result of this combination of ideological escalation and mass hedonism.

For this reason, one must make a careful distinction between the spirit of May and revolutionary movements guided by an eschatological faith and an all-powerful party. Revolutionary ideology is actually one facet of the modern ideology of individualism. Revolution is only possible when it is based on a certain conception of society as consisting of free and equal individuals and treats them as the ultimate source of power and orientation. Revolutionary ideology sets out to secure the great individualist values of equality and liberty for all. However, the logic of revolutionary organization denies the supremacy of the individual. It demands perfect sacrifice and complete subordination of its members to the party, the proletariat, or the revolution. While revolutionary discourse affirms individualist values in theory, in practice it destroys their underlying principle in the name of collective action, history, and the construction of the future society.

May '68 undid this duality because it was a revolt in the present tense, a "celebration of communication" as much as a rejection of state bureaucracy and authority. The May movement had no single vision of the future, no predetermined plan. An orgy of endless discussion and argument exhibiting a fascination for the spontaneity and initiative of the masses, the movement's only demand was to live without restraints. Unlike traditional revolutionary thinking, which is unmistakably oriented toward the future, here the temporal axis remained the present. In this sense, May '68 represented a compromise between the revolutionary age, with its view to the future, and the individualistic, narcissistic age of the present, focused on the individual's immediate concerns. With its barricades and general strikes it symbolized a revolutionary break with the past. At the same time, it brought forth aspirations typical of the contemporary withdrawal into private life, where subjectivity rules supreme, and where mass discipline and constraints are rejected in the name of hedonism and relaxed moral standards.

May '68 thus effected a compromise that furthermore hastened the dissolution of participation in politics and championed private life. While its influence hardly compares to the effects of mass consumption, the May movement contributed in its own way to the advent of contemporary narcissistic individualism. In France, it paved the way for women's and homosexuals' liberation movements of the early 1970s. But while these movements may have taken the form of collective struggles, they too magnified the desire for individual autonomy by stressing the need for immediate emancipation and the attainment of individual identity. Certainly, radical feminism tried to increase group consciousness and group solidarity, but its harshly militant and Manichean discourse continued this larger transpolitical process by refusing to separate politics from sexuality, or collective from individual liberation. Otherwise, radical feminism also addressed itself to "real life," personal needs, and the practice of self-awareness and self-help. After May, women began increasingly to speak out and to make demands. Their discourse of the personal and private spread to society as a whole, effectively blurred the lines between the sexes, and bolstered the supremacy of subjective individuality. In one stroke this transpolitical movement managed to confuse previously well-defined roles and identities, making personal subjectivity a legitimate political issue.

May '68 furthermore gave rise to a peculiar process of political disaffection through its "revolutionary" legitimation of cultural deviance and alternate lifestyles. The revolution yielded to a euphoria of microscopic, minority subversions: communes, squats, living on the fringes of society, psychedelic drugs, and unusual sexual practices. May '68 had made people so wary of the politics of politicians and parties, of programs and ideologies, that militancy came to seem a kind of alienation, a means of avoiding intimacy. By miniaturizing the revolution this movement emptied it of content, rendering it nothing more than a fad subject to the demands of pure individuality. As the face of individualism, the transpolitical moment contributed to the decline of political passions as well as the glorification of the individual, all in the name of revolution. Just as Tocqueville once observed that the French Revolution only extended the centralization of the Ancien Régime, in a different way one might argue that the spirit of '68 exacerbated the ominous tendency toward the privatization of postwar French life.

Alain Touraine, a sociologist sympathetic to the revolution, explored the meaning of its "utopian communism" in the midst of the events of May. For Touraine, the essence of May '68 was the way it revealed both the new forces challenging authority and the new sources of conflict growing out of postindustrial society: it was the harbinger of future class struggles rooted in the demands of new social strata for full citizenship. In rejecting techno-bureaucratic domination, these new strata sought to control the basic direction of society, Touraine believed. In a confused fashion May '68 therefore represented the future claims of civil society against prevailing power, and the birth of new social movements requiring more democracy and less technocratic intervention. As Touraine remarked: "The May movement has no tomorrow; it has a future."[1]

Twenty-five years later, after the exhaustion of these political opposition movements, we can see that May '68 had no future. It was not the avant-garde of social conflicts yet to come but a final mass irruption, haunted by an obsolete revolutionary imagination inherited from the past. In no way did May announce the restructuring of the society; indeed, it signaled the very opposite. It was a psychodramatic and parodic end to the revolutionary age. It augured the victory of individualism and the irreversible privatization of the social sphere. For revolutionary consciousness, May '68 was the last stand. Taking the long view, we can see that

May '68 was less an antitechnocratic movement struggling for collective self-determination than a wild moment in our relentless descent into the world of modern individualism and personal autonomy.

—Translated by Lisa Maguire

Note

1. Alain Touraine, *The May Movement: Revolt and Reform*, trans. Leonard F. X. Mayhew (New York, 1971).

CHAPTER 17

The End of Alienation?

ANNE GODIGNON AND JEAN-LOUIS THIRIET

WHY DISCUSS a notion whose time so clearly seems to have passed? After all, the concept of "alienation" no longer enjoys much favor among intellectuals, and philosophy has already pronounced it dead. As we all know, the demise of this idea owes a great deal to the decline of Marxism and the triumph of liberal principles; Marxism appears to have carried the concept of alienation to its grave. But while Marxism and alienation are historically linked, one must be careful to distinguish between them. In fact, this idea is now most likely to appear outside any explicit reference to Marxist theory. Although contemporary philosophers and sociologists are apt to ignore it, common opinion still employs the term when trying to understand the captivating power of consumption and fashion. Even those intellectuals who rightly see modernity as the advent of individual liberty still resort to the idea of alienation in order to explain less transparent aspects of social reality. Although discredited, the concept of alienation refuses to disappear.

The reason for this is clear enough. Modern man is commonly portrayed as stupefied by advertising, bedazzled by false needs, stirred by desires dictated by the fashion world, the dupe of an illusory happiness offered by the media. He is, in sum, the pitiful product of a consumer society. However threadbare this image may seem, something in it rings true. The simple fact that the concept of alienation is currently out of fashion is therefore hardly a reason to spare it critical evaluation. Indeed, to the degree that alienation presents itself as a viable idea, it challenges our own view of modernity. This view portrays the modern era as one of triumphant individualism marked by the achievement of freedom, freedom understood here as the individual's ever-growing independence from external objects and discourses. In short, modern freedom means the end of alienation. The following critique of the theory of alienation aims to support this view of modernity by examining one of its especially striking features, which has been accorded great importance in the theory of alienation: mass consumption.

In both its practices and its objects, mass consumption must be understood as the fundamental outcome of individual freedom—that is, as arising from *within*, and not outside, the consuming subject. Gilles Lipovetsky has already shown how consumption has become increasingly personalized, constantly calling upon individuals' capacity to choose and consequently putting their freedom into action.[1] Yet Lipovetsky's correlation between consumption and choice has hampered further reflection on the more important link between consumption and freedom. The issue of choice is, in our view, less important than that of the radical independence that now defines modern individuals. If our hypothesis is correct, consumption must be seen as an outcome of individual emancipation, and an outcome of far greater consequence than the capacity to choose arising from that emancipation. Consuming may set us free, but freedom leads us to consume. The theory of alienation can only be disproved by approaching the problem in this way, since choice does not exclude the possibility of alienation.

It has often been remarked that modern pleasure is fleeting, continually requiring new objects for its always deferred satisfaction. Impermanence of this sort can only be seen as the expression of the subject's freedom, for becoming attached to an object would mean attributing a definitive value to it, thereby limiting and denying this freedom. The act of consuming therefore negates and destroys the object, which merely furnishes the opportunity for his self-affirmation. In other words, consumption serves as a pretext for the self and is never directed toward the object itself. This is why the object is always changing. The repeated pursuit of the same object, any "loyalty" or attachment to it, would imply a degree of recognition dangerous to the subject's freedom. If he lingers, he is lost. Although he will continue to experience sudden infatuations, he will no longer experience true passion. His wanton consumption goes hand in hand with a profound indifference to the objects consumed. No object can claim superiority over others, since to form a hierarchy among them would accord value to the external world. And, as we have seen, such valuing threatens individual freedom. All things must be equal; the insatiable consumer can desire everything, precisely because he desires nothing in particular. Hence this hyperactive consumption, whose sole purpose is to reaffirm his being and freedom. "I consume, therefore I am": this existential affirmation is modern man's first principle.

It is thus incorrect to view consumption as the logical outcome of production, that is, as behavior imposed by the outside world. Consumption is essential for the individual to establish his individuality and independence. By reducing the world to a stock of ready material for fulfilling every desire, consumption assures the definitive triumph of an all-powerful and all-consuming subjectivity over the nature of the object. In this sense, consumption-as-praxis fulfills the nihilism of modernity, which rejects values, meaning, and tradition.

Moreover, the freedom expressed in consumption also reveals something distinctive about consumer products. Although the object is itself unimportant, it does not necessarily follow that it can be just anything. Given that the ego seeks only itself through consumption, the object must be irresistible, offering immediate pleasure and demanding no effort—which is in fact what occurs. The subject turns away from anything that is not immediately attractive or that might require reflection, education, or culture. Freedom demands nothing more than primal, unrefined animal sensation. Taste, the product of initiation or education, is a thing of the past because it is too restrictive of our freedom.

Cooking provides a good example. We now prefer weak flavors to strong, sweet to salty, and liquid to solid—in short, we like foods that do not assault the senses. Instead of seeking out acute sensations, we heighten our dining enjoyment by increasing the portions. The pleasure of eating has become the pleasure of eating a lot; the object's quality, its mark of distinction, has disappeared, to be replaced with its quantity, which is easier to master. Americans have taken consumerism to its logical conclusion in this realm, and the French are following in their footsteps. It is easy to understand how this way of eating has quickly spread throughout the world. We are here dealing with a substance that is universal from the start because it is based on pure sensation, and thus pure individuality. But our sensations are raw and uneducated; it does not mean that we are regressing back to nature. On the contrary, nature is an origin and as such competes with another origin, which is the self. As a result, we turn away from nature whenever possible today: we denature our food and make it artificial. Synthetic foods have replaced natural ones; we now drink Coke instead of wine. Although modern consumption is supposed to serve hedonism, it actually dulls the senses. Anything resisting the senses is too solidly real and requires effort on the part of the subject, and this creates disharmony. In the end, the empire of the senses renders the world less real. The modern individual prefers to float outside that world, renouncing ecstasy.[2]

Now we see how individualism creates the consumer, and how consumption then generates production. Since the individual seeks nothing beyond himself, worldly aims disappear, leaving nothing behind but infinite desire. The individual constantly reaffirms his own existence through the infinite desire sustained by consumption. Similarly, advertising successfully manipulates the consumer by conforming to his individual desires. Advertising offers the consumer not just any image, but an image that expresses his individuality; it can create the individual's desire for a product provided that it satisfies his expectations. Seduction, the privileged realm of advertising, presupposes the complicity of the one seduced.

Consumption and consumer products are thus indeed products of freedom. But if consumption contributes to individual freedom, how can it nonetheless constitute a mass phenomenon? Partisans of the theory of alienation here seem to have a compelling argument. Claiming that we are not free, they link the inherent uniformity of mass consumption to the economic demand for maximum profits and return on investment. Yet, paradoxical as it may seem, individual freedom is actually the source of this uniformity. For although individuals are not forced to conform, they will do so as long as they are left to form their identities by themselves. Today individual identities are formed independently of external culture and history. Becoming fully human now demands only that the individual ward off all outside influences. In this way, the external world is drained of its meaning, and reality loses its significance. As the world undergoes what has been called "the death of meaning," freedom for the subject has arrived, since nothing external defines him any more. He is reduced to a timeless, insubstantial, and empty subjectivity. Only two possibilities remain: activity (primarily work) or stagnation (the modern form of hedonism). Any residual "self" resembles any other, and like the world on which it is modeled, this self is empty, insignificant, uncultivated, and without history. Colorless and unmysterious, it is as blank as a California beach. Since they are identical, free individuals form a mass, and since they want the same things and make the same choices, they consume as a mass. The coexistence of individual freedom and mass consumption is no paradox.[3]

Partisans of the theory of alienation will nonetheless argue that the consumer's desires are determined by values imposed on him without his knowledge. But in fact he experiences nothing of the kind. It is not a question of "values" but of specific acts of valorization that confer significance and appeal to individual objects. While an alienated individual is motivated by the intrinsic qualities of the desired object, modern man is motivated only by his desire. He is made aware of his subjectivity in action, saying: "It is good because I want it." Thus the modern ego is not only in itself, but for itself; it thus escapes the trap of alienated consciousness. By submitting to its own shifting, spontaneous, and capricious whims, desire rejects mediating forces. The pleasant alone is master.[4] Some semblance of normative discourse persists, but it does not deal in objective qualities. Instead it bandies subjective feelings about, which become casual, vague, diffuse, and consequently limited in scope. In any case, the primacy of private desire guarantees a certain respectful indifference toward tastes that are not one's own.

By positing itself solely through desires, modern consciousness no longer satisfies the fundamental requirement for alienation, which is reference to the real. Modern consciousness shuts out structured external reality, and along with it any concern for truth. It has no set purpose for objects, only the simple desire for them. Therefore, the real has been reduced to whatever value the individual has accorded it and now merely comprises another of his desires. Modern consciousness abandons any objective representation of the world; drained of meaning, that world simply disappears. Because we do not confront the world in its reality, we can have neither true nor false consciousness of it. In this era of triumphant consumerism, we are no longer dealing with a restrictive, objective world but an impermanent, splintered, factual exteriority. An alienated consciousness would be unequipped for modernity because it would still be trying to interpret the real world. The dedicated modern consumer does not interpret reality but fashions it after his own desires.

Therefore the consumer is not alienated. If by some accident he happens to become alienated, he would no longer be a consumer. Consumption must relieve itself of any hindrance in order to be total, and alienation is just such a hindrance. Alienation directs choices along certain channels, narrowing the field of possible objects of desire, and therefore desire itself. Our utterly frantic, unbounded consumption cannot exist unless it is free, animal, and unalienated. Not only does the theory of alienation fail to explain modern consumption, it conceals its very essence.

Individualism and freedom, not alienation, are the keys to understanding modernity. However we cannot help but feel unsatisfied with this conclusion. Certain uncomfortable facts remain. However free the modern individual may be, we still have the impression that he is generally passive and conformist. Uniform masses of wholly interchangeable individuals, given to idolizing the same media heroes, zombies that are buffetted by the whims of fashion—such images hardly resemble freedom and seem to support the theory of alienation. How is it possible that the individual is truly free when this freedom so closely resembles alienation?

The modern individual has indeed been liberated from religious, cultural, economic, social, and political determinations. Yet his consciousness accepts this freedom the way it accepts anything else, without questioning it or understanding it. Consequently, this attitude is not radically different from that of an alienated consciousness—the same lack of critical reflection, the same passive acceptance. Such an unknowing, unthinking freedom is ultimately reduced to the status of an object, which his consciousness relates to as something external to himself. That is why the free individual appears to be alienated: he has no authentic experience of freedom, or any real understanding of either his world or himself. The free individual could not be said to be alienated, since modernity has nothing to do with alienation. Nonetheless, freedom today is not pure freedom. Pure freedom excludes all attachment and renounces all substance, even the emptiest, most insignificant thing of all, the self.

—Translated by Lisa Maguire

Notes

1. Gilles Lipovetsky, *L'ère du vide: Essais sur l'individualisme contemporain* (Paris, 1983).

2. One can argue that there are acute sensations specific to modernity, which some would call barbarous: we have witnessed an escalation in violent images, for example. But strong images do not necessarily elicit strong sensations. Someone who enjoys such images may not perceive them in all their intensity. Force-fed images and sounds, the modern individual has become desensitized, and because he has a higher threshold needs to intensify his sensations. It should also be noted that the violent object does not present itself directly to the viewer but requires the artifice of the image, a screen. It is unlikely that a modern individual would enjoy crude entertainments such as live circuses. Modern violence is certainly barbarous, but it reflects more the absence of culture than the violent expression of our own instincts.

3. We reject completely Gilles Lipovetsky's argument that mass consumption is entirely a thing of the past. Certainly, we have "exchanged restrictive conformity for free choice, an homogeneity for plurality" (Lipovetsky, 21). But for all that, it does not follow that "consumption is a vector for differentiating between human beings," or that "it accentuates their uniqueness" (121). Alongside the increase of world wealth is a growing poverty of the individual, to the point where it is possible to speak of a "process of depersonalization." However great the range of choice in products might become, they remain meaningless if they are incapable of bringing about real differences in individuals. More striking than the diversity of available goods is the increasing similarity of tastes. Furthermore, the value of this alleged range of consumer choice is questionable, since more often than not it simply consists of endless variations on the same popular item.

4. The evolution in advertising from the full-fledged campaign to the promotional "spot" is more easily understood in light of this fact. While the former tries to convince, the latter simply aims to please—and to inspire a pleasant feeling in the consumer either through humor or beautiful imagery. In the best examples of the genre, any link to the product seems purely accidental. Contrary to the widely held belief inspired by theories of alienation, advertising does not increasingly penetrate the mind of the buyer. Advertising has not improved its techniques but has simply adapted to the evolution occurring in human consciousness, that is, its progressive dis-alienation, both in and through consumption.

CHAPTER **18**

The Rebirth of Voluntary Servitude

ANNE GODIGNON AND JEAN-LOUIS THIRIET

THE MODERN ERA has accorded tremendous value to work. As the vehicle for self-fulfillment and personal growth, work has quickly become the focus of individual freedom, as its impure origins in physical subjugation and subsistence needs have been forgotten. At one time it was believed that humanity would finally be released from its hard labor through mastery of the physical world. These enthusiastic visions belong to another age. Modern society now accords a wholly positive value to work, transforming it from a means to an end in itself.

The reasons for this phenomenon, as well as the modern attitude favoring compulsive activity in general, deserve reflection.

One obvious and definite fact about modern society is that all values now begin and end with the individual. But looking beyond this sociological fact, we find an underlying ideal of freedom, which goes beyond the traditional liberal notion of independence. This ideal cannot be met simply by living according to our own whims within social constraints; it manifests itself more clearly in our desire for total emancipation, allowing the individual to alone define himself.

Yet ideally, in order to be a self and nothing but a self, the individual must evade all material responsibilities; to assert his identity, he must discard externally imposed ones. In other words, he must define himself as devoid of definition. For the self to be free it must be empty. But it cannot reduce itself to nothing at all, to an absolute void. Instead, because the self no longer derives meaning from external reality, it now figures as the source and first principle of that reality. Since it remains entirely undefined, the self becomes nothing but the act of its own definition. This definition immediately dissolves into a new one, and so on, into infinity. As a free entity, the self has therefore become activity and nothing but activity.

Self-affirmation can therefore only be achieved through pure action. It must take the form of an endlessly self-renewing project, in which we set ourselves goals that are later deemed unnecessary and discarded. All that truly matters is the exercise of power for its own sake. Goals have no fixed, attainable ends because these would destroy the self's reified powers and, with that, its freedom. Instead, one goal must give rise to further goals, and so on, continuing indefinitely until death. The free individual has neither taken on nor kept any baggage. Nothing more than his force of will, he only exists through the continual deployment of his own capacity for nonstop work, which becomes the ultimate measure of his being. Only through work can he valorize his own "potential," which he vainly wishes were inexhaustible. Freedom demands that the human will remain in perpetual motion so that it may continually reassert its presence; rest or reflection are prohibited; independence becomes something that one cannot, strictly speaking, "enjoy." Independence only really exists within the drive to complete this unending project, and to prevent this fluctuating will from taking solid form in any completed task. Independence must therefore constantly reactualize itself in activity and overachievement. Freedom can only exist in ceaseless self-surpassing—that is the final upshot of individualism.

We can now understand why work has become the individual's most important, all-consuming activity. Its exactions constantly feed the willful appetites that haunt the modern world. If freedom must remain permanently unrealized, work is the perfect place to exercise it. Whereas the unceasing demands of work once made it so abhorrent, today work creates the necessary space for the infinite expansion of the human will. The western myth of human progress and its project of mastering the living world are also signs of the infinite task we have set for ourselves. Our unremitting labor is performed with zeal precisely because it never ends. We are witnessing a strange reversal of perspective, in which servitude—be it voluntary or forced—becomes freedom in action, freedom realized. Certainly, work's ultimate ends—to produce, to consume, to live—remain, but they have long since been relegated to the background. Although it continues to serve needs, work in fact exists independently of them today. For the individual, work has become an end in itself. The idea of self-sufficiency reaches its logical conclusion in work, in which the individual's relationship to the world is exchanged for the exclusive relationship of the self to itself.

Simply working is not enough, though. One must always work harder and better, since the power to act cannot be limited. We accord the greatest value to those endeavors which offer the individual endless opportunities to surpass his own goals and make ever-increasing psychological investments in himself. The meaning now attached to labor has made "nonwork" activity seem inconsequential. In this way, work has lost its traditional defining characteristics. Try as bureaucrats might to fulfill their duties, they will never be rid of a lazy public image, since bureaucratic tasks remain fixed and circumscribed. Were factory workers' working conditions not so pitiful, we might conclude that they, too, do not really "work."[1] The ideal type of worker today is the entrepreneur or, better yet, the yuppie. His work is done privately, independently, and at a breakneck pace. It is indissociable from the drive to succeed; as in games, "winning" at work is now the real goal. Because labor has dropped its connotations of drudgery, servitude, and subsistence, it can—paradoxically—transform itself into a game. Yet we can never "win" this game; we can only reach certain temporary stopping points. Moreover, anyone who limits himself to past achievements recognizes in them his failure to attain more. Power is ephemeral, disappearing in the gap separating the personal project from its completion. But since power has an entirely subjective worth, the effort exerted to achieve a goal becomes far more important than the goal itself. The completed task, presumably the end result of this existential project, is simply eclipsed by the next goal. Thus, our constant drive to excel is gratified in the requirements of microprojects and momentary challenges. Modern success is an entirely private affair, with no need for social recognition. The era of the established, respectable bourgeois is over; a good "position" and its accompanying prosperity now have little meaning. The image of the happy, prosperous bourgeois has now given way to the evanescent silhouette of an overly preoccupied, excessively cautious, business-minded yuppie unwilling to sit still long enough to pose for a snapshot.

We live in an age of goal inflation. The only way to evaluate the superiority of one goal over another is therefore to reduce them both to numerical categories—in other words, to something quantifiable. Work goals must be not only varied but also placed on a continuum of personal growth and degree of performance. Overachievement requires that we homogenize our objectives in this way, since the successive attainment of a variety of unrelated goals would make us doubt our belief in progress. The goal of continual growth, the touchstone of individual overachievement and personal progress, eventually subsumes any truly productive ends. Work, now cleansed of its original, impure material goals, is put in service of an abstract quantifiable form of progress and thereby ennobled.

The primacy of power, and through power, subjectivity, is translated into the glorification of money. On the one hand, wealth connects us to the world and thereby limits us; on the other, it opens an infinite field of possibilities. Individual freedom finds a more satisfying expression in wealth than it had in objects. As the most minimal form of materiality, money is nothing more than the material form of subjectivity in action. The individual's pursuit of money through work does not invalidate the idea that work is an end in itself, since the freedom to work and the goal of accumulating capital are one and the same.

To sum up, work in its modern form can no longer be defined only in terms of production and exchange. It must also be understood as a form of, but also formed by, modern consciousness; only work can meet modern man's existential needs. The fundamental changes that have affected work have largely bypassed the kind of upheavals that ushered in postindustrial society. Instead, they now occur in the consciousness of its actors.

But if work is the most immediate and tangible manifestation of the power of the individual, it is not the only one. We engage in activities outside of work. Yet what is most striking about modern man is how his other activities ultimately acquire all the characteristics of work. Everything becomes a matter of effort, everything becomes a duty to oneself. In other words, everything turns into work. As work loses its forbidding, menial connotations and is experienced as power, leisure time similarly loses its original function of pleasant relaxation. Instead, leisure becomes the opportunity to address oneself to real tasks, to submit once again to the draconian demands of overachievement. Here as elsewhere, we assign ourselves goals and then work toward them, only to fix more challenging ones once they have been attained. And so on, into infinity.

Sports provide a good example. Sports are now only considered from the standpoint of performance. We always try to best ourselves, even to suffer; our arid, solitary, and entirely personal discipline excludes any reference to others, that is, the competition. The inherent pleasure of the activity has been relegated to the background; the only thing that counts now is pleasure derived from effort, breaking obstacles, and self-mastery. At this point, pleasure and pain converge, as do work and leisure. Both become forms of pure action without specific goals and intentions. From morning to night, modern man knows only one mode of existence, work; he is incapable of enjoying his leisure. Calling a halt to this constant activity would be too distressing—he would grow bored and empty, feeling weak and useless. If modern consciousness ever pauses to rest, it only finds a void that serves to fuel its own anxieties. We have no choice except activity or void, work or anxiety.

It is true that there is room for a different type of recreation. At first glance, television, amusement parks, and shopping malls all appear to provide the relaxation absent in this "active leisure." Yet these passive kinds of leisure, by their very nature, can provide only a release. They do not exist for the sake of pleasure but instead guarantee a certain peace of mind. Complacent strolls along the prescribed routes of amusement parks and the stupefaction of a trip to a shopping mall only prolong our television-induced hypnosis. This type of leisure achieves its purpose each time an inconsistent and pliable consciousness, having transported itself to the world of make-believe, regresses to a tender and entirely artificial childhood.

Although this narcotic state is the opposite of work, it nevertheless serves the purposes of both labor and activity in general. Such "passive leisure" is merely part of a larger marshaling of our productive forces. In order to satisfy its own imperatives for high performance and overachievement, the human machine cannot dissipate its energies in a steady, regular rhythm of work. It must concentrate its efforts by alternating between total rest and intense activity. Only this practice of "all or nothing" can guarantee maximum release of individual "potential." Thus, relaxation necessarily takes the form of absolute inactivity. Any amount of slackening off is only temporary, a latency period. We conserve our energies in order to spend them more freely. Far from being worthwhile in itself, passive leisure is nothing more than a momentary lull in activity so that work can then reclaim us. In the last analysis, everything in the daily life of modern man serves one master. Relaxation always serves the purposes of further activity.

One might argue that sleep provides a simpler and more natural means to obtain total rest. But since sleep sacrifices vigilance and eclipses consciousness, it only detracts from the sleeper, who has momentarily escaped the demand for constant activity. Modern man wants to remain ready to work, even at the deepest levels of relaxation. To sleep more than necessary is bad form, a mistake, an anomaly. The modern era has transformed not only our experience of sleep but also the value it once held for us. If sleep was previously sought as a refuge and a pleasure, we have now reduced it to its purely biological function. Modern man, if he does indeed sleep, does not like to do so. Moreover, he sleeps badly, because he is haunted by this program of total self-control. "Passive leisure" thus becomes indispensable because it assures the peace of mind that sleep cannot guarantee. After all, sleep has dangers of its own—the night and its ghosts open an abyss that casts the helpless sleeper adrift and allows him to slip out of control. If we must dream, we prefer sterilized and stereotypical dreams manufactured by leisure professionals.

Modern society is not hedonistic. Neither working or consuming nor inactivity gives us pleasure. We were mistaken to think that the emancipation of the individual would lead to the liberation of all desires and passions, to hedonistic self-fulfillment. Far from responding to the call of pleasure, modern man is entirely focused on the realization of his power to act, which is the sole indication that he is free. His activities and their accompanying tasks prevail over all else. Modern man experiences no inner conflict, since he has nothing inside to overcome. This absolute freedom, having created an utterly abstract individual who can only exist as pure will and pure drive to overachieve, has rendered useless anything sensual or corporeal. Hedonism as traditionally understood is an outmoded anthropological category and thus does not adequately describe modern individualism. In fact, the rise of individualism has entirely transformed humankind, something that many of us still have not realized and perhaps will not realize for a long time to come.

Only through the undivided rule of pure action can modern man express his own power, achieve independence, and perfect his individualism. He is no longer curious about the outside world or capable of aesthetic enjoyment. He has no time to wander freely, no time to waste in wonderment, reflection, or diversion. The self has dispensed with the outside world, and its tireless activity has now forbidden any intrusions. The imperatives of power and success, of hyperprofessionalism and the total mobilization of personal energies to a single project, sound the death knell not only of dilettantism but also art. Only the most utilitarian ways of thinking can triumph within such narrow forms of activity.

Freedom has now shown its true face: it robs us of art, leisure, and pleasure. Freedom today takes the form of voluntary servitude to an absent master. Modern man is his own master, yet he has all the characteristics of the slave. Although he is hyperactive, excessively vigilant, and extremely driven, it is entirely by choice. He works frantically because he is free; not because he is held in bondage. This is not a sign of madness; it is the logical outcome of modern freedom.

—Translated by Lisa Maguire

Note

1. The various interpretations of the meaning of work that successively held sway were, in each case, inseparable from the dominant image of production at the time. In the agricultural era, work was understood as insurmountable servitude, while the industrial revolution gave work its Promethean dimension. But all such interpretations are based upon the importance accorded one activity as paradigmatic of the age (as in Hegel's apologia for the state bureaucrat). This is also what occurs today, when "real" work is considered the lot of the happy few. Work has become an aristocratic privilege!

Notes on the Authors

JEAN-MARC FERRY (b. 1946) is instructor in philosophy at the Free University of Brussels.

LUC FERRY (b. 1951) is professor of philosophy at the University of Caen. He founded the Collège de Philosophie in 1974 with Alain Renaut.

MARCEL GAUCHET (b. 1946) teaches at the École des Hautes Études en Sciences Sociales in Paris, is editor of the journal *Le Débat*, and coeditor of *La Pensée Politique*.

ANNE GODIGNON (b. 1958) teaches philosophy in Paris.

BLANDINE KRIEGEL (b. 1943) teaches philosophy at the University of Lyons and edits the journal *Philosophie Politique*.

GILLES LIPOVETSKY (b. 1944) teaches philosophy in Grenoble.

PIERRE MANENT (b. 1949) teaches at the École des Hautes Études en Sciences Sociales in Paris and is coeditor of *La Pensée Politique*.

BERNARD MANIN (b. 1951), formerly of the Institut d'Études Politique in Paris, is currently professor of political science at the University of Chicago.

PHILIPPE RAYNAUD (b. 1952) teaches political science at the University of Lille.

ALAIN RENAUT (b. 1948) is professor of philosophy at the University of Paris (Sorbonne). He founded the Collège de Philosophie in 1974 with Luc Ferry.

STÉPHANE RIALS (b. 1951) teaches law at the University of Paris (II).

JEAN-LOUIS THIRIET (b. 1949) teaches philosophy in Paris.

TZVETAN TODOROV (b. 1939) is currently associated with the Centre National de la Recherche Scientifique.

Selected Bibliography

Note: This short bibliography lists some of the main books and essays written by the authors featured in this anthology, as well as other authors whose work has been particularly important to them. Whenever possible I have listed English translations rather than the French originals. Following this list is another of general reference works in post-war French intellectual history which some readers may find useful as background reading.

PRIMARY WORKS

Aron, Raymond. *The Committed Observer*. Chicago, 1983.
———. *In Defense of Political Reason*. Edited by Daniel J. Mahoney. Lanham, Md., 1994.
———. *Introduction to the Philosophy of History*. Boston, 1961.
———. *Main Currents in Sociological Thought*. 2 vols. New York, 1965–67.
———. *Marxism and the Existentialists*. New York, 1969.
———. *Memoirs*. New York, 1990.
———. *The Opium of the Intellectuals*. New York, 1957.
Bergounioux, Alain, and Bernard Manin. *Le régime social-démocrate*. Paris, 1989.
———. *La social-démocratie ou le compromis*. Paris, 1979.
Bouveresse, Jacques. *Le philosophe chez les autophages*. Paris, 1984.
———. *Philosophie, mythologie et pseudo-science*. Paris, 1991. [Translation forthcoming, Princeton, N.J.]
———. *Wittgenstein: La rime et la raison*. Paris, 1973.
Bruckner, Pascal. *La mélancolie démocratique*. Paris, 1990.
———. *The Tears of the White Man*. New York, 1986.
Castoriadis, Cornelius. *Cornelius Castoriadis, Political and Social Writings*. 2 vols. Minneapolis, 1988.
———. *Le contenu du socialisme*, 1979.
———. *Crossroads in the Labyrinth*. Cambridge, Mass., 1984.
———. *L'expérience du mouvement ouvrier*. 2 vols. Paris, 1974.
———. *The Imaginary Institution of Society*. Cambridge, 1987.
———. *Philosophy, Politics, Autonomy*. New York, 1992.
———. *La société bureaucratique*. 2 vols. Paris, 1973.
Clastres, Pierre. *Society against the State*. New York, 1977.
Descombes, Vincent. *The Barometer of Modern Reason*. New York, 1993.
———. *L'inconscient malgré lui*. Paris, 1977.
———. *Modern French Philosophy*. Cambridge, 1980.
———. *Objects of All Sorts*. Oxford, 1986.

Dumont, Louis. *Essays on Individualism*. Chicago, 1986.
———. *From Mandeville to Marx: The Genesis and Triumph of Economic Ideology*. Chicago, 1977.
———. *Homo aequalis 2: L'idéologie allemande*. Paris, 1991.
———. *Homo hierarchicus*. 2d ed. Chicago, 1980.
Dupuy, Jean-Pierre. *Ordres et désordres*. Paris, 1982.
———. *Le sacrifice et l'envie*. Paris, 1992.
Engel, Pascal. *The Norm of Truth*. Toronto, 1991.
Ferry, Jean-Marc. *Habermas: L'éthique de la communication*. Paris, 1987.
———. *Les puissances de l'expérience: Essai sur l'identité contemporaine*. 2 vols. Paris, 1991.
Ferry, Luc. *Homo aestheticus*. Chicago, 1990.
———. *Le nouvel ordre écologique*. Paris, 1992.
———. *Rights*. Chicago, 1990.
———. *The System of Philosophies of History*. Chicago, 1992.
Ferry, Luc, and Alain Renaut. *68–86: Itinéraires de l'individu*. Paris, 1987.
———. *French Philosophy of the Sixties: An Essay on Antihumanism*. Amherst, Mass., 1990. [A weak translation of *La pensée 68* (Paris, 1985).]
———. *From the Rights of Man to the Republican Idea*. Chicago, 1992.
———. *Heidegger and Modernity*. Chicago, 1990.
———. "The Philosophies of '68," *Partisan Review* (1989:3).
———. *Système et critique: Essais sur la critique de la raison dans la philosophie contemporaine*. Brussels, 1985.
Ferry, Luc, and Alain Renaut, eds. *Pourquoi nous ne sommes pas nietzschéens*. Paris, 1991.
Finkielkraut, Alain. *The Undoing of Thought*. London, 1988.
Furet, François. *La gauche et la Révolution française au milieu du XIXe siècle*. Paris, 1986.
———. *In the Workshop of History*. Chicago, 1984.
———. *Interpreting the French Revolution*. Cambridge, 1981.
———. *Marx and the French Revolution*. Chicago, 1988.
———. Préface. In Alexis de Tocqueville, *Démocratie en Amérique*. 2 vols. Paris, 1981.
———. *Revolutionary France, 1770–1880*. Oxford, 1992.
Furet, François, Jacques Julliard, and Pierre Rosanvallon. *La république du centre*. Paris, 1988.
Furet, François, and Mona Ozouf, eds. *A Critical Dictionary of the French Revolution*. Cambridge, Mass., 1989.
———. *Le siècle de l'avènement républicain*. Paris, 1993.
Furet, François, and Denis Richet. *The French Revolution*. New York, 1970.
Gauchet, Marcel. *Le désenchantement du monde*. Paris, 1985.
———. "Les Droits de l'homme ne sont pas une politique." *Le Débat* (July–August 1980).
———. "L'expérience totalitaire et la pensée de la politique." *Esprit* (July–August 1976).
———. *L'inconscient cérébral*. Paris, 1992.
———. Préface. In Benjamin Constant, *De la liberté chez les modernes*. Paris, 1980.

———. *La révolution des droits de l'homme*. Paris, 1989.
Gauchet, Marcel, and Gladys Swain. *La pratique de l'esprit humain*. Paris, 1980. [Translation forthcoming, Princeton, N.J.]
Glucksmann, André. *The Master Thinkers*. New York, 1977.
Kriegel, Blandine. *Les chemins de l'état*. Paris, 1986.
———. *Les droits de l'homme et le droit naturel*. Paris, 1986.
———. *L'état et la démocratie*. Paris, 1986.
———. *L'état et les esclaves*. Paris, 1979. [Translation forthcoming, Princeton, N.J.]
———. *Les historiens et la monarchie*. 4 vols. Paris, 1988.
Lefort, Claude. *Democracy and Political Theory*. Cambridge, 1988.
———. *Eléments d'une critique de la bureaucratie*. Paris, 1979.
———. *Les formes de l'histoire*. Paris, 1978.
———. *L'invention démocratique*. Paris, 1981.
———. *The Political Forms of Modern Society*. Cambridge, Mass., 1986.
———. *Le travail de l'oeuvre*. Paris, 1972.
Legros, Robert. *L'idée de l'humanité*. Paris, 1990.
Lévy, Bernard-Henri. *Barbarism with a Human Face*. New York, 1977.
Lipovetsky, Gilles. *Le crépuscule du devoir*. Paris, 1992.
———. *The Empire of Fashion: Dressing Modern Democracy*. Princeton, N.J., 1994.
———. *L'ère du vide: Essais sur l'individualisme contemporain*. Paris, 1983.
Manent, Pierre. *An Intellectual History of Liberalism*. Princeton, N.J., 1994.
———. *La cité de l'homme*. Paris, 1994.
———. *Naissances de la politique moderne*. Paris, 1977.
———. *Tocqueville et la nature de la démocratie*. 2d ed. Paris, 1993.
Manent, Pierre, ed. *Les libéraux*. Paris, 1986.
Mongin, Olivier. *La peur du vide*. Paris, 1991.
Morin, Edgar, Claude Lefort, and Cornelius Castoriadis. *Mai 1968*. 2d ed. Brussels, 1988.
Nora, Pierre, ed. *Les lieux de mémoire*. 8 vols. Paris, 1984–93.
Philonenko, Alexis. *La liberté dans la philosophie de Fichte*. Paris, 1966.
———. *L'oeuvre de Fichte*. Paris, 1984.
———. *L'oeuvre de Kant*. 2 vols. Paris, 1969–72.
———. *Théorie et praxis dans la pensée morale et politique de Kant et de Fichte en 1793*. Paris, 1968.
La Philosophie qui vient. Parcours, bilans, projets. Special issue of *Le Débat* (November–December 1992).
Raynaud, Philippe. "Feminism and the *Ancien Régime*." *Partisan Review* 4 (1991).
———. *La fin de l'École républicaine*. Paris, 1990.
———. *Max Weber et les dilemmes de la raison moderne*. Paris, 1987.
———. Préface. In Benjamin Constant, *De la force du gouvernement actuel de la France*. Paris, 1988.
———. Préface. In Edmund Burke, *Réflexions sur la révolution de France*. Paris, 1989.
Renaut, Alain. *L'ère de l'individu*. Paris, 1989. [Translation forthcoming, Princeton, N.J.]
———. *Sartre, le dernier philosophe*. Paris, 1993.

Renaut, Alain. *Le système du droit: Philosophie et droit dans la penseé de Fichte.* Paris, 1986.
Renaut, Alain, and Lukas Sosoe. *Philosophie du droit.* Paris, 1991.
Rials, Stéphane. *La Déclaration des droits de l'homme et du citoyen.* Paris, 1988.
Rosanvallon, Pierre. *Le capitalisme utopique.* Paris, 1979.
———. *L'état en France.* Paris, 1990.
———. *Le moment Guizot.* Paris, 1985.
———. *Le sacre du citoyen.* Paris, 1992.
Todorov, Tzvetan. *Les morales de l'histoire.* Paris, 1991.
———. *On Human Diversity.* Cambridge, Mass., 1993.
Yonnet, Paul. *Jeux, modes et masses: 1945–1985.* Paris, 1985.

REFERENCE WORKS

Bénichou, Paul. *Le temps des prophètes: Doctrines de l'âge romantique.* Paris, 1977.
Caute, David. *Communism and the French Intellectuals: 1944–1960.* New York, 1964.
Chebel d'Appollonia, Ariane. *Histoire politique des intellectuels en France, 1944–1954.* 2 vols. Brussels, 1991.
Dosse, François. *Histoire du structuralisme.* 2 vols. Paris, 1992.
Droz, Jacques. *Histoire des doctrines politiques en France.* Paris, 1956.
Griffiths, A. Phillips, ed. *Contemporary French Philosophy.* Cambridge, 1987.
Hirsh, Arthur. *The New French Left.* Boston, 1981.
Howard, Dick. *The Marxian Heritage.* London, 1977.
Jardin, André. *Histoire du libéralisme politique.* Paris, 1985.
Judt, Tony. *Marxism and the French Left.* Oxford, 1986.
———. *Past Imperfect: French Intellectuals, 1944–1956.* Berkeley, 1993.
Kelly, Michael. *Modern French Marxism.* Oxford, 1982.
Khilnani, Sunil. *Arguing Revolution: The Intellectual Left in Postwar France.* New Haven, Conn., 1993.
Lichtheim, George. *Marxism in Modern France.* New York, 1966.
Mahoney, Daniel J. *The Liberal Political Science of Raymond Aron.* Lanham, Md., 1992.
Martin, Kingsley. *The Rise of French Liberal Thought.* 2d ed. New York, 1954.
Montefiore, Alan, ed. *Philosophy in France Today.* Cambridge, 1983.
Nicolet, Claude. *L'idée républicaine en France.* Paris, 1982.
"Notre histoire. Matériaux pour servir à l'histoire intellectuelle de la France, 1953–1987." Special issue of *Le Débat* (May–August 1988).
Ory, Pascal, and Jean-François Sirinelli. *Les intellectuels en France, de l'affaire Dreyfus à nos jours.* Paris, 1986.
Pavel, Thomas. "Empires et paradigmes." *Le Débat* (January–February 1990).
———. *The Feud of Language: A History of Structuralist Thought.* Oxford, 1989.
Pavel, Thomas, ed. *France-Amérique: Dialogue and Misreadings.* Special issue of *Stanford French Review.* Vol. 15, nos. 1–2 (1991).
Pierce, Roy. *Contemporary French Political Thought.* London, 1966.

Poster, Mark. *Existential Marxism in Postwar France*. Princeton, N.J., 1975.

Rieffel, Rémy. *La tribu des clercs: Les intellectuels sous la Ve République*. Paris, 1993.

Roth, Michael. *Knowing and History: Appropriations of Hegel in Twentieth-Century France*. Ithaca, N.Y., 1988.

Simonin, Anne, and Hélène Clastres, eds. *Les idées en France, 1945–1988: Une chronologie*. Paris, 1989. [Much of the material in this volume is taken from the special issue of *Le Débat* (May–August 1988) mentioned above.]

Soltau, Roger Henry. *French Political Thought in the Nineteenth Century*. New York, 1959.